AMERICAN CINEMATOGRAPHER VIDEO MANUAL

Edited by

Michael Grotticelli

THE ASC PRESS
HOLLYWOOD, CALIFORNIA

American Cinematographer Video Manual

Third Edition

ISBN 0-935578-14-5

Cover design by Charles Mark-Walker
Production by Marion Gore and Martha Winterhalter
Printed in the United States by Larry Brown Litho

AMERICAN CINEMATOGRAPHER VIDEO MANUAL

Contents

How To

Introduction

The advent of digital technology has forever changed the way in which video production is approached and completed. Although it's clear the analog videotape will be around for a long time to come (¾-inch U-Matic still maintains a presence in many areas), if you aren't shooting with a digital camera and are not archiving on digital tape, you're missing out on the immense possibilities and limiting the future viability of your work.

Digital technology began to infiltrate the professional production environment in the mid-to-late Eighties. Today, the consumer electronics world has gone digital, the transmission architecture for television in the United States is going digital, and literally thousands of young amateurs are shooting with digital cameras every day and distributing it themselves on the Internet (creating an impact that has yet to be fully realized).

"Digitizing" the traditional analog signal into a series of ones and zeroes has made all the difference for videographers in the world. Video "segments" or scenes are now looked at as data files that can be manipulated and duplicated with an ease only dreamed about in the Seventies and early Eighties. Material can be repurposed and output to various different media (print, video, CD-ROM, film, etc.) all from the same data.

Digital video cameras produce better pictures, carry more features and cost less than their analog counterparts. Digital audio equipment produces sounds and effects previously only possible after much effort and expense. Editing systems now put the creative decisions into the hands of the editor sitting at the console, freeing them to experiment in a variety of ways.

Basically, digital technology has opened the doors to a wider user base that is still realizing its full potential. Digital has broken down the barriers of cost and high-end equipment availability and allowed "the Everyman" to produce high-quality work previously only seen from the most sophisticated professionals.

That being said, high-quality content remains the domain of the most talented among us. For it's still about the artist and his inherent abilities. While digital technology has allowed many to get involved, it still is only a tool in the person's hand. What they do with it is entirely up to their skill level and their grasp of what it is they (or their client) is trying to accomplish with the project at hand. It's always been true that digital effects can be stunning. It's also true that too many digital effects can get in the way of the message and sometimes be downright annoying.

When I was approached to edit this, the third edition of the ASC Video Manual, I was immediately honored. The manual, like its sister Film version, has a history with videographers that can't be denied. Video professionals from around the world have come to rely on its contents to inform and educate. It's been used as a reference tool on some of the highest profile and most successful video productions ever created. It has also been used by corporate and industrial videographers whose work is no less important to the people directly involved.

It is with this in mind that we present this third edition of the ASC Digital Video Manual. The format here is slightly different than its predecessors. In developing new material for this edition, it is assumed that the reader is at least familiar with analog video production and its intricacies. In it, I've tried to assemble a selections of writers who are well versed in the specific areas of production they write about here. It is hoped that this edition will serve as a starting out point for further exploration into a digital world that is still evolving and is constantly advancing.

Due to the nature of this constantly evolving technology, we're planning periodic updates as they become necessary. This is particularly the case with the "How-To" section, where you'll see emerging areas discussed as on a continuing basis.

As with previous ASC Manuals, we've decided to focus on acquisition and "front-end" production methods, while avoiding post-production and creative issues. Again, what's described within these pages are simply methods and tools for an artist to utilize as they see fit. How you use them is entirely up to you.

I, as Editor, hope that you find it helpful and that it clears up some of the "mysteries" that go along with being digital. A new generation of digital processing, high-definition equipment and the Internet have created opportunity that's there for the taking. Virtually anything's possible. Let's see what you can do.

—Michael Grotticelli

Michael Grotticelli *has been covering the professional video industry for more than 12 years. He is currently Technology/New Media Editor at Broadcasting & Cable magazine, published by the Television Group of Cahners Business Information. He previously served as Editor of TelevisionBroadcast magazine, and has worked as News/Technology Editor for TV Technology magazine and Managing Editor at Videography magazine as well.*

The End of NTSC: We Were Shafted

by Mark Schubin

Before considering the future of television, it may be worth a peek into its past. After all, it was about three-quarters of a century ago that we got shafted.

At that time, a gaunt figure strode through the dark streets of London, his bloody ghoulish treasure wrapped in a handkerchief: a freshly extracted human eyeball. He later sliced it open, attempted to extract something valuable from inside, and then threw it into a canal.

The ghoul's name was John Logie Baird. He is considered by many (with just cause) to be the inventor of television. He also gave us the shaft.

That is, he quite *literally* gave us the shaft. In Baird's first implementation of television, both the camera and the remote display device utilized perforated spinning disks for image scanning, an idea patented in Germany in 1884.

Each perforation traced a line across the image as the disk rotated, and each succeeding perforation was one hole-width closer to the center of the disk. After all the perforations spun by, the entire image had been scanned from top to bottom and was broken up into sequential scanning lines. The next revolution captured the next frame of motion. The perforations in the camera disk allowed light to hit a photosensitive surface; those in the display (TV monitor) allowed light to reach a viewer's eye.

Baird thought that extracting visual purple (rhodopsin) from the human retina would improve his camera's sensitivity. Unfortunately, he couldn't figure out how to perform the extraction, so the eyeball, freshly obtained from a hospital, was discarded, and TV has yet to make use of biochemical enhancements.

Camera sensitivity, however, wasn't Baird's only problem. As video had yet to be invented (in any practical sense), there was no standard for synchronization signals.

To keep the scanning lines synchronized between camera and display, Baird ran a rotating shaft through a hole in a wall. The camera's scanning disk was attached to one end; the display's disk was attached to the other. In October of 1925, through the use of this apparatus, it became possible, for the first time, to transmit a recognizable image of a human face electronically from one room to another.

Within the next few years, Baird came up with an astounding range of video inventions: broadcast television, color television, transatlantic television, see-in-the-dark television, 3-D TV, network television, video telephony, videodiscs, theatrical giant-screen video, mobile production trucks, film-to-video transfer systems, and more. He also came up with televised drama, televised sports, televised interviews, televised movies, and many other forms of programming still recognizable today. Yet, even though he stopped using it almost immediately, his greatest legacy may have been that shaft.

Baird's physical shaft disappeared quickly because it put the lie to the *tele* of television. With camera and display separated by any appreciable distance, it would, of course, be impractical to connect them with a rotating shaft. And the idea of connecting all viewers of a broadcast to the transmitting station by rotating shafts was just plain ridiculous.

Instead, Baird (and other video pioneers of the 1920s) developed the concept of electronic synchronization. The camera and display could be physically separated, but the scanning lines still needed to occur in lock step. When the first scanning line in the camera crossed the top of the image, the same had to happen in the display.

Early attempts at synchronization were less than perfect. There are photos of General Electric's chief television researcher, Dr. Ernst Alexanderson, sitting in front of a TV set in the late 1920s with what appears to be a primitive, wired remote control in his lap. It *was* a remote control of sorts. One knob controlled the speed of the spinning disk. Another adjusted its angular position relative to the camera disk. Only when both parameters matched perfectly did a stable, complete picture appear.

If that seems like a lot of effort to watch TV, consider what was required for changing channels. First, tools were necessary to remove one station's scanning disk and replace it with another's. One television broadcaster might have chosen to transmit, say, 30 scanning lines per frame at 12 frames per second (fps); another might have chosen 48 lines at 30 fps. Only after the display apparatus was changed could the task of tuning in the new channel begin.

One of Baird's early systems had just eight scanning lines per frame at just eight fps. A later system had 30 lines at 12.5 fps. That's still very poor definition, especially when compared to current television's roughly 480 active (picture-carrying) scanning lines per frame and 30 frames per second. When 60 lines replaced 30, a new term began to be used in video (in the early 1930s): high-definition television (HDTV). Sixty lines soon yielded to 120 and 120 to 240.

Consider "The Report of the Television Committee," presented to the British Parliament in January 1935. The section labeled "High Definition Television" defined it as follows: "not less than 240 lines per picture, with a minimum picture frequency of 25 per second."

The following year, the British government arranged for a shoot-out between Baird's latest mechanical (rotating components) system—by then improved to the requisite 240 lines at 25 fps—and a competing Marconi-EMI electronic system offering 405 lines. The two systems broadcast on alternate weeks. According to a report in *The Economist* on August 29, 1936, "At the moment, there is little to choose between them."

In fact, consumers *couldn't* choose between them. To do so, they'd have had to have purchased two completely incompatible television systems. Professionals and bureaucrats, however, *did* make a choice. On February 6, 1937, they announced that only the electronic system would continue. For the first time, a nation chose a single television standard.

By May of that year, with broadcasts only in London, about 2,000 TV sets had been sold; by 1939, it was 20,000. Those numbers may seem trivial, but they are comparable to (and perhaps exceed) the number of digital television (DTV) sets that were been sold in a similar period in the U.S.

The DTV standard adopted by the Federal Communications Commission (FCC) in 1997 was not the first U.S. television standard. That honor belongs to the specification developed by the first National Television System Committee (NTSC). Its final report was issued on January 27, 1941 and was adopted by the FCC. That so-called 525-line system (not all of the lines carry picture information) is, in essence, the one still used today.

The 1997 DTV rules, however, weren't even the second U.S. television standard. On October 10, 1950, the FCC selected another mechanical (spinning-disk-based) television system as a U.S. standard. It called for 405 total lines, instead of 525, and 24 fps, instead of 30. It also called for a spinning filter wheel to change monochrome images on a black & white picture tube into color.

After a series of judicial actions, the U.S. Supreme Court upheld the FCC's decision and set the date to begin broadcasting what came to be known as CBS color as June 25, 1951. The system lasted only until October 19 of the same year, when the Mobilization Director of the United States asked that spinning-wheel color-TV manufacturing cease in order to aid the requirements of the U.S. intervention in the Korean conflict. Broadcasts of spinning-wheel color never restarted.

What was wrong with the system? One may point to such technical issues as varying colors in fast motion or the mechanical nature of receivers, but incompatibility with an existing base of millions of black & white TVs may have been more significant. RCA research engineer George Brown described the problem in his 1979 book *and part of which I was* (Angus Cupar Publishers, Princeton).

"Any black & white receiver in the New York area which happened to be tuned to channel 2 [the

CBS-color transmissions] produced either sixteen little black & white pictures moving rapidly upward in unison or a batch of hash, depending upon the particular model of the receiver. Naturally, the potential audience turned to more exciting television entertainment. Apparently this audience lost between four and five in the afternoon did not bother to return to Channel 2 after five o'clock. As a result, the sponsors of the five to six o'clock programs soon discovered that the potential audience was lost and in turn the sponsors were lost."

A second NTSC was organized to create a color television system compatible with existing receivers and broadcasts. The FCC adopted NTSC color on December 17, 1953, and we still watch it today.

That is, we still watch NTSC color in the U.S. (and many other countries). In Britain, viewers watch a different form of color television, PAL (phase alternation by line), with a transmission method totally incompatible with the 1937 British television standard.

That first-in-the-world standard was given the designation System A by the International Telecommunications Union. Not only was it strictly black & white, but it also used VHF channels and had AM sound, only 405 total scanning lines per frame, and only 3 MHz of video bandwidth (a measure of how fine detail can be in the horizontal direction), among other characteristics.

It was replaced not only by PAL color but also by transmission in System I, with UHF channels, FM sound, 625 total scanning lines, and a 5.5 MHz video bandwidth. Clearly, System A transmissions were incompatible with System I receivers, and vice versa. Nevertheless, aside from DTV, all terrestrial television broadcasts in the U.K. are currently System I. The change was made.

Ah, but how long did the change take? System I transmissions in the U.K. began in 1964. They offered color and better clarity of both pictures and sounds. Nevertheless, the last System A transmitter wasn't shut down until 1985, 21 years later, at which point it was probably easier to buy new TVs for any remaining System A viewers, rather than continue to transmit to their older receivers.

That was a case of an incompatible system replacing an older one. In the U.S., NTSC color was compatible with black & white TVs and transmissions, but it still took 24 years before the number of color TVs in U.S. households first exceeded black & white, and even longer—until 1981—before there was a color TV in at least 85 percent of them. There was at least one VCR in at least 85 percent of U.S. households sometime in 1994. If the VCR were dated just from the introduction of VHS in 1976, that would be still be 18 years.

What's the significance of 85 percent U.S. household penetration? It may have something to do with determining when NTSC broadcasting ceases.

Section 3003 of the Balanced Budget Act of 1997 prohibits the FCC from extending the license of any U.S. NTSC broadcast station beyond December 31, 2006 unless one of three conditions occurs.

First, if a single outlet for one of the top four networks is not transmitting digitally in a particular market (broadcasting region) by that date but has "exercised due diligence" in trying to get on the air with DTV, then no broadcaster in that market need turn off its NTSC transmitter. Second, if "digital-to-analog converter technology is not generally available in such market," then, again, no station in the market need turn off its NTSC transmitter.

Lawyers may have a field day interpreting what "exercised due diligence" or "not generally available" means, but the third Congressional NTSC escape clause may be the best. The FCC may continue to renew the NTSC television transmission license of any broadcaster if:

(iii) in any market in which an extension is not available under clause (i) or (ii) [the two previously described escape clauses], 15 percent or more of the television households in such market—

(I) do not subscribe to a multichannel video programming distributor [cable TV, direct-to-home satellite service, "wireless cable" (MMDS), etc.] that carries one of the digital television service programming channels of each of the television stations broadcasting such a channel in such market; and

(II) do not have either—

(a) at least one television receiver capable of receiving the digital television service signals of the television stations licensed in such market; or

(b) at least one television receiver of analog television service signals equipped with digital-to-analog converter technology capable of receiving the digital television service signals of the television stations licensed in such market. [from Section 3003 of the Balanced Budget Act of 1997]

In other words, until more than 85 percent of the households in a U.S. television market either own a DTV receiving setup or subscribe to a cable-TV or satellite service that carries at least some DTV programming from every DTV broadcaster in that market, NTSC broadcasting need not cease. To put things into perspective, as this is being written [in Summer 1999], the combined subscriber bases of all U.S. multichannel video programming distributors (cable TV, satellite, wireless cable, telephone company video service) have yet to exceed 85 percent.

Furthermore, practically no DTV broadcast programming is being carried by any of them. One of the nation's largest cable-television systems, Time Warner Cable of New York City, is experimentally carrying the DTV signals of WCBS-DT to some subscribers, but it doesn't meet the Congressional criteria because it's not carrying WNYW-DT, another DTV broadcaster in the market, it isn't providing service to all of its subscribers, and DTV-to-NTSC conversion isn't being supplied to any subscribers.

The FCC has yet to issue any rules requiring any cable-television systems to carry any DTV broadcasts; it is by no means certain that they ever will. Meanwhile, both houses of Congress have passed legislation regarding the carriage of local television broadcasts by satellite multichannel video programming distributors. This legislation doesn't even consider DTV.

Only five consumer-electronics products have ever achieved 85 percent U.S. household penetration: telephones, radios, TVs, color TVs, and VCRs, and, of those, VCRs moved fastest. If DTV moves as fast, it will hit 85 percent household penetration sometime around 2016. But, thus far, DTV is moving nowhere near as fast as VCRs.

Thanks to loophole number three, therefore, it's unlikely that NTSC broadcasters will ever be forced off the air, but could there come a time when they will want, *voluntarily*, to cease NTSC broadcasting? Again, history may provide some insight.

The FCC authorized NTSC color broadcasting to begin on January 22, 1954. Like DTV and 1997 (when the FCC issued its digital television rules), color TV took a long time getting to 1954 (aside from Baird's work, there was even an optical color videodisc system for which a patent was applied in 1929). And, just as DTV receivers didn't go on sale to consumers immediately after the FCC rules, so, too, with color.

In March of 1954, Westinghouse sold the first post-spinning-wheel color TV set. It had a 12-inch screen and cost $1,295 at a time when one could buy a new Ford automobile for $1,695. Nevertheless, Fortune magazine predicted one in three homes (18 million) would have color TV by 1959.

Early adopters raced to retailers. Westinghouse sold 30 TV sets the first month, pretty close to one manufacturer's estimate for its DTV sets in November 1998.

Despite the Fortune prediction, by 1962 there were only a million color TV sets in homes. That's when NBC announced that it would air 2,000 hours of color in the 1962-3 season, the end of which would mark the beginning of the tenth year after commercial NTSC color transmission was authorized.

There were 1.4 million color sets in use as of January 1, 1964. One year later there were 2.8 million. A year after that it was 5.5 million, and the following year there were roughly 11 million. The number of color sets in use was doubling annually.

It stopped doubling after that, so there were just 15 million as of 1968, and, again, the number of homes with color didn't exceed the number with monochrome until 1978. Will DTV follow a similar path?

Thanks to some subsidies from receiver manufacturers, it may be running ahead of schedule on the programming side. Mitsubishi paid for CBS to transfer its film-based series to HDTV [in the 1999-2000 season]; Panasonic provided a mobile production facility so that ABC could air *Monday Night Football* in the same season; and Sony initially subsidized NBC's HDTV production of *The Tonight Show*." All of that is in addition to PBS's monthly HDTV shows, ABC's twice-weekly HDTV movies, and Fox's 15 hours per week of non-HDTV DTV programming.

Non-HDTV DTV programming? Yes. Digital technology has finally broken the shaft that forced receivers to march in lock step with cameras.

When the first NTSC came up with the 525-line, 30-fps television system, they noted that not even 30 frames per second were sufficient to prevent pictures from flickering. Film may be shot at 24 fps, but dual-bladed shutters in movie-theater projectors have ensured that audiences view 48 images per second, each frame being projected twice.

Such dual projection is possible because film is an image-storage medium. Before digital technology, there was no equivalent storage in TV sets. If a TV set were to show 60 flicker-free images per second, the camera would have to generate them at the same time (although NTSC television was first broadcast in 1941, the first successful videotape recorder wasn't introduced until 1956).

Unfortunately, 525 lines at 60 fps would require channels roughly twice as large as 525 lines at

30 fps, so the NTSC turned to an old principle called interlaced scanning. The 525 lines were divided into fields of odd-numbered and even-numbered scanning lines, each forming a complete image with half as much vertical detail as the complete frame. Those fields were then transmitted sequentially, creating the requisite 60 images per second and theoretically providing the full 525 lines of vertical resolution (actually closer to 480, when only active, image-carrying lines are considered).

Given the quality of cameras and TV sets in 1941, the interlace compromise worked well. At the end of this century, however, we've found some flaws in interlaced scanning. It's true that large-area flicker is effectively eliminated by the transmission of 60 images per second, but horizontal edges that appear in only one scanning line (as might be generated in computer graphics) are seen only 30 times a second and produce a small-area flickering called twitter.

Then there's the issue of whether interlaced scanning truly does offer the full vertical resolution of the number of scanning lines in the complete frame. An interlace coefficient multiplied by the total number of lines is now generally accepted to reduce perceived resolution. Its value has been estimated from about 0.5 to 0.9. If the former, there was no resolution-adding value to the NTSC's 1941 decision; a 263-line non-interlaced system would have offered the same detail as 525 lines interlaced.

In the U.S., the ABC television network has chosen to transmit non-interlaced HDTV, using 720 active lines (out of 750 total) instead of the 1080 active (out of 1125 total) of interlaced HDTV, with 60 complete frames per second. The interlaced system is abbreviated as 1080i; the non-interlaced system is abbreviated 720p, the p standing for progressive scanning (in which the lines progress from 1 to 2 to 3, and so on, instead of interlace's 1, 3, 5,..., 2, 4, 6,...).

CBS and NBC have chosen 1080i HDTV. There are good reasons to choose either 720p or 1080i. Fox has chosen 720p for those programs it will transmit in HDTV, but it has chosen forms of 480p for its other DTV programming.

Ordinary NTSC video may be characterized as 480i (480 active lines out of 525 total). A 480p that was analogous to 720p would have 60 fps and introduce the same problems that led the NTSC to choose interlace in 1941.

Much of primetime U.S. network programming, however, originates on film shot at 24 fps. Fox has chosen, therefore, to transmit 480p at only 24 fps (or, sometimes, 30). What about flicker?

All DTV receivers must include image storage memories. Those memories allow a 24-fps transmission to be viewed at 60 fps. Indeed, many of the receivers will also allow 1080 lines to be viewed as 480—or vice versa.

The shaft has been broken. The DTV standard of the Advanced Television Systems Committee (ATSC) lists 36 different video formats, and many DTV receivers will be able to decode any of them and, perhaps, display something completely different. And, when the FCC approved the ATSC's standard, they eliminated even that restriction; broadcasters are free to transmit any form of video acceptable in the compression standard used.

Changing from one form of video to another may happen often. Suppose that ABC chooses to use some CBS HDTV football footage in one of its

HDTV Monday Night Football shows. It will have to be converted from CBS's interlaced format to ABC's 720p (an imperfect process) prior to network distribution.

ABC's Dallas-Fort Worth affiliate is WFAA, a station owned by a group that has decided to standardize on 1080i. The station must, therefore, convert 720p to 1080i, a second conversion for the CBS material.

If AT&T's Dallas cable-television system chooses (or is forced) to carry WFAA's digital signals, it may convert them back to 720p, a format the system's owner was said to favor (because it was said to be easier to compress and, therefore, take up less channel space). That, however, is not the end of the conversion processes.

Many DTV receiver/decoders have only 1080i HDTV outputs. Thus, the signals will be converted once more. And some displays, such as Pioneer's 50-inch HDTV plasma panel, can handle only 720p HDTV—a fifth format conversion.

Indeed, different display technologies favor different forms of HDTV. Texas Instruments' digital light processing (DLP) projectors need non-interlaced signals. Ordinary picture tube and projection tube displays have a hard time dealing with the very high scanning rate of 720p (45,000 lines per second) and can more easily deal with 1080i (33,750).

Thus, broadcasters no longer know what viewers will see after the signal leaves the transmitter. One viewer might watch a 720p show as 720p, others as 1080i, 480p, or 360i—a figure automatically arrived at when a widescreen HDTV program is shown in a letterbox (shrunken) format on an ordinary TV set. Viewers might see 60 fps, 30 interlaced, or even, perhaps, 75 on a computer monitor. The shaft has clearly been broken.

What does this have to do with reaching the magic 85 percent? Well, the fact that viewers have an option of viewing DTV on NTSC TV sets (or computers) may provide an incentive for them to purchase decoders without expensive HDTV displays.

The FCC, however, requires broadcasters to simulcast some NTSC programming on DTV beginning in 2003 (rising to 100 percent in 2005), with such simulcasting to continue until NTSC is shut down. If viewers can watch the same programming without an adapter, why buy the adapter—at any price?

Remember, however, that the shaft is now broken. Not only can DTV broadcasters transmit different formats of video, but they can also transmit multiple video programs simultaneously in a single transmission. If an NTSC broadcaster is transmitting, say, a quiz show, that show must be simulcast on the same broadcaster's DTV transmission, but the DTV transmitter could also be carrying a movie, a kid's show, and weather updates at the same time. The only way to see that movie, kid's show, or weather program is to have a DTV receiver—or, perhaps, a cable-television system carrying all four programs.

In fact, DTV transmissions need not be used exclusively for video. PBS may be transmitting very little HDTV, but they are pioneering in data-enhanced TV, e.g., blueprints transmitted as data accompanying a home-building program, player statistics with a sports show, etc.

Perhaps these enhancements will drive DTV receiver sales; perhaps not. If they do, and

TV stations find the vast majority of their audience watching DTV, they may voluntarily turn off their NTSC transmitters. Of course, no one can predict the future.

When the VCR was introduced in the 1970s, its primary function was to have been time shifting of broadcast programming. Today it appears that its primary function is to play tapes obtained from a video retailer, a business category that didn't exist when the first VHS recorders were sold.

If NTSC is turned off in 2006, something no longer expected in any quarter, it will have reached the traditional retirement age of 65. How much longer can it go on? Remember the now-ancient predictions of commuting by personal aircraft? Of robots performing housework?

A centennial of NTSC in 2041? It's possible.

Mark Schubin *is an engineer, historian, teacher, forensic analyst, consultant, expert witness, researcher, and judge. He is a Fellow of the Society of Motion Picture and Television Engineers(SMPTE), a multiple Emmy award winner, and a recipient of many other honors. His clients range from the Children's Television Workshop to IBM to the Metropolitan Opera to Hong Kong's STAR-TV. He also serves as Technical Editor for* Videography Magazine *and is a regular contributor to* Television Broadcast Magazine.

Video Standards and Committees

Standards are the technical criteria used to specify the operational characteristics and tolerances that a device or system may work under. They are an important part of the electronics and communications industry. Committees have been established that write standards for use in the U.S. and throughout the world.

Many committees and groups worldwide such as the Institute of Electrical and Electronic Engineers (IEEE), Society of Motion Picture and Television Engineers (SMPTE) and the International Telecommunications Union (ITU) have developed standards that provide a reference point for industry.

Sometimes these committees are renamed, adding to confusion where the standards are concerned. The International Radio Consultative Committee (CCIR), for example was renamed as the International Telecommunications Union (ITU) in 1993. As a result, standards with a CCIR heading now bare the ITU label.

The standards developed by these committees are generally titled with the name of the authoritative unit and an alphanumeric designation number. Some commonly known digital television standards are SMPTE 259M, which specifies a 10 bit serial digital interface for video, and ITU-R601-4 (formerly known as CCIR-601 and now commonly referred to as "601"), which recommends the encoding parameters for digital television studios.

It is not uncommon for standards to be revised over time as new technologies and formats become available. Such revisions will sometimes create subdivisions of existing standards, such as when Rec. 601 was split into Parts A and B, which refer to 4:3 and 16:9 (widescreen) video, respectively.

Standards for color television were developed in the in the early 1950's by the National Television System Committee (NTSC). NTSC standards were developed for use by TV stations in the US. NTSC is also the standard used in Japan, Canada, and Mexico.

Going Digital

by Joseph Fedele

The Principles of Moving Pictures

Any discussion of video must first begin with an understanding of moving pictures and how the limitations of the human eye have been exploited by engineers to render "perceived" motion. We say that motion is "perceived" in film or video because it is not possible to convey motion in its true or natural form. This is due to the infinite and minute increments of which they consist.

For example, motion exists as a millionth of a second, but our visual senses cannot perceive it. Thus, it would be impractical and wasteful to record such information. Rather, a more practical method of recording motion would be to select "snapshots" over time at a rate that will convey the perception of motion while the intervals between those snap shots remain virtually invisible.

This inability to see minute changes in motion can be traced to how the human eye operates. Light passing through the human eye lands on the retina which then transfers the light information to the brain for processing. But images captured by the retina tend to linger for a brief instant until they fade and allow more images to be processed. An exaggerated form of this lingering effect is experienced when you are temporarily blinded by the sun and continue to see its form for a few seconds after covering your eyes.

The principles of moving pictures or movies are based on this phenomena. Testing on human subjects found that sequential pictures flashed at a rate approaching 48 frames per second tended to appear seamless. Thus, the minimum "flicker rate," or the rate at which pictures may be presented in sequence before the eye can detect the gap between them, was established at 48 frames per second (fps).

In film, these snapshots in time are recorded at 24 fps but played back at twice the rate. This is facilitated through the use of a special shutter that flashes the same picture twice. Thus, the perceived picture rate equals 48 fps.

However, it should also be noted that the flicker rate is directly related to the ambient light intensity around the subject matter and changes accordingly. For instance, a movie shown in near dark conditions at 48 fps would tend to flicker if the theater lights were turned up to a bright level.

In the home, where television sets operate at higher rates of between 50 or 60 fps, light levels are brighter, but remain relatively average. These slightly higher frame rates offer better immunity to flicker in this average light environment. But in offices, where bright white neon lights are the norm, computer screens must operate at rates exceeding 70 fps.

Understanding Analog Video

Any understanding of video must begin with a discussion of its components and how it is captured by both the human eye and electronic equipment. Scientists have spent years researching how we see and hear. Our ability to perceive visual and audible information has, in fact, dictated the standards by which some production equipment is designed and manufactured.

Our eyes are capable of vision because of photoreceptors located at the back of the retina called rods and cones. Rods are responsible for what is called "night vision," but are not sensitive to colors. Cones are the color sensing part of the retina that are responsible for the identification of color. Three different types of cones are each sensitive to different visible light wavelengths and thus recognize the primary colors of red, green, and blue.

All colors can be produced simply by mixing the appropriate amount and intensity of red, green, and blue. Color can thus be defined as a linear combination of the three primary colors. These three components of light are also referred to as RGB.

Component and Composite Video Signals

Color video cameras act in a similar manner as the human retina by capturing light and converting its red, green and blue components into electrical impulses that may then be recorded or displayed on a monitor. When these components are recorded or distributed individually the signal is referred to as component video.

Maintaining video is its original component form is highly desirable because its quality can be maintained at a high level. But maintaining video in its components can prove to be very expensive. Distribution of component video requires the use of one cable for each of the three components. Component monitors, routers, switchers and recorders are also expensive to purchase, operate and maintain.

When these components are mixed together they form composite video. Composite video is used in the transmission of the NTSC signal and is is far more cost effective than component because it requires the use of only one cable to carry the signal. However, video quality is not maintained at the high level that it would be had it remained in the component domain. When compared to component video, the quality of composite is marginal at best. The results of converting to composite are color bleeding, low clarity and high generational loss.

Given the choice between composite and component, the latter is always preferred. Component is by far the more superior format than composite. However this higher quality comes at a premium price.

Color Difference Signal Formats

A component signal may also be expressed in other forms known as a color different format. Color difference formats are often referred to as component signals but this is technically incorrect.

Y R-Y B-Y	Y I Q	Y Cr Cb	Y Pr Pb

Figure 1 - Color Difference Formats

RGB remains the only true component signal, but for our purposes, we'll informally refer to these formats as component signals.

A composite video signal is composed of several elements. The chrominance signal, also called the chroma, contains a picture's color information such as hue and color saturation. The luminance, or luma portion contains the luminous intensity (brightness) or the monochrome part of the video signal. Prior to the development of color TV standards, the luminance signal was sometimes thought of as the video signal itself.

Studies have shown that the human eye perceives spatial and temporal changes of luminance much more than chrominance variations. This becomes an important factor in the development of digital video sampling methods (see Sampling).

Color difference signals can be thought of as mathematical representations of RGB. If we let the letter "Y" represent 'luminance' a better explanation of the color difference signals may be obtained.

We know that three values added together yields a sum containing information from each of the original values. From algebra we learned that if the value of the sum and only two of the three original values are known then the third value can be found by simple arithmetic.

Hence, in the case of Y R-Y B-Y, R and B may be derived by adding Y to R-Y and B-Y respectively. The value for G may then be derived by subtracting RB from Y R-Y B-Y (the sum).

Broadcast equipment such as VTRs and digital

disk recorders generally offer a number of inputs and outputs (I/O) for video. The most common is a composite I/O. Y R-Y B-Y is generally the component I/O provided and used in most high quality broadcast applications. RGB is rarely used in broadcast recording because it requires more bandwidth in order to achieve a similar subjective quality when compared to color difference formats such as Y Cr Cb.

Consumer or "prosumer" (one step between professional quality and consumer grade) equipment will sometimes offer Y/C or S-Video I/Os as well.

Y/C is a quasi-component video format. Y/C maintains a separate luminance (Y) and chrominance (C) but is not considered to be true component video. While it is superior to composite, Y/C is still lacking in quality when compared to RGB or even any of the color difference video signals like Y R-Y B-Y.

U.S. Analog Video Formats

NTSC has been the analog color TV format used in the U.S. since 1953. The format consists of specifications for a number of technical criteria, including the number of lines, definition of color, and the rate a which the picture frames are transmitted.

The NTSC picture consists of 525 lines of video information that is scanned from left to right. Scanning of the picture is performed in two sweeps called "fields". The first field consists of all the odd numbered line while the second field contains the picture information of the even numbered ones (see Figure 2).

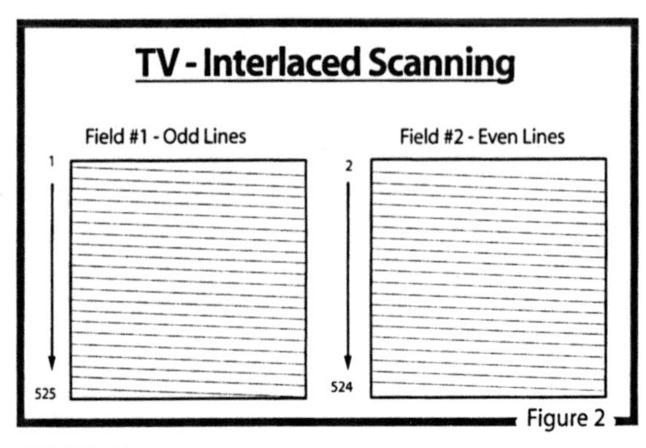

NTSC Fields

When messed or interlaced together these fields make one frame of video. So a frame can be thought of as "snapshot" or image of NTSC video that is composed of two fields (see Figure 3).

In the original monochrome TV standard a frame rate of 60 frames per second (fps) was established as the "field scanning rate." The field scanning rate was based on the alternating current (AC) line frequency of a standard electrical outlet. But when color was added in 1953 a small adjustment was made to the field rate and it was changed to 59.94Hz.

The reasons for this dates back to a decision made by the Federal Communications Commission (FCC) which attempted to deal with interference between the audio and color subcarriers in the final NTSC transmission standard. The details of this are very technical and beyond the scope of this book.

But this change in the field rate created a serious shortcoming when timecode was introduced into the video domain because video fields of 59.94

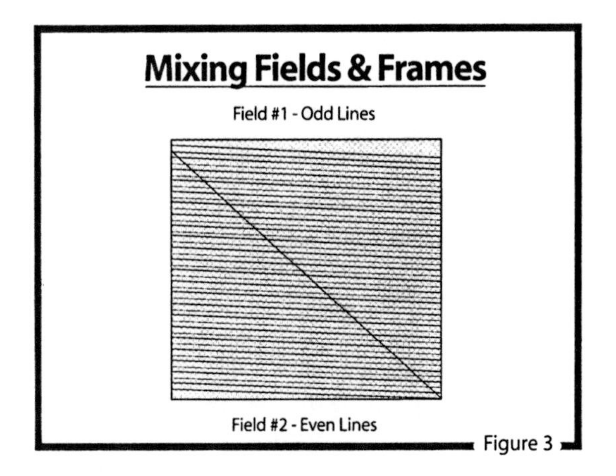

Figure 3

Hz could not be measured against a 60 second clock. Consequently "drop frame" video was developed where 108 frames per hour are automatically eliminated from video to match the 59.94 Hz rate.

Using drop frame video, two frames are cut every minute (except on every 1/10th minute) to compensate for the uneven frame rates. This effect is similar to "leap years," where a day is added to the calendar every fourth year, but not at the beginning of some centuries, in order to compensate for the fact that a year is actually composed of 365.24 days (not an even 365).

Interlaced scanning was the method chosen due to its inherent ability to produce a flicker-free picture at such a low scanning rate. Maintaining a low scan rate was important because higher rates required more "bandwidth" for TV transmissions. Broadcasters were limited to a 6 MHz wide channel by the Federal Communications Commission (FCC) standards.

Another means of scanning pictures is in the

progressive method. Progressive scanning is used in computers and is also available for use in the digital television standards. In a progressive system each frame is scanned in only one field. This eliminates the need to merge two fields together as in the interlaced scanning method. Progressively scanned systems are sometimes called "non-interlaced" due to this fact. The advantage of progressive scanning is that it is immune to "picture artifacts" or distortions, such as varying hue, that interlacing sometimes produces in a picture.

A disadvantage in the use of progressive scanning is that it requires true scanning rates higher than 70 fps for computer applications and 60 fps for video (as opposed to the 30 fields per second of interlaced video). This increase in the scanning rate necessitates the use of a wider bandwidth for transmission. Put simply, progressively scanned pictures take up more spectrum.

Because interlaced scanning is much more spectrally efficient in its use of the airwaves it was chosen as the TV standard for broadcasting worldwide. Computer systems, on the other hand, did not have to deal with the restrictions imposed by bandwidth requirements so they were free to develop progressive systems.

Aspect Ratio

The height and width dimensions of an image are used to define the aspect ratio. The aspect ratio selected for use in the early development of television was a 4:3 image, which is slightly wider than it is tall. In moving pictures, wider images allow for better tracking of motion, such as people walking and general movement.

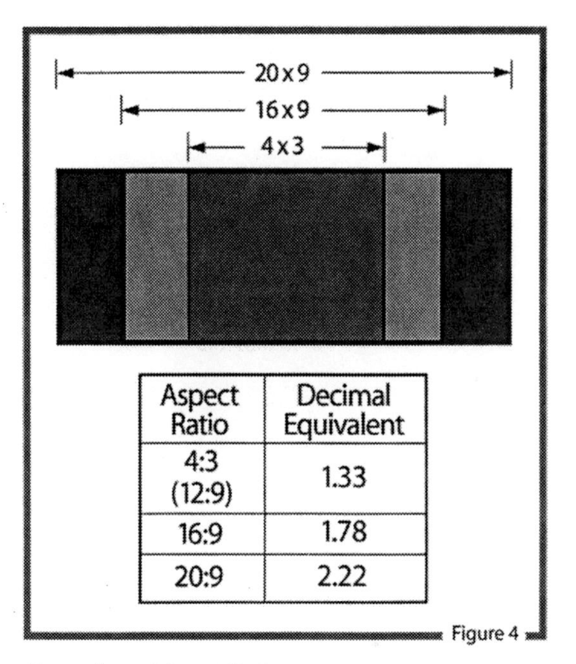

Aspect Ratio	Decimal Equivalent
4:3 (12:9)	1.33
16:9	1.78
20:9	2.22

Comparison of Aspect Ratios

Aspect ratios were originally set at 4:3 for television to match those used by the film industry. Later, the film industry began to utilize wider screen ratios of 16:9, 20:9 and more. In recent years, and with the introduction of DTV with its multiple aspect ratio capabilities, aspect ratios have become an important new part of digital video production.

Due to the confusion of trying to visualize ratios like 4:3 and 16:9, decimal numbers are sometimes used instead. Figure 4 allows for a simple comparison of several aspect ratios:

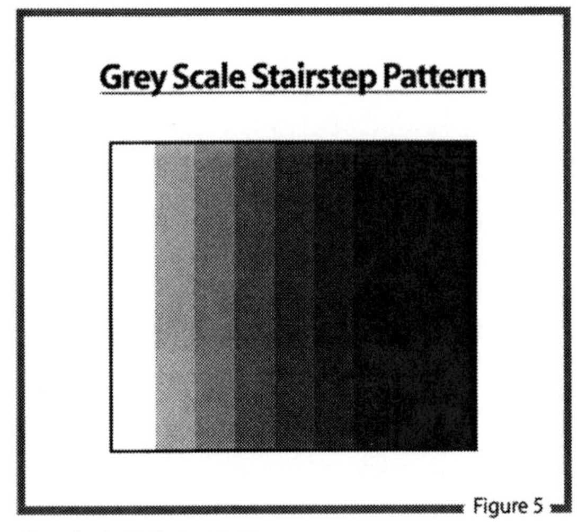

Gray Scale Stairstep Pattern

Measuring Video

Video measurements are performed with two basic instruments, called waveform monitors and vectorscopes. Waveform monitors are used primarily to measure the luminance portion of video while the vectorscope examines the chrominance signals. Various waveform patterns, such as color bars, stairstep, multiburst and other video signals are also used as test images to accurately measure and adjust video signals.

Figures 5 & 6 show what a gray scale stairstep pattern would look like on video and waveform monitors, respectively.

A video signal is made up of several important portions that include pulses used to synchronize the lines within a frame and limits that define its luminance boundaries. The overall amplitude of a

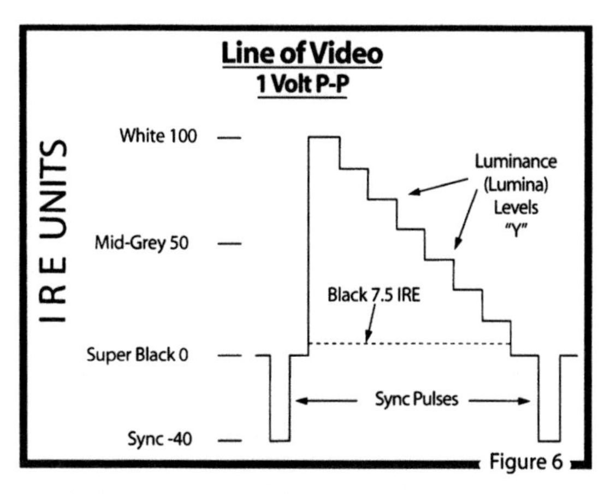

Gray Scale Pattern as Viewed on a Waveform Monitor

video signal is measured on a waveform at one volt peak-to-peak from its white peak to the lower tip of the synchronous or "sync" pulse.

Video measurements are made using Institute of Radio Engineers (IRE) units. The IRE scale is shown on a waveform monitor to reflect 100 units for the visual information and 40 units of sync. The baseline of a video signal is at the zero reference point while the white level is seen at 100 units. The black reference is also called the setup level and is set at 7.5 IRE units. Any video that lies between the black and white levels corresponds to the different shades of gray in a monochrome picture.

The 7.5 unit setup allows for a buffer zone between the black limits and the sync that was originally meant to prevent image information from entering into the synchronous pulses. This area is sometimes referred to as superblack and is often used with various post production equipment to develop interesting special effects.

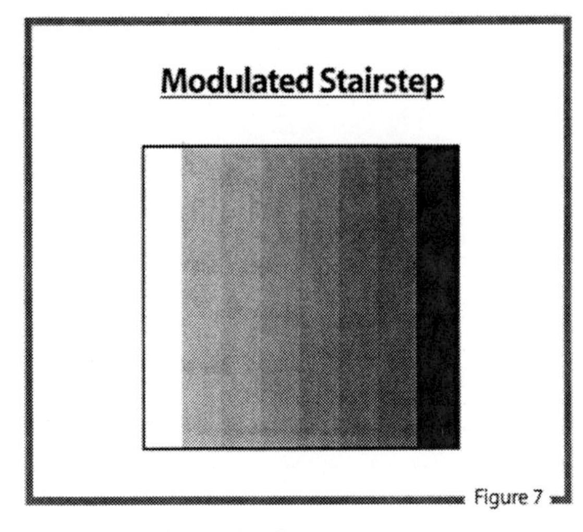

Modulated Stairstep Signal

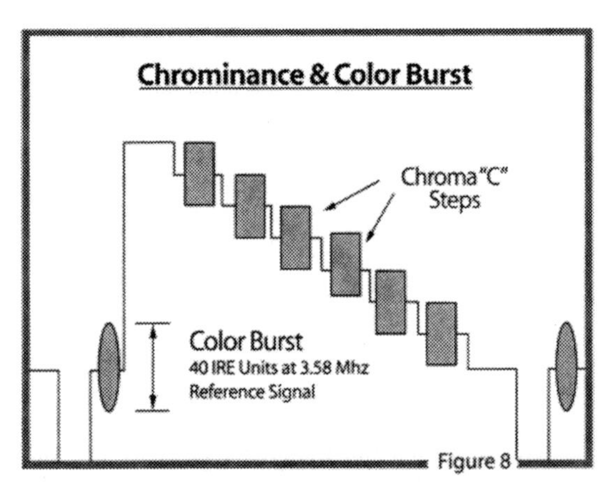

Modulated Stairstep as Viewed on a Waveform Monitor

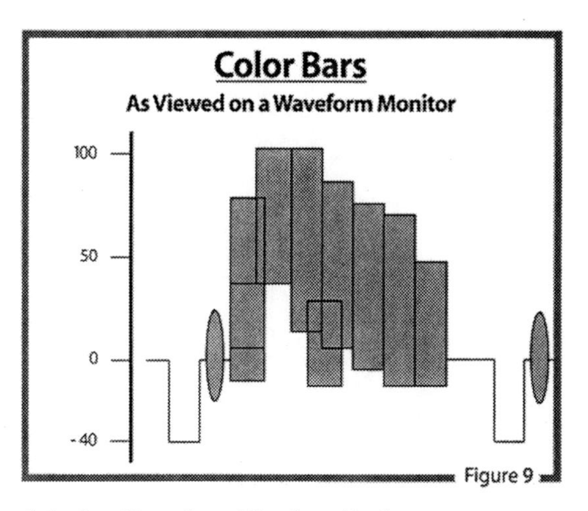

Color Bars Viewed on a Waveform Monitor

When color information is added to the stairstep signal it is referred to as modulated stairstep. An example of this is shown in Figures 7 and 8. In the stairstep signal the color burst or simply the burst signal is inserted after each sync pulse. The burst is set to 40 IRE units on the baseline. This important signal provides the color reference signal for video. Without it the signal would turn to monochrome.

Figures 9 and 10 show what color bars would look like on a waveform monitor and vectorscope. Except for the amplitude of the color burst, virtually no color information is measurable with any degree of certainty on the waveform monitor. However, on a vectorscope, each of the color components is clearly visible.

In measuring the chrominance information, the further a point extends from the center of the scope, the more chroma it contains. Hence, a

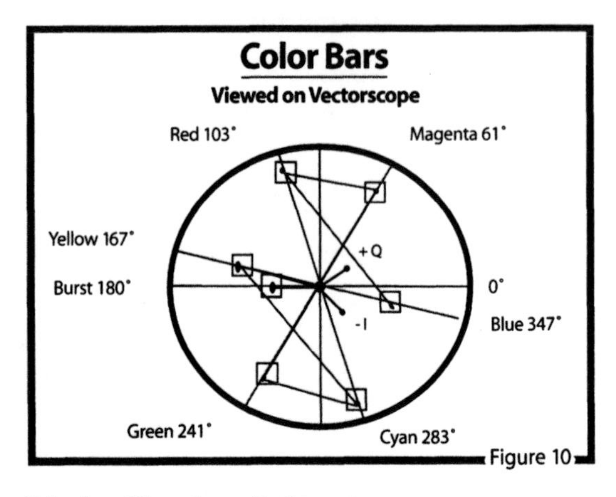

Color bars Viewed on a Vectorscope

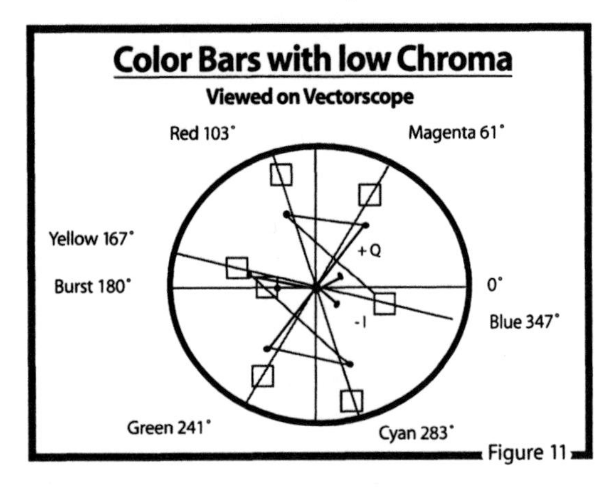

Color Bars with Reduced Chroma as Viewed on a Vectorscope

colorbar signal with not enough chroma would be seen as shown in Figure 11.

For more on this, see Video Test and Measurement chapter.

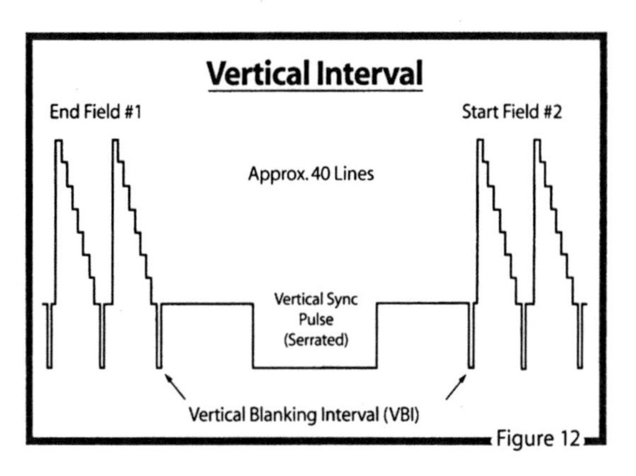

The Vertical Blanking Interval

Vertical Blanking Interval

Another important portion of a video signal is called the Vertical Blanking Interval or "VBI." The VBI (shown in Figure 12) is the part of video that lies between the frames and is used to retrace the picture from the bottom of the screen to the top.

The VBI also includes the first 20 lines of video. This area is used to insert video test signals like color bars, VITS, VIRS and the Ghost Canceling Reference Signal. But the actual picture information region of video in an NTSC signal lies between lines 21 to 262 ½ (field #1) and 282 ½ to 525 (field #2).

The VBI is also a convenient place to "hide" other information that may or may not be used along with the picture information. Closed captioning information is one example of how ancillary data may be inserted into the VBI and then used for the hearing impaired. Other data streams totally unrelated to the program material may also be inserted into the VBI for delivery within the video signal.

The VBI is also an important area used by video switchers to cut from one video program to another. This region is used as the cut point because it is the best place to interrupt a signal without causing the video to "jump." If video were to be switched in the middle of a line, for example, the picture would temporarily loose synchronization and the image on the screen would momentarily jump until sync is found. Hence, Vertical Interval switchers are so named because of their ability to switch at the beginning of the VBI and maintain picture synchronization.

International Analog Video Formats

The reason why different standards were developed internationally can be traced primarily to that fact that the AC line frequencies are not the same worldwide. While North America, Japan, and most of South America utilize a 60Hz AC standard, a large part of the world uses 50Hz. This immediately divided the world's television systems in two. Countries with a line frequency of 60Hz developed television standards based on 30 fields per second and those 50Hz based countries used a 25 field rate.

Although NTSC remains the primary standard for television in the US and some countries worldwide, the more dominant format used in Europe and elsewhere is PAL. SECAM is not as widely used and confided mostly to French speaking countries, the former Soviet Republics and their allies prior to its breakup.

The PAL standard is actually a modified version of NTSC that was developed to remedy the problem of color artifacts produced by the interlaced scanning.

The number of lines used in PAL was also increased from 525 in NTSC to 625 lines. PAL is considered to produce a better quality picture, but at a higher price.

SECAM was developed in 1962 by the French to primarily protect their domestic TV set manufacturing industry. SECAM is also based on the 50 Hz AC power system and uses interlaced scanning at 25 fields per second. Technically speaking the SECAM systems is considered to be the simplest television standard in the world.

Because SECAM is incompatible with NTSC or PAL systems, it was adopted as the TV standard in the former Soviet Republics and Eastern Block countries in an attempt to prevent the reception of transmissions from non-communist countries.

The conversion of video from one format to another is performed through the use of a "standards converter." Standards converters are available for use that can convert video between any of the formats. The cost of these devices varies widely and depends largely on the technology used and the required quality level of the finished product.

Understanding Analog and Digital

What is Analog?

In electronics, the word analog refers to a signal, wave, or other electronic information that is continuously variable and whose dimensions form a contiguous shape of infinite points that are "analogous" or in-step with a reference. One example of an analog signal is an audio wave where the shape of the signal varies with the amplitude and phase of the vibrations produced by an instrument.

These audio waves can then be captured by the diaphragm of a microphone whose reciprocating motion, which is caused by the energy in the wave and is analogous to the waves actions, is then used to drive an electrical current through wire. Because the electrical current varies in accordance with the motion of the diaphragm, the signal flow through the wires is also said to be an "analog" interpretation of the original sound wave.

An analog wave is assumed to possess an infinite number of points with no discernible limits in between them. Nature itself is said to operate in analog form. Light rays from the rising sun, for instance, gradually increase in intensity in an infinite number of steps.

What is Digital?

In electronics the word digital refers to a process where some value is expressed as a finite number in accordance with a predetermined scale. In contrast, you may recall that in an analog signal there are an infinite number of points that form a contiguous shape.

In order to understand digital one must first understand a process called sampling. Sampling is a procedure where a value is obtained from a signal in a predetermined and regular pattern. Sampling may also be considered as a "snapshot" in time of a signal. Samples taken at regular intervals may then be laid end to end to form a representation of the original signal.

An example of this is a movie where 24 frames or "snapshots" of a scene are taken in each second. Each frame may be considered as a "sample" in time. When shown individually each frame displays a

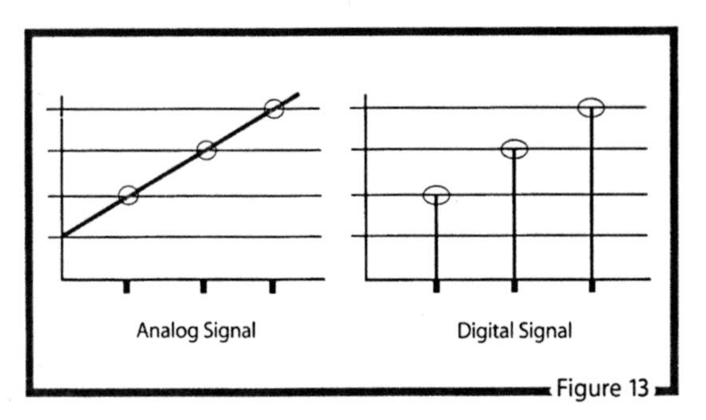

Figure 13

Understanding Analog and Digital through the use of Graphs

limited amount of information. But when played back in sequence at a rate of 24 frames per second these samples provide the viewer with the illusion of contiguous motion.

This "illusion" is possible because an image projected on the retina of the human eye lingers for a period of time before fading. Hence, a faster sampling rate would yield information that is of no value to the viewer under the same conditions.

Another way to understand the difference between analog and digital is through the use of two simple graphs. In Figure 13 a line graph is used to represent an analog signal and a bar graph provides the visual representation of samples taken from the original signal.

Each graph depicts identical information but in different forms. This bar graph can be thought of as having sampled information from the line graph at predetermined and regular intervals. If the bar graph were used to represent visual information, the missing segments may not be useful and discarded. As in the case of the film shot in segments of 24 frames per second, any picture information between the frames serves no purpose because the eye cannot even detect the difference beyond a certain sampling interval.

Note that sampling intervals occur at a predetermined rate that is constant throughout the process. This is an important part of sampling. The final step in the formation of digital information is to convert the sample to a number. The analog signal is then converted to a set of numbers that represent a numeric version of the original signal.

Bits, Bytes and Binary

In our example above, the digital information is represented in decimal number form. However, a far more useful way to work with these numbers would be to convert them to "binary" form. The binary numbering system uses ones and zeros to represent its values. Binary numbering is the system primarily used in computers and communications systems to store, process and transmit information. Hence, it is the preferred method of working in the digital domain.

In a binary numbering system a single digit of information is represented by a bit. Bits are abbreviated with the small letter "b". Bits are then grouped into "bytes", which are abbreviated with a capital letter "B." The distinction between the two is very important and will become immediately apparent.

Figure 14 provides an example of how the decimal numbers zero through 10 are represented in a 4 bit binary byte. Here the decimal number has been converted to binary digits represented by a 4 bit byte. It should be noted that binary numbers are often represented in 8 bit bytes. Generally speaking, however, bytes are assumed to contain 8 bits unless otherwise noted. But it should also be pointed out that computers and other electronic equipment sometimes work with bytes that are 4, 16, 32 and 64 bits long.

Decimal Number	Binary Form
0	0000
1	0001
2	0010
3	0011
4	0100
5	0101
6	0110
7	0111
8	1000
9	1001
10	1010

Figure 14 - Decimal Numbers in 4 Bits

Serial Digital

Serial digital is the process where digital information is laid end to end to form a continuous stream of binary information. Our example of frames shown in rapid succession to form a moving picture is an example of how digital information is relayed.

An advantage of working in a serial digital environment is the ability to transmit several streams of information using only one transmission. Multiplexing is when several distinct bit streams are interleaved into one contiguous line of information.

In broadcasting, for example, multiplexing may be used to transmit several audio, video and ancillary digital data sources simultaneously onto a single stream of information.

Figure 15 shows how binary information from different sources are systematically segmented and assembled to form a multiplexed line of information.

	Digital Stream Segmented into 4 Bit Bytes		
Program Source	**Byte 1**	**Byte 2**	**Byte 3**
V - Video	0010	1101	0000
A1 - Audio 1	0110	0011	0110
A2 - Audio 2	1111	0110	0101
D - Data Channel	0011	1111	0001

A Multiplexed Bit Stream

Header	V B1	A1 B1	A2 B1	D B1	Header	V B2	A1 B2	A2 B2	D B2	Header	V B3	A1 B3	A2 B3	D B3	Header
0100	0010	0110	1111	0011	0101	1101	0011	0110	1111	0100	0000	0110	0101	0001	1101

Figure 15 - Multiplexing

These individual segments are assembled to form words which are separated in the bit stream by headers. These headers act as markers that delineated the start and end of each word. In our example, 4-bit bytes are used to show how this might work. In reality, however, video or audio information is typically saved in 8 or 10 bit bytes. Headers, data packets and other synchronizing information are also sent in the serial bitstream (not all shown in this example) which vary considerably in length and could reach up to 188 bytes long.

On the receiving end of the transmission, audio, video and data information is removed from the multiplexed bit stream by separating the words and their individual elements. The original streams of information may then be reassembled and used accordingly.

The rate at which this transmission occurs is known as the data rate. The data rate is an important barometer of the amount of information that may be transported. Data rates may be expressed in either bits (b) or bytes (B) per second. Earlier in this chapter a distinction was made between the abbreviation of the words bits and bytes. It should now be clear how a mislabeled data rate would cause great confusion.

The Essence of Digital Video

Although digital television transmissions to the home are a relatively new form of video delivery, the concept and implementation of digital video has been around for many years. Digital video is rooted in the analog system of producing moving pictures and can be considered, for the most part, to be a conversion of analog information to the digital realm. Hence, digital video is merely a binary representation of analog moving pictures.

It is important to understand that, regardless of how a "real" moving image is stored or transmitted, its original picture information was captured in analog form and later converted to digital. More specifically, the image of a person walking is a natural or "real" occurrence whose moving picture information enters the camera lens as analog light waves. Those analog light waves may then be stored on film, recorded electronically or transmitted to some other medium.

In any case, a conversion to the digital domain is necessary in order for it to be considered as such. On the other hand, some forms of moving pictures—such as digitally produced computer animations—remain in binary form throughout.

Regardless of how images are produced, transmitted or stored, the final viewing of moving pictures is made possible by monitors that present those signals in analog form for our eyes. Hence, the primary reason to convert video from analog to digital in the first place is to allow for quality improvements in transmission or storage and for the inclusion of other visual information that may not be reasonably added given the desired level of quality.

Making Digital From Analog

The process by which information is converted to or from analog and digital is a complex series of events. But converting an analog video signal to digital can be organized into two overall steps of Sampling (which includes the analog-to-digital [A/D] conversion process) and Quantizing.

Sampling

The results of different sampling methods are expressed in ratios, such as 4:4:4, 4:2:2, 4:1:1 and 4:2:0, that describe the pixel resolution of both the luminance (luma or Y) and chrominance (chroma or C). Except for 4:4:4, which is generally used in high end graphics applications, the remaining sampling methods exploit limitations of the human eye to reduce the volume of information that is stored. The reason for this will become very apparent latter in this chapter.

It should be pointed out that different sampling types have been chosen for specific applications. Chart A lists some of the generally accepted uses for the different sampling methods.

Scientists have long known that our eyes have the ability to perceive subtle changes in luminance to a higher degree than in color information. Consequently, it was determined that if color information was sampled at rates less than that of the

Chart A

Sampling Rates	Typical Use
4:4:4 or 4:4:4:4 *	High-end Graphics
4:2:2	Professional production and post production
4:2:0	Video distribution (primarily to the home)
4:1:1	Lower quality production and post production

*** Note: The 4th digit in 4:4:4:4 is commonly used to denote 4 samples of the key channel in graphics**

luminance portion of light, efficiencies in digital signal processing and storage methods could be realized. These efficiencies translate into substantial savings in the price of manufacturing equipment and in the cost of storage mediums and transmission bandwidths.

Testing of various sampling methods with human subjects determined that if half of the color information was discarded, no significant perceptible video impairments were visible. If the color was reduced to ¼ of its original resolution, some impairments were visible but the quality of the video remained acceptable for certain applications. These reductions in color resolution are noted in the ratios previously stated.

Sampling ratios are used to describe the number of times an individual picture element (pixel) is analyzed when groups of four pixels are compared in succession over each line of video. The numeric value in each ratio describes the number of times that the luminance (Y) and the color difference signals Cr and Cb are sampled, respectively (See Figures 16, 17 and 18).

The first digit in a 4:2:2 video signal, for example, indicates that the Y portion is sampled on each of the

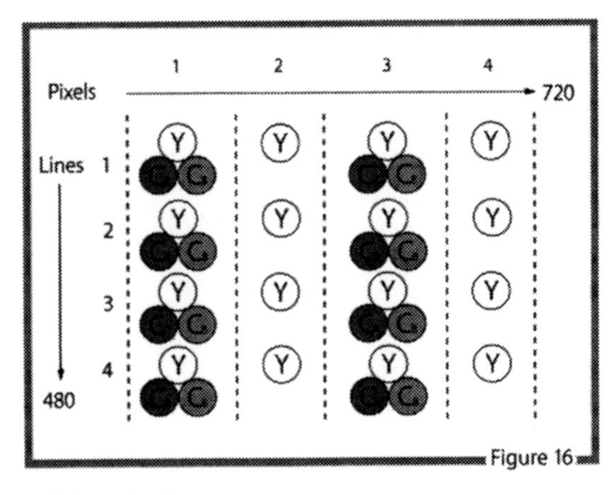

4:2:2 Sampled Video

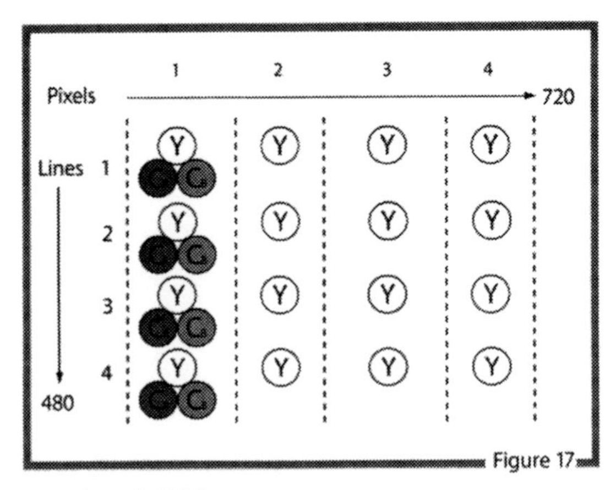

4:1:1 Sampled Video

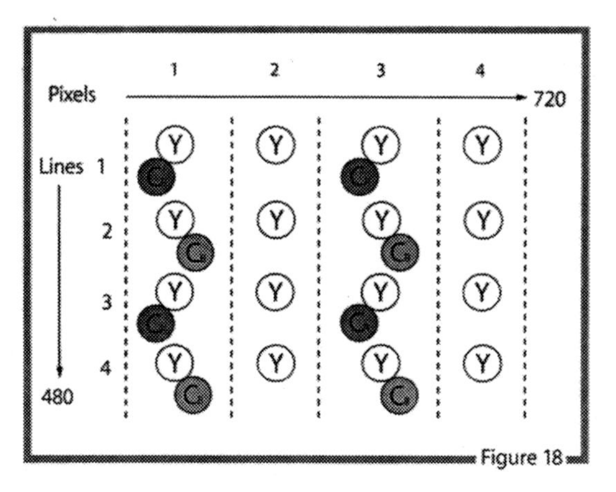

4:2:0 Sampled Video

four pixels. The second and third digits denote that Cr and Cb are only sampled twice in the grouping of four.

A derivation of the sampling ratio can be seen in 4:2:0 where the second digit denotes that the two chroma samples are taken, but the third digit implies that they are staggered over two individual and adjacent lines.

Another aspect of sampling is the sampling rate or sampling frequency. This is the rate at which sampling takes place. The commonly stated sampling frequencies for standard 4:3 video and 16:9 widescreen are 13.5 Mhz and 18 Mhz, respectively.

Quantizing

Quantizing is the next step in the conversion to digital and consists of transforming the sampled information into either 8- or 10-bit words. The quantizing process itself is actually performed

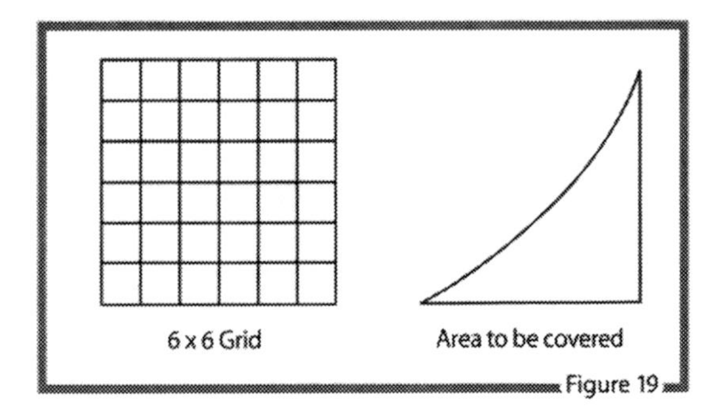

Grid and Area

during the sampling operation as information from each pixel is first sampled and then quantized. The process starts at the upper left hand side of the picture and samples each picture according to the type of sampling specified (4:2:2, 4:1:1, etc).

Information collected in the analog sample is then compared to a chart of digital steps and assigned a numeric value that most closely matches the scale. That information is then saved in binary form and eventually used accordingly. The number of steps in the digital scale is set by the number of total bits that

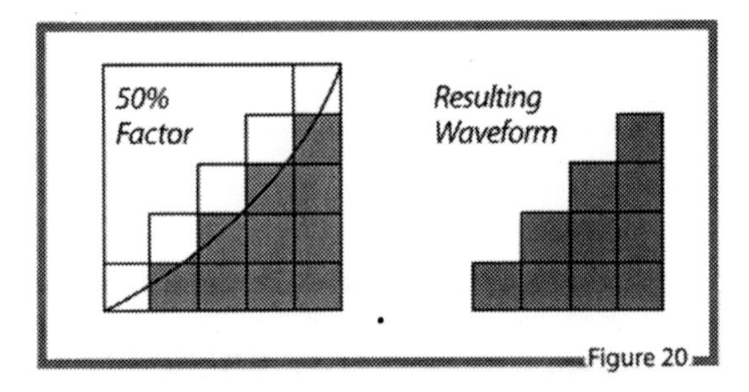

Quantizing Results

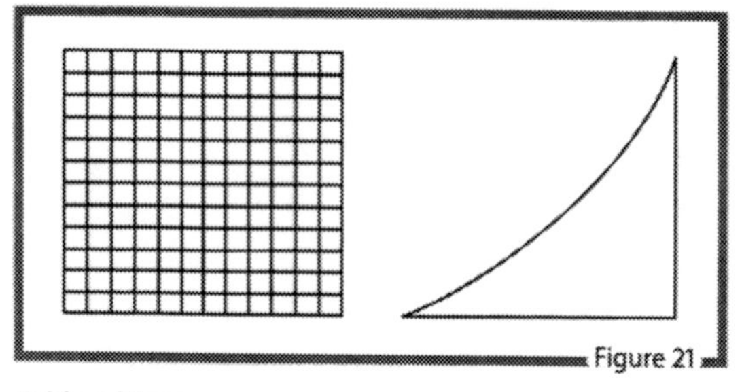

Grid and Area

are specified in the process. As previously mentioned, video sampling methods quantize in either 8 or 10 bit words. Consequently the digital scale will utilize 256 or 1024 steps to quantize the analog sample.

An example of how quantizing works is in Figures 19 through 23. A relatively simple way of understanding how the quantizing process works is by using the installation of floor tiles in a room as an example. For the sake of simplicity, a 6 x 6 step grid is used to demonstrate how an analog signal is quantized. A 50 percent factor is then applied where only areas of the analog waveform that cover one half

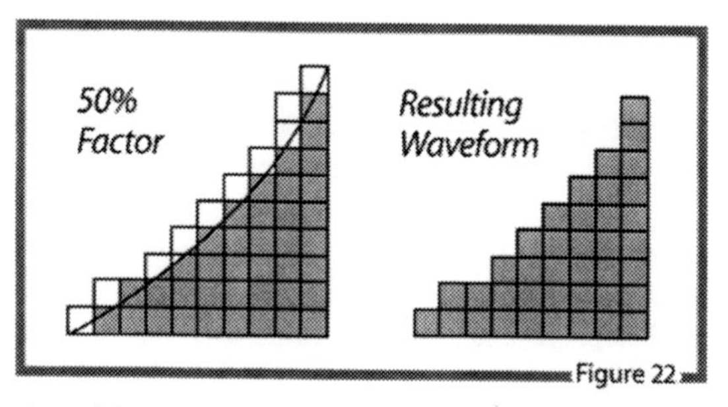

Quantizing Results

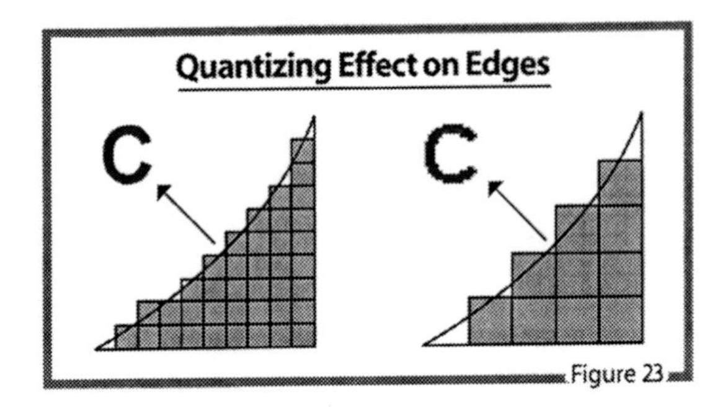

Quantizing Effect

or more of a tile are kept and the remaining sections are discarded.

You will note that when a scale with twice the number of steps (in this case 12 x 12 tiles) is used the resulting pattern more closely resembles the original analog form. Hence, the information derived from 10-bit quantizing would be more accurate (and contain less visual artifacts) than that obtained from 8-bit levels.

In Figure 23 we see the effect of different quantizing levels if the visual information in our example was taken from the letter "C." This example clearly demonstrates how different quantizing levels can effect picture quality in the conversion process. The jagged edges seen in each picture illustrates how higher quantizing levels result in smoother images as well. This stairstep effect is also called aliasing.

Once every pixel has been sampled and quantized the digital information for the subject video frame is now ready for use and the next picture frame is then analyzed. The information obtained can then be transferred to either a frame buffer—where it may remain until needed—saved on videotape, disk or other record media, or distributed elsewhere for further processing.

Digital Data Rates

Once a video signal has been converted to digital, the process of saving and distributing the information begins. The amount of data derived from the sampling and quantizing processes is directly related to a number of factors that include the video format, the aspect ratio and the number of quantizing steps.

The formula below is used to calculate the data rate for each of the sampling methods. The values given for the picture width corresponds to the number of horizontal pixels in each frame of video. The value of Cr and Cb, respectively, are derived from the picture width and sampling method. So, for instance, if the sampling method were 4:2:2 the values of Cr and Cb would each equal half of the picture width (W). When the same formula is applied to 4:2:0 sampling, the values of Cr and Cb would be the same. If 4:1:1 were used, Cr and Cb would equal ¼ of the picture width.

The number of lines (L) in the specified picture frame, the quantizing levels (Q)used and the number of frames per second (fps) account for the remaining values in the formula.

<u>Formula:</u>

(W + Cr + Cb) x L x Q x fps = Serial Digital Data Rate

<u>Example:</u>

4:2:2 Sampling with 8-bit Quantizing & 480 Horizontal Lines @ 30 fps

(704+352+352) x 480 Lines x 8 bits x 30 frames = 162 Mbps

A comparison chart of the different NTSC

DTV Video Format	Pixel Resolution	Quantizing Levels	Sampling	Scanning	Data Rate
NTSC Component	720 x 486	8 bits	4:4:4	30 fps - Interlaced	252 Mbps
NTSC 601 Component	720 x 486	8 bits	4:2:2	30 fps - Interlaced	168 Mbps
NTSC 601 Component	720 x 486	10 bits	4:2:2	30 fps - Interlaced	210 Mbps
NTSC Component	720 x 486	8 bits	4:2:0	30 fps - Interlaced	126 Mbps
NTSC Component	720 x 486	8 bits	4:1:1	30 fps - Interlaced	126 Mbps
SDTV 4x3	704 x 480	8 bits	4:2:2	30 fps - Interlaced	162 Mbps
SDTV 4x3	704 x 480	8 bits	4:1:1	30 fps - Interlaced	122 Mbps
SDTV 4x3	704 x 480	10 bits	4:2:2	30 fps - Interlaced	203 Mbps
HDTV	1280 x 720	10 bits	4:2:2	60 fps - Progressive	1.1 Gbps
HDTV	1920 x 1080	10 bits	4:2:2	30 fps - Interlaced	1.24 Gbps
HDTV	1920 x 1080	10 bits	4:2:2	60 fps - Progressive	2.5 Gbps

Figure 24 - Data Rate Comparison Chart

DTV component formats and data rates is provided in Figure 24. The chart compares several of the quantizing methods to illustrate the wide ranging data rates that result from each.

It should be noted that all of the data rates included in the table above do not include any video synchronization, control, the vertical blanking interval or other information normally associated with a video signal.

Although the current NTSC video standard specifies 525 horizontal lines, 39 of them are not used for picture information at all. This area, normally referred to as the Vertical Blanking Interval, is reserved for such things as test signals, closed captioning and other data information.

Hence, the data rates may appear to be somewhat smaller than expected. For example, SMPTE 259M, which specifies the serial digital interface standards, designates a 270 Mbps data rate for 4:2:2 component video with 10 bit quantizing (commonly referred to as the "D1 standard" or ITU-R601) rather than the 210 Mbps rate as stated in the chart.

The same holds true for the HDTV standards, such as those that specify 1125 horizontal scanning lines but the actual picture information resides in only 1080 of them.

Changes in the ITU-R601 standard are also reflected in SMPTE 259M to include the 16x9 wide screen formats. Accordingly, a 360 Mbps data rate has been specified for 16:9 SDTV video. Simply put, 270 Mbps refers to a 4:3 aspect ratio while 360 Mbps implies 16:9 video with ITU-R601 Part A specifying the former and Part B the later.

Video Compression and Standards

Compression Standards

A number of video compression standards are in use today that were designed for various and specific purposes. The formats range in use from compressing individual still photos to moving pictures and video conferencing. Updated versions of these formats are constantly underway and some of the standards have even been modified over time to perform functions that were not part of their original intent.

The two primary standards setting groups of interest to the videographer are the Joint Photographic Experts Group (JPEG) and the Moving Picture Experts Group (MPEG).

The JPEG standard was originally designed to compress still images, but several variations of JPEG have been designed in the last decade to work on moving images. Motion JPEG or M-JPEG is one of many variants of the original that have been included in several non-linear editing and video file storage systems. However, no official M-JPEG standard exists.

The MPEG group began its work in 1988 and has specified several standards which they have numbered as MPEG-1, MPEG-2, etc. MPEG-1 is now used primarily for Compact Disk (CD) video applications while MPEG-2 is the main compression engine used in most quality video applications. Although early adopters of MPEG used version 1 for professional video distribution, most have switched in favor of the greatly improved MPEG-2 series.

In 1994 development on MPEG-3 became redundant because its HDTV subject matter was folded into the MPEG-2 standard. Consequently a completed MPEG-3 standard does not exist. MPEG-4 is intended for use in video conferencing applications.

What is Compression?

All compression systems reduce the size of signals by eliminating or reducing redundant and unnecessary information that take up valuable bandwidth or storage capacity. As we will see, sometimes these reductions are transparent and do not impair signal quality while other times they cause all sorts of problems.

The distinction between each of the compression methods discussed herein generally lies in the approach taken by its creators and the levels of complexity used in its design. The commonality of all compression schemes is that they attempt to reduce the size of video (or audio) signals while sometimes sacrificing varying degrees of fidelity from the original.

The terms lossy and lossless compression methods

are used to distinguish between the perceptibility of signal degradation in the final product.

An example of lossless compression is when computer files are compressed onto a disk without the loss of any information. In computer data the loss of a single digit could yield catastrophic consequences. Hence, any compression techniques used for such applications merely eliminate unused data bits inherent in all computer generated files.

In video, relatively large portions of the signal are used exclusively to convey timing, synchronization and blanking pulses that do not include any picture information at all. In fact, only 78 percent of the information contained in an analog video signal is devoted to carrying picture information. Thus, a video signal could be reduced by nearly a quarter of its original size without sacrificing any visual picture information.

Unlike lossless compression, however, lossy methods reduce the amount of information by also discarding some of the picture data. This results in varying degrees of picture degradation; that is directly related to the amount and type of data which is removed. Thus, it follows that greater reductions in picture information result in poorer picture quality.

In lossy compression techniques artifacts (distortions in the visual picture) are produced when this data is discarded. These picture distortions may be categorized into three basic groups called contouring, pixellation and aliasing.

Contouring is when adjacent pixel information is incorrectly coded in a similar manner, even though they may have been very different in the original image. Compressed images that appear to have a blocky structure and do not conform to the subject image are said to have been pixellized or suffer from pixellation. The jagged edges or stairstep pattern seen on smooth images is called aliasing. Pixellation and aliasing are caused by course or insufficient sampling and quantizing methods.

Compression Ratios

The level of reduction in the size of a file that is achieved through the use of a specific compression method is gauged by its compression ratio. The compression ratio is used to compare the size of a video file before and after it has been compressed.

So, for example, a video file that may have originally consisted of 100 MB of data that is compressed down to only 25 MB would yield a ratio of 4:1. While most of the time whole integers are used in representing compression ratios, decimal fractions are sometimes also used.

The format developed by Sony for Digital Betacam, for example, compresses video by a factor of 2.3:1 Hence, a video file consisting of 4:2:2 sampled video would normally require 95 GB of storage capacity. The same video stored on Digital Betacam would occupy only 41 GB.

Compression ratios can also be used to specify the level of reduction in a bit stream. As again, in the case of Digital Betacam, its 210 Mbps video source is reduced to only 91 Mbps.

The JPEG Standard

JPEG is considered an intra-frame or spatial method of compression, developed originally for use with still images, where each frame is compressed individually and without relation to any other.

JPEG is, by nature, a lossless compression scheme that reduces picture information by exploiting the limitations of the human eye and removing redundant information whose absence is not perceptible to the viewer. This is the key element in JPEG compression engines.

Most of this data reduction comes in the form of minimizing the amount of information used to describe color information. This may be done successfully because our eyes are not able to process color information as acutely as changes in luminance. Consequently, the removal of the extra color information will not result in any appreciable loss in picture quality if those reductions are performed within reasonable limits.

Obviously there comes a point where too much information is removed (e.g., too much compression). At this point the picture begins to show signs of noticeable degradation. This generally comes in the form of a blocky picture that lacks details and color information that misrepresents the original image. As compression is increased beyond reasonable limits the image may become unrecognizable.

Further reductions in signal size may be realized by reducing the amount of picture information of the luminance portion of the image. However the degree to which that information is removed will impact the image more forcefully than that of the color.

JPEG systems also utilize Discrete Cosine Transfer or DCT compression techniques, that further reduce picture information. DCT is a complex formula of bit reduction that analyzes

Chart B

Picture Quality	Compression Ratios
Lossless	2:1
Visually Identical to Original	11:1
Good Quality	22:1
"Useful" Image	64:1
Recognizable Image	160:1

Courtesy of Sony.

pixel blocks with regard to their amplitude and frequency characteristics to yield high compression ratios.

The amount of lossiness can also be impacted by reducing the accuracy of the sampling method used to capture this information. However, regardless of which methods are used, the degree of compression realized is directly related to image quality. Hence, a trade-off of image quality for signal size is achieved.

Chart B above compares how higher compression ratios impact picture quality.

In Figure 25, the easily recognizable photograph of a cooked turkey is JPEG compressed to a ratio of about 140:1. The resulting image is barely intelligible with severe blocking and contouring effects present. Without the original to compare the image with, it might be difficult for most to determine what the subject in the photograph was.

Another form of JPEG encoding used in video applications is called Wavelet coding. Wavelet is a non-DCT coding scheme that utilizes complex mathematical algorithms (formulas) to compress images.

Wavelet technology has been used in some video applications but its inherent inability to produce quality images at higher compression ratios

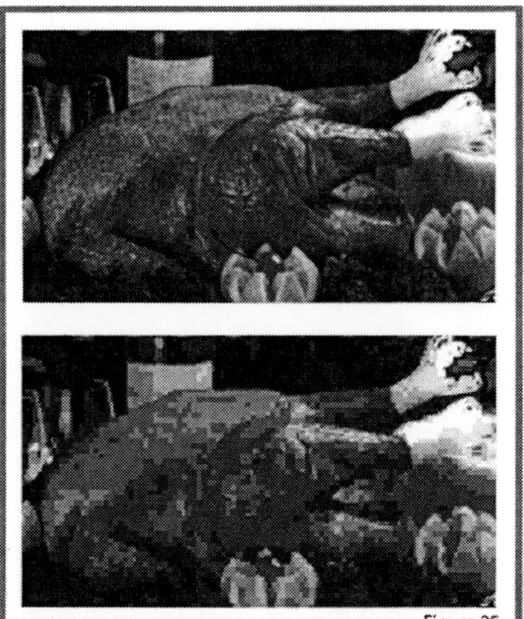
Figure 25

Effect of High JPEG Compression Ratios

has somewhat limited its widespread use.

Motion JPEG or M-JPEG

Although originally developed for use with still images, JPEG has also been used in server technologies and editing systems to compress video and audio. Using JPEG for such purposes is possible because the coding scheme compresses each image individually with no relation to other frames . Since video is merely a series of still images, this concept remains consistent with its original design.

Over time, variations of the JPEG format have

been created by a number of vendors for editing and storing moving pictures that make these processes more efficient where video applications are concerned. ASC, Avid Technology, and Tektronix are just some of the many hardware makers that use these variations to power their disk-based systems and editors.

The term Motion JPEG or M-JPEG is often used to describe compression formats that have been optimized for use in storing and editing video. However, no single or official M-JPEG "standard" actually exists. Rather, each coding scheme has its own proprietary feature, making them all unique onto themselves. Consequently, none of these systems are compatible between vendors.

The MPEG Video Standard

Since its inception in 1988, the Motion Pictures Experts Group has issued several revisions of the MPEG standard with different end uses in mind. MPEG-1 was originally intended for use in compressing audio and video for CD-ROM applications. With compression data rates of up to 1.5 Mbps, MPEG-1 video is considered to be VHS-like quality and not suitable for broadcast applications.

Over the years several satellite distribution equipment manufacturers have attempted to improve MPEG-1 quality by introducing proprietary systems that have sometimes been referred to as MPEG-1+ or MPEG-1++ based compression schemes. These systems showed a vast improvement over the original MPEG-1 standard but remained inferior in quality to the next generation of MPEG-2 products.

MPEG-2 debuted in 1994 and was designed to

process "broadcast-quality" television signals. Although the MPEG-2 standard includes both audio and video compression schemes, only the video portion was selected for use in digital television (DTV) applications by the FCC for digital transmissions. (Dolby's AC-3, also known as Dolby Digital, was selected for use as the DTV audio compression engine.)

The inclusion of high definition television (HDTV) into the MPEG-2 standard late in its developmental stages allowed for the committee to discontinue work on MPEG-3, which had originally been earmarked for the new high-quality and widescreen video medium.

MPEG-4, the compression technology designed for very low bit rate video conferencing.

How MPEG Works

MPEG video coding is considered an inter-frame or temporal compression scheme. Unlike JPEG systems—where each frame is analyzed and compressed individually—inter-frame compression systems compare adjacent frames in order to determine how they differ from one another over time. These changes are then used to predict and build new frames further down the line.

This, along with many of the same techniques used in JPEG compression that exploit the limitations of human vision and utilize DCT coding, is combined to provide a powerful standard for reducing file sizes. Thus, the amount of data that must be stored and distributed is greatly decreased, resulting in higher compression ratios than would otherwise be possible in JPEG type coding.

MPEG-2 is the second variant of the MPEG standard that was developed by the Moving Picture Experts Group. MPEG coding techniques utilize three components called the "I," "P" and "B" frames.

The I frames are similar to JPEG compressed images that are "intra-frame" compressed and which contain information about only a single frame of video. P frames are predictive frames that take information common among adjacent frames into account. This is used to predict motion by comparing it to the closest preceding I frame or P frame. B frames are "bi-directional" and also provide inter-frame compression. The B frames derive data from the preceding and subsequent I and P frames. B frames encode the current frame, based on the differences between the current, previous, and the next frame.

By restricting the level of information saved in B and P Frames to only the changes between them and the original I Frame, which the comparisons were based on, the amount of data in these frames is lessened considerably. Comparing this to JPEG video, where all of the images in the sequence are I frames, it is easy seen how MPEG can provide far more compression ratios for comparable or better video quality.

An MPEG video sequence of frames is collected into a Group of Pictures (GOP) consisting of all three types of frames. A typical sequence might look like that shown in Figure 26.

The key element that MPEG systems rely on to derive their compression power is motion estimation. The amount of compression offered by the intra-frame coding found in an I frame pales in comparison to that achieved by the motion

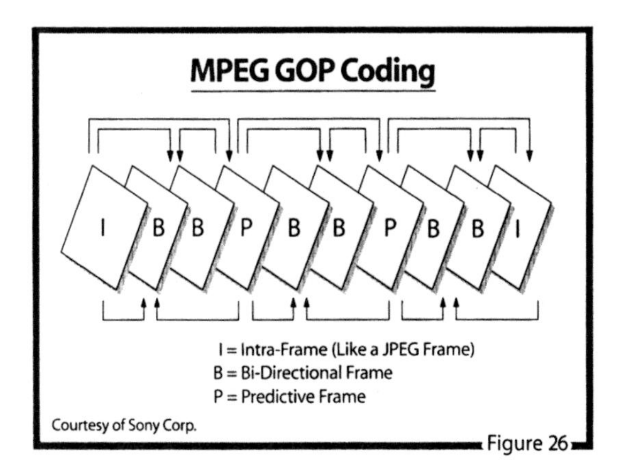

Figure 26

MPEG Group of Pictures

estimation capabilities that result from the additional use of B, and P frames.

An example of how motion estimation works can be seen in Figure 27, where a series of four still images are laid out in sequence. Proceeding from left to right, an empty blue image changes when an arrow enters into left side of the frame and finally is seen to be existing the picture on the fourth.

Using the first image as a reference, then analyzing the next two frames, anyone viewing the sequence could logically predict that the fourth would show the arrow exiting the picture. This is called motion estimation.

In this example, the first frame could be considered as the I Frame, with frames two and three being B Frames and the final image as the P Frame. As the reference image, it was necessary to evaluate the entire I Frame. In the B Frames information gathered looking forward and backwards became the basis for the conclusion that

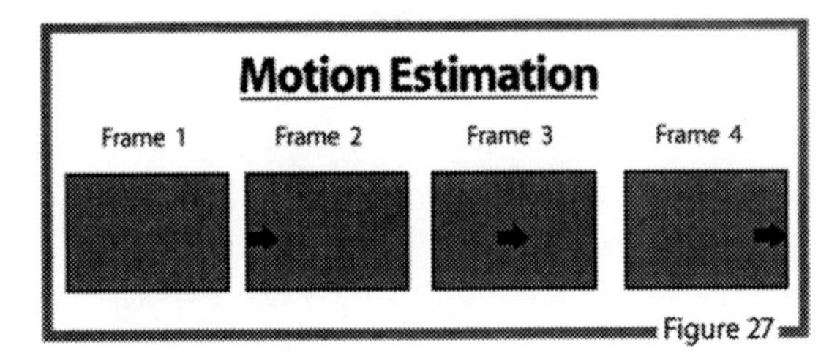

Predicting Motion

the last frame would contain the blue background from the I Frame with the same arrow contained in the B Frames, but merely at a different location on the screen.

The unique part of motion estimation is that only a small amount of information is needed in the B and P Frames to describe what is occurring. Whereas in the I Frame the entire image had to be analyzed.

Remembering, that I Frames are merely JPEG compressed images, it becomes clear that MPEG coded video could be compressed to a higher degree than when using the intra-frame method.

Profiles and Levels

The MPEG standard was written to include several subsets to meet a wide range of applications. These subsets have been defined using profiles and levels to distinguish the technical characteristics and scope of each. Profiles are used to define limits on the coding syntax, while levels provide guidelines on sampling rates, frame dimensions and coding bitrates. Thus, a decoder's ability to handle a particular bitstream has been defined

LEVELS		PROFILES						
		Spatial Resolution	Simple 4:2:0 IP Non-Scalable	Main 4:2:0 IPB Non-Scalable	4:2:2 Profile 4:2:2 IPB	SNR 4:2:0 IPB SNR Scalable	Spatial 4:2:0 IPB Spatially Scalable	High 4:2:2 IPB Spatially Scalable
HIGH		Enhanced		1920x1152 60@80Mbps				1920x1152 60@100Mbps
		Lower						960x576 30@25Mbps
HIGH -1440		Enhanced		1440x1152 60@60Mbps			1440x1152 60@60Mbps	1440x1152 60@80Mbps
		Lower					720x576 30@15Mbps	720x576 30@20Mbps
MAIN		Enhanced	720x576 30@15Mbps	720x576 30@15Mbps	720x608 30@50Mbps	720x576 30@15Mbps		720x576 30@15Mbps
		Lower						352x288 30@2Mbps
LOW		Enhanced		352x288 30@4Mbps		352x288 30@4Mbps		
		Lower						

Figure 28

MPEG Profiles and Levels

using profiles and levels.

Figure 28 shows that there are six MPEG profiles. These profiles define the colorspace resolution and scalability of the bitstream. Under the MPEG guidelines, decoders and encoders need not be comparably matched with each other in their technical performance. In other words, an MPEG bitstream created by a very high-quality encoder may be read using an inexpensive or low-quality decoder.

Scalability can be defined as the ability of a decoder to decode a bitstream that produces a reconstructed sequence of equal or lesser quality to the original. This would be comparable to taking an HDTV video signal and down converting it to NTSC. In this example, scalability refers to the fact that the quality of the signal has been reduced (in both line number and aspect ratios) but remains viewable in the low resolution format.

Four levels were originally defined by MPEG

but later revisions established sublevels of spatial resolution to include enhanced and lower points. The levels define the maximum and minimum image resolution, luminance (Y) samples per second, the number of video and audio layers supported for scalable profiles, and the maximum bit rate per profile.

Levels also confine the syntax parameters. For example, Main Level at Mail Profile (also written as ML@MP) provides for a maximum bit rate of 15 Mbps. By contrast HL@HP (High Level at High Profile) permits data rates of up to 100 Mbps.

More and more equipment manufacturers are using the L@P (a Level at some Profile) designations to denote the level of performance that a specific piece of equipment has been designed to meet. So, for example, a unit stated to be compliant with HL@MP would be of superior quality to one labeled ML@MP.

Another commonly used L@P is the "4:2:2 Profile @ Main Level" or 4:2:2P@ML. This designation was established in 1996 to denote a higher quality standard above ML@MP. This new designation extended ML@MP from 15 to 50 Mbps and allows for the inclusion of both 4:2:0 and 4:2:2 sampling.

JPEG vs. MPEG

The unique approaches used in the two formats to compress image information directly effects each in their ability to perform certain tasks with varying degrees of acceptability. These differences often dictate which compression scheme may be more appropriate for a given job.

One major difference between JPEG and MPEG, for example, is in their ability to compress video files. JPEG can typically achieve 10:1 to 20:1 compression ratios without any appreciable loss in quality or the inclusion of unacceptable numbers of visual artifacts. Beyond this the pixels become blocky. MPEG, on the other hand, is capable of achieving typical compression ratios of 25:1 or better, making it a superior digital scheme when file reduction is of paramount concern.

However, editing an MPEG sequence becomes complicated because, unlike JPEG where each frame can stand on its own, MPEG frames rely on adjacent pictures. If, for instance, the edit point on an MPEG stream were taken between two B frames, the corresponding I and P Frame information would be lost, making the sequence unusable. Thus, JPEG-compressed video is seen to be much more conducive to editing video than MPEG.

This might lead you to believe that editing MPEG video is simply not possible. However, with some coding modifications, an MPEG stream can be made to allow for limited editing functions. By shortening the length of GOPs and by increasing the number of I Frames, an MPEG bitstream may be edited, but only at the I Frame junctions.

This approach mimics JPEG compression but reduces some of the efficiencies gained by the use of MPEG. It also makes editing more complex and does not allow for many of the video effects that videographers have come to expect, such as fades, crawls and wipes.

Due to the fact that JPEG compressed stills do not rely on the information contained in adjacent frames, such video can be easily edited with absolute frame accuracy. A typical video editing session consists of numerous cuts at specific frames that are then mixed with other footage and assembled into a final product.

Since JPEG information is stored on a frame-by-frame basis, the editing process is not hampered by compression—as picture frames may be regrouped in any order without interaction. This has contributed to its widespread acceptance and success in such applications.

But the limitations imposed by characteristics favorable to editing also translate into relatively low compression ratios and higher storage costs. And, when used at high compression rates, its video quality is poor in comparison to that found in MPEG systems.

In recent years a wide variety of JPEG-based compression techniques have been developed by a number of equipment manufacturers for use in both nonlinear editing and disk-based storage systems. JPEG has, in fact, outpaced MPEG to become the dominant compression standard used in most of these systems today. This is due to the limited editing capabilities of MPEG.

MPEG-based systems on the market today are generally aimed at digital storage/playback needs used for on-air applications—such as spot insertion, multi-channel broadcasting, program playback, archiving, network delay and Near Video on Demand (NVOD). These systems typically offer "cuts-only" editing and the "splicing" of program material for delivery to air in a Master Control type of environment.

But, unlike JPEG-based systems such as

nonlinear editing stations, MPEG equipment is not capable of performing complex editing functions unless the program material is reprocessed by external methods. This would include decoding the program material back to analog, creating the effect with component or composite equipment and then re-encoding it back to MPEG-2. This process is identical to the one used in edit suites that utilize videotape machines in conjunction with outboard switchers and effects equipment.

Another important limitation in MPEG systems is the matter of latency or delay caused by the buffering of video frames. Unlike JPEG systems, which compress on a frame-by-frame basis, MPEG encoders must look ahead at future frames in order for them to code the B and P Frames. This requires the decoder to store entire fields which, in turn, cause the same type of delay found in frame synchronizers commonly used in many video applications.

In 1996 the FCC chose standards developed by the Advanced Television Systems Committee (ATSC) for DTV. The ATSC standard includes the MPEG-2 system for compressing video in the 19.39 Mbps raw bit stream encompassed by a 6 Mhz-wide TV channel. But, while MPEG-2 is now the official compression system for the transmission of DTV, JPEG has maintained its commanding lead in nonlinear editing and disk-based storage systems.

There are some people who firmly believe that operating in a full MPEG environment offers broadcasters many benefits. Unlike the many M-JPEG standards, MPEG-2 is independent of any one manufacturer and is scaleable across applications. It was designed to offer one of the highest data compression ratios and best image quality while maintaining a more cost-efficient storage capability. And, because it was selected as the transmission standard for DTV, it is more effective in a shared media environment.

Figure 29 (below) shows the common advantages and disadvantages of JPEG and MPEG systems with regard to editing and file storage:

JPEG & MJPEG		MPEG	
Advantages	**Disadvantages**	**Advantages**	**Disadvantages**
Simple to edit Complex editing function such as fades, wipes & other effects	Low compression ratios Higher capacity disk space needed	High compression ratios Low capacity disk space needed	Editing is difficult "Cuts-Only" and "splicing" editing capabilities only
Large selection of equipment available	Lower video quality at high compression ratios	Higher video quality at high compression ratios	Relatively small selection of available equipment
	Non-Uniform standardization of Motion-JPEG	Universal standardization of Motion-JPEG	

Figure 29

__Joe Fedele__ is technical consultant, writer, lecturer and the owner of the Fedele Group of companies. The Fedele Group includes Fedele and Associates, a technical consulting and broadcast systems integration firm, A2D Solutions, a discount equipment supplier for the video and broadcast production industries, and Close-Up, an Internet News Magazine for broadcast professionals.

Prior to building the group, Fedele held several senior level engineering management positions at two major television networks in New York and Miami. As Managing Director of Network Engineering for Telemundo in Miami he was instrumental in rebuilding the nation's second largest Spanish language television network. While in New York City Mr. Fedele spent nearly 10 years at CBS television, working the last 5 years as

Chief Engineer for WCBS-TV, the flagship station of the CBS television broadcast group.

With a degree in electronics and over twenty five years experience in radio and television broadcast engineering Mr. Fedele continues to further expand the Fedele Group of companies to meet the needs of a digital future.

Digital Videotape Formats

by John Rice

There was a time, not all that long ago, when the idea of using digital videotape meant the highest possible quality, and most often a high price tag. But as digital technology expands and excels, there are now a myriad choices that fall under the banner of "digital." And we are only talking about videotape here, let alone the servers, hard drives and other "tapeless" devices that are being used to record professional and broadcast signals for acquistion, postproduction and distribution.

Digital videotape, once the domain of the high-end, high-budget production, has now become the mainstream with over 15 formats or versions of formats currently available. But in that selection process there are an ever increasing variety of applications and cost-points that make different formats more viable for different uses.

In the following list and chart, we will attempt to identify the primary formats available on the market today and to point out the differences in recording technique, and application.

To say that there is a leading digital videotape format in today's production and postproduction market is virtually impossible. Some formats are succeeding on their technical strength and the marketing muscle of their makers. Others, while having good arguments for their benefits, have been caught at higher pricing levels than newer competitors. And it is safe to say that there are more iterations on the horizon as manufacturers can adapt formats with processors, tape pitch, speed and various sampling rates to make their products more efficient, and more cost effective.

There is no simple decision on what digital format is best. For some, quality is, and will always be the primary consideration. But quality does not in and of itself make for a successful format. (It happened in consumer video with Betamax vs.VHS, and in professional analog, and it will happen again in digital videotape formats.)

Price considerations must also be taken into account. And price goes to more than the cost of purchasing or renting a given deck. Tape cost must be factored in. And maintenance will impact the long-term cost of any new equipment purchase.

To try to address the best format for any given use, the first step should be to identify the application strength of the product. If the primary goal is to shoot in digital, then there are formats that provide quality and cost benefits, as well as weight and operational considerations that make them strong contenters to take into the field. Some of these also have viable applications in post-production.

But other formats shine brighter in post-production. They may be too big (in equipment weight or tape size) to make them reasonable for field work, but they may best serve in a linear postproduction environment. Some others may best serve specific types of post-production work, such as graphics and film transfer, where quality is arguably the primary concern.

Another issue is one of compatibility and generational impact on the image. At the high end, uncompressed formats promise the highest quality over multiple passes in an edit or processing environment. When creating graphics, for example, a multigenerational uncompressed format may be the only choice. But more and more of the compressed formats are finding ways of maintaining high quality (if not quite as high as uncompressed) by maintaining the digital information as data during the passes.

That would eliminate concerns over concatination (the issue of uncompressing and recompressing a signal with each editorial pass). Such a scenario gives strength to "closed" systems where all equipment operates in the same compression mode. But again, that may be unrealistic for any facility or operation that needs to integrate newer gear into an existing system.

Again, the choices are many, and there can be good and valid arguments for selecting almost any format included here.

Here we've broken down the formats into two fundamental categories: Standard definition (525/625 lines of resolution) and high definition (720 lines and above). Even with this break down, be careful. Many of the standard definition formats are capable of widescreen recording (16:9 aspect ratio) although the signal remains in the realm of current NTSC and PAL signals. To be honest, any format can record a 16:9 aspect ratio if the wide image is anamorphically squeezed.

High definition formats will record higher resolution images. Most of the initial offerings operate using 1080 lines interlaced. But these formats and their VTRs are already promising to record the broad range of high definition signals; including 720 progressive, 480 progressive (arguably not high definition) and even 1080 progressive. As these decks emerge, some will be capable of recording multiple formats while others will most likely be offered in different models.

One thing is for sure. We aren't done yet. The standardization process has already confirmed eight different digital videotape formats (from D1 to D9, skipping D4). And there are more entering or in the midst of the formal standardization review. Some of the formats listed will likely fade as they are usurped by better and/or cheaper variations. And there is a good chance the new formats will emerge sooner than later.

If we could tell you which would slip away and what is yet to come, we would. But we can't. The choice, I'm afraid to tell you, is yours.

Standard Definition Formats

D-1

The first digital videotape format to come to the broadcast and video market was D-1, developed by Sony Corp. in 1986. At the time, it offered the first capabilities for multi-generational editing without degradation associated with analog tape passes. The D-1 format uses 19 mm (or æ-inch) metal particle videocassette tapes with a maximum recording time of 94 minutes.

The format records component video signals with a resolution of approximately 460 lines of horizontal resolution. The advantage of component recording is that chrominance and luminance signals remain separate. In this manner, the signals maintain their maximum bandwidth and thereby maintain a higher quality.

Unlike future digital formats, D-1 does not compress the video signal. Although this maintains the highest quality, it also impacts the cost of machinery and tape stock. Early testing of D-1 offered that nearly 100 passes (playback and re-recording of an image) could be accomplished before seeing any noticable difference or degradation in the signal.

The initial, and still probably the most widely used application, for D-1 is in graphic production where multiple recording passes for layering and effects are required. The introduction of such capabilities opened up new levels of creative and technical capabilities for such work.

But D-1 has always been limited in its application, primarily due to the high cost of equipment and tape stock. More recent format introductions have proven to be more cost-effective for postproduction and graphics applications, although D-1 decks continue to be sold and used.

D-2

Shortly after the introduction of D-1, Ampex Corp. unveiled a composite digital format, called D-2. Composite recording, where chrominance and luminance information are combined, allowed for lower cost of decks in the format. However, the composite process does not maintain image quality at the level of component recording.

The D-2 format was quickly adopted by Sony, which began marketing its own decks under a licensing agreement with Ampex. D-2 also uses

19mm (or ¾-inch) metal particle videotape cassettes but they are not compatible with D-1.

D-2 recording provides a resolution of approximately 450 (horizontal) lines. Maximum recording time on a cassette is 208 minutes. D-2 decks were used to a great extent as a replacement for 1-inch open reel analog decks for postproduction recording.

Although the composite signal does not allow for the depth of generational passes as D-1 will, this format was more broadly adopted in postproduction because of its digital quality. A key feature for the format and its decks is "pre-read," allowing for the signal to be read from the tape, passed through a switcher or edit control system and recorded back on the identical tape. What minimal degradation that might be introduced by multiple passes is still well within generally acceptable standards.

D-2 also found applications in program playback, particularly when configured into robotic cart systems.

D-3

A comparable, but incompatible format to D-2 was developed by Matsushita in 1991 and was standardized by SMPTE as the D-3 format. Using composite digital signals and metal particle tape as well, D-3 also provides horizontal resolution of around 450 lines. Matsushita, which is marketed in the U.S. under the Panasonic brand, was a strong manufacturer of ½-inch tape formats, including consumer VHS. This in no small part contributed to D-3's use of ½-inch videotape cassettes. The format is capable of recording at lengths of up to 245 minutes on a single tape.

Although D-3 was worthy competition for D-2 in edit configurations (except, perhaps, in the Hollywood postproduction community), the strength of the format came from the ½-inch tape, which allowed for a broader line of equipment—including the first digital videocassette camcorder.

Although D-3 did not make its mark on the Betacam SP camcorder market like some had expected, it did move Panasonic/Matsushita into a much stronger market position with broadcasters and production facilities. That would prove to be very important as subsequent digital formats would come to the marketplace.

D-4

There is no SMPTE D-4 format. The explanation most often offered is that the Japanese word for "death" is very similar to "D4."

D-5

In 1993, Panasonic made a strong entry into the high-end world of video recorders with the introduction of the D-5 format, an uncompressed, component (10-bit) digital videotape format using 4:2:2 8-bit sampling. Initially offered as a studio format to compete with D-1, D-5 provided strong competition to Sony's high-end, uncompressed format and provided the additional benefit of playback and record compatibility with D-3. Using ½-inch metal particle tape, it can record up to 124 minutes on a single cassette.

D-5 was initially accepted as a replacement for D-1 because of lower cost. It has taken a reasonable hold in the high-end postproduction, graphics and film transfer markets. The compatibility with D-3 may have been responsible for some of its early strength, but Panasonic also let it be known early on that D-5 would contain a direct migration path to high definition recording. (See HD D5).

D-5 was introduced around the same time as Digital Betacam, setting off fierce positioning over the issue of compression. Targeted for high-end film transfer, graphics and compositing work, D-5 demonstrated its strength in the post-production environment.

D-6

Both Philips and Toshiba introduced the D-6 digital format several years ago, but hasn't found many takers. The format uses a 19mm helical-scan cassette tape to record uncompressed high definition television material at 1.88 BGps (1.2 Gbps). D-6 accepts both the European 1250/50 interlaced format and the Japanese 260M version of the 1125/60 interlaced format that uses 1035 active lines. It does not accept the ITU format of 1080 active lines. Although many people like the idea of uncompressed HDTV recording, only a few VTRs actually exist because they are extremely expensive to own and operate (the machine's 32 heads are said to be warranted for only six months).

DVCPRO (D-7)

With the development of the small sized, digital video (DV or DVC) format for consumer use, manufacturers looked to expand the fundamentals

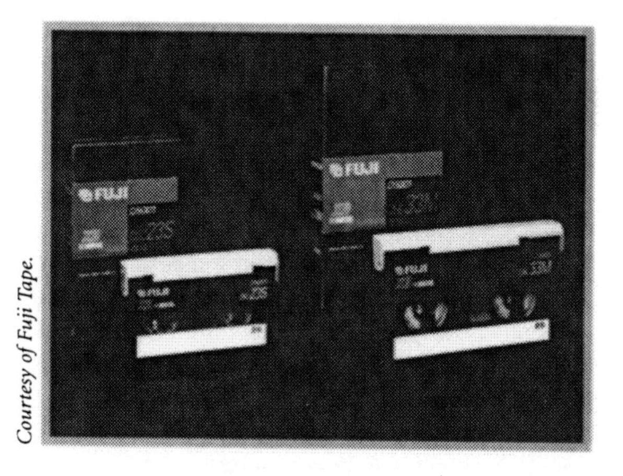
Courtesy of Fuji Tape.

of the format for professional and broadcast applications. Matsushita/Panasonic's answer became DVCPRO, which was standardized by SMPTE as D-7.

Using the same sampling rate and compression as DV, DVCPRO operates with 4:1:1 quantization and a compression ratio of 5:1 at 25 Megabytes per second (Mpbs). It is important to note that DV, DVCPRO and Sony's DVCAM all record using the same fundamental quantization and compression scheme. Differences in the format are limited to tape speed (and therefore recording time) and features such as time code—as well as equipment configurations based on the markets which are using the formats.

DVCPRO tape speed runs at twice the speed of DV tape, allowing for recording of control track and time code that is necessary for professional applications. DVCPRO is also differentiated from DV and DVCAM in its use of metal particle tape (as opposed to metal evaporated for the other formats). Metal Particle is a more robust formulation that reduces drop-outs often associated with multiple passes of a piece of tape—for example in editing.

The DVCPRO cassette is a 6mm tape, with cassette sizes up to 123 minutes. DVCPRO decks can playback all DV-based formats (DV, DVCAM, etc.).

All three DV-based formats record component digital signals and provide horizontal resolution of just under 500 lines, putting them in a league with D-1, D-2, and D-3 for quality, while they're superior to analog formats.

Another key feature of the DVCPRO format is 4x playback. This is being implemented for input into computer-based non-linear systems utilyzing DVCPRO cards for direct input of data. Although the format does offer a "laptop" cut-only linear edit system, the primary applications of DVCPRO have been for news and acquisition.

DVCPRO 50

The second generation of the DVCPRO family answered many concerns voiced over the first manifestation. DVCPRO, the original, sampled at 4:1:1, raising concerns over applications such as chroma key. By modifying the format for 4:2:2 sampling at a data rate of 50 Mbps, chroma resolution is enhanced and the format performs on a level comparable to other 4:2:2 formats, such as JVC's Digital-S (D-9).

Faster tape speed and a lower compression ratio (3.3:1 compared to DVCPRO's 5:1) account for better image quality. But the speed also reduces recording lengths for cassettes. Most decks, camcorders and cameras can record both DVCPRO50 and DVCPRO signals.

Although DVCPRO has found its niche in acquistion and news, DVCPRO 50 is much better positioned as an all-around format including post-production applications. The format's related equipment also allows for 16:9 as well as 4:3 aspect ratio recordings.

The DVCPRO50 format can also be configured for progressive recording, with a horizontal resolution of 700 lines in 16:9 format.

DVCAM

Sony's professional adaptation of the consumer DV format is named DVCAM. It operates at a higher tape speed than DV, but again uses the same component digital signal and sampling rate (4:1:1 in NTSC, 4:2:0 for PAL). DVCAM uses Metal Evaporated (ME) tape comparable to DV, and at a lesser cost than Metal Particle (MP). DVCAM tape moves at a higher speed than DV, but slower than DVCPRO.

Product configurations for DVCAM equipment include emphasis on "iLink" (IEEE-1394) for integration into computer-based edit systems. With higher-end digital formats from Sony (Digital Betacam, Betacam SX, etc.), the positioning of DVCAM in the marketplace is oriented much more toward mid-range corporate and small broadcast production.

Products include a widescreen camcorder and studio VTR. Decks are also capable of playing back all DV formats including DVCPRO. Expanded offerings of DVCAM products now include low-cost camcorders (under $4,000) and VTRs designed specifically for non linear applications.

DCT

The offering from Ampex into the high-end digital video arena is DCT, which stands for Digital Component Technology (not discrete cosine transfer as used in the Digital Betacam format). DCT technology is targeted almost exclusively to post-production and film transfer applications.

Ampex DCT records compressed (2:1) digital component signals and boasts error correction as opposed to other formats error concealment processes. Decks are switchable from 525 to 625 and can record more than three hours on a single, 19mm (3/4-inch) tape.

DCT may be more in line with data recording machines (a current strength of Ampex's offerings) than in comparison with digital videotape decks. Processes of error correction put it more in this realm, although the products do offer error concealment as well. Interestingly, Ampex has never strongly referred to its machines as VTRs, preferring to call them "tape transports." It may be more semantic than technical, but it is an indication of the company's position on the gear.

Digital Betacam

Introduced by Sony in 1993, Digital Betacam is the digital successor to the popular Betacam SP line. Using cassettes that resemble Betacam SP, Digital Betacam offers backwards compatibility—thus allowing Betacam SP tapes to be played back, but not recorded on Digital Betacam decks.

The initial product offerings for Digital Betacam looked to replace Betacam SP in acquisition and post-production environments. More recent

Courtesy of Quantegy Corporation.

products have highlighted the format's capabilities to record widescreen 16:9 imagery for digital television (DTV) and to emulate popular film stocks.

One strength of the Digital Betacam format has been the familiarity of the marketplace with Betacam SP. However, concerns over cost of the digital manifestation led to development of other formats from Sony, including Betacam SX.

Although Digital Betacam uses component digital signals, it compresses the digital signal by a factor of 2:1, using discrete cosine transfer (DCT). The format records component digital at a sampling rate of 4:2:2, 8- or 10-bit..

One advantage of DCT over other compression systems is that each frame is compressed individually (intra-frame), allowing for cleaner and more precise decompression—especially in editing scenarios. Other compression schemes that are inter-frame actually compress data from a number of frames simultaneously. This hampers efforts to accomplish frame-accurate editing without decompressing and recompressing with each edit pass.

Digital Betacam also uses metal particle tape and provides horizontal resolution of just under 500 lines. Many Digital Betacam decks are backwards compatible, allowing analog Betacam and Betacam SP tapes to be played.

Betacam SX

Apparently in reaction to limited acceptance of Digital Betacam within the Betacam SP community, Sony offered Betacam SX beginning in 1996. SX uses MPEG-2 compression at a compression ratio of 10:1, and sampling at 4:2:2.

Initial offering of the Betacam SX line were oriented toward recording and playback, especially for broadcast, but later equipment announcements broadened the market for acquisition (news and production) and even a field edit configuration. Products have also been offered at lower cost levels, more in line with the company's DVCAM products.

However, MPEG-2 compression, requires all production and post-production systems to operate within an MPEG-2 environment in order to maintain image quality.

D-8

The SMPTE committee members responsible for naming formats felt that, to avoid confusion, no format would be given the "D-8" name. This is due to the fact that it was too close to Tascam's "DA-88" audio tape format, which is used extensively for archiving and transporting audio and video data.

Digital-S (D-9)

Digital-S is JVC's first offering in the digital videotape arena, which has been standardized by SMPTE as the D-9 format. Recording component digital signals and using 1/2-inch tape similar to S-VHS, the format uses 4:2:2 sampling, leading to image quality comparable to Digital Betacam and judged by many to be superior to DV-based formats. Horizontal resolution is in line with the DV formats and Digital Betacam and Betacam SX at just under 500 lines.

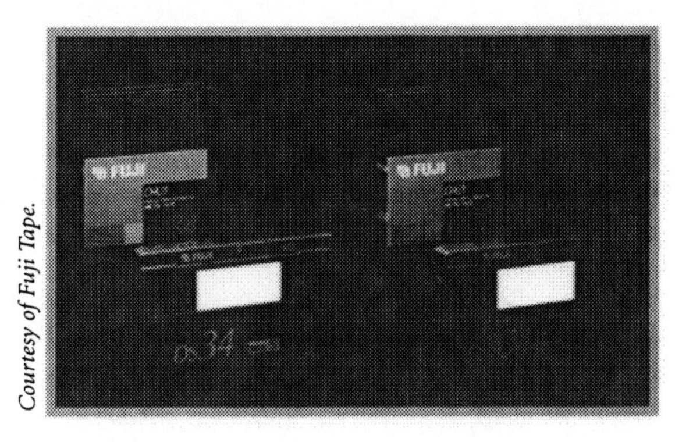

Courtesy of Fuji Tape.

Digital-S also provides pre-read, a unique feature in digital formats. Pre-read allows for a single deck to playback and record simultaneously, making it possible to configure A/B roll systems using only two decks. Price points of Digital S equipment put it in line with Betacam SP gear.

Although originally positioned as a digital upgrade for existing S-VHS users (corporate, industrial, small broadcast), Digital-S has found acceptance in the broadcast community as well. The full product line provides camcorders, record and edit decks and equipment for integration into non-linear edit packages.

DV

In the early 1990s, a number of manufacturers gathered to create a new consumer format to replace VHS. The result was Digital Video Cassette (DV or DVC). Shortly after development of the format, it was supported by 17 different manufacturers who planned to offer DV and related products. To date, however, the idea of a new consumer format has not taken off, in the face of competition from disk-based playback formats like DVD.

The professional community took notice of the format's 4:1:1 digital signal and soon Panasonic/Matsushita and Sony unveiled their upgraded version of the DV format for professional applications (see DVCAM and DVCPRO).

But DV's digital signal, ability to record widescreen images, and upward compatibility with both DVCAM and DVCPRO, have made the format a popular acquistion tool for broadcast and higher-end productions. Because the compression and digitization processes of all DV-based formats are the same, the only perceivable difference in image quality between the three is usually associated with the optics of the camera. The digitization is identical.

Although there is little if any activity in developing complete production systems based exclusively on DV, the small, lightweight cameras have found a role in news, corporate, and documentary production.

High Definition Digital Formats

HDCAM

Sony was the first company to offer a high definition digital videotape recorder, the HDD-1000. It is a full-bandwidth, uncompressed recorder using 1-inch open reel tape. While it is still available in the marketplace, equipment cost and tape cost ($1,300 for a one-hour reel) have limited its use.

Sony's current foray into high definition production and postproduction equipment comes under the banner of HDCAM. Initial offerings of studio and record decks have been fleshed out with camcorders and additional production gear. Further expansion of the product line includes VTRs that can playback Betacam SX and Digital Betacam, in some cases allowing for upconversion of Digital Betacam signals to high definition (1080/60i).

HDCAM records using 3:1:1 quantitization (10 bit) at a compression ratio of just under 4.5:1. (If you consider the difference between 4:2:2 and 3:1:1, the compression works out to about 7:1).

In 1999, the ITU adopted a global HDTV standard for both production and program production (ITU-R BT 709-3) that includes picture capture rates of 60/50/30/25 and 24-frame progressive as well as 50/60 interlace. New equipment that would record in both 50/60 interlace and 24-progressive was brought into the HDCAM line in 2000 including camcorders and VTRs.

FORMAT	Signal/Compression	Sampling	Tape Size	Tape Type	Resolution	Equipment	Primary Applications	Compatibility with other Formats
D-1	Component Digital/Uncompressed	4:2:2 8 bit	3/4-inch (19mm)	Metal Particle	460 lines	Recorders	Post, Graphics, Film Transfer	None
D-2	Component Digital/Uncompressed	8 bit	3/4-inch (19mm)	Metal Particle	450 lines	Recorders	Post	None
D-3	Component Digital/Uncompressed	8 bit	1/2-inch (12.65mm)	Metal Particle	450 lines	Recorders, Camcorders	Post, Acquisition	D-5 decks will play back and record D-3
Digital Betacam	Component Digital/2:1	4:2:2 8/10 bit	1/2-inch (12.65mm)	Metal Particle	500 lines	Recorders, Camcorders, Field Edit Package	Acquisition, Post	Decks will play Betacam SX, Betacam (analog) and BetacamSP (analog)
D-5	Component Digital/Uncompressed	4:2:2 8 bit	1/2-inch (12.65mm)	Metal Particle	500 lines	Recorders, Camcorders	Post, Acquisition, Graphics, Film Transfer	Swicthable Decks record and play back D-3 (see also HD-D-5)
DVCPRO (D-7)	Component Digital/5:1	4:1:1	1/4-inch (6mm)	Metal Particle	500 lines	Camcorders, Recorders, Field Edit Package	Acquisition (News), Post	Decks play back DV and DVCAM
DVCPRO 50	Component Digital/3.3:1	4:1:1	1/4-inch (6mm)	Metal Particle	700 lines	Camcorders, Recorders, Field Edit Package	Acquisition, Post	Decks play back DVCPRO
DVCAM	Component Digital/5:1	4:1:1	1/4-inch (6mm)	Metal Evaporated	500 lines	Camcorders, Recorders	Acquisition, Post (especially as source for computer-based edit systems)	Decks play back DV and DVCPRO
DCT	Component Digital/2:1	4:2:2 8 bit	3/4-inch (19mm)	Metal Particle	500 lines	Recorders	Film Transfer, Post, Graphics	

Betacam SX	Component Digital/10:1	4:2:2	1/2-inch (12.65mm)	Metal Particle	500 lines	Recorders, Camcorders, Field Edit Package	Post, Acquisition	
Digital S (D-9)	Component Digital/3.3:1	4:2:2	1/2-inch (12.65mm)	Metal Particle	500 lines	Camcorders, Recorders	Acquisition, Post	Decks play back S-VHS (analog)
DV	Component Digital/5:1	4:1:1	1/4-inch (6mm)	Metal Evaporated	500 lines	Camcorders, Recorders, *especially for use in* computer-based edit systems)	Acquisition	
HDCAM	Component Digital/4:5:1	3:1:1 10 bit	1/2-inch (12.65mm)	Metal Particle	1080 lines (interlace) 720 lines (progressive)	Camcorder, Studio and Field Recorders	Acquisition and Post	
D-6	Uncompressed		3/4-inch (19mm)	Metal Particle	500 lines	Recorders	Post, Graphics, Film Transfer	
HD D-5	Component Digital/4.5:1	4:2:2 8 bit	1/2-inch (12.65mm)	Metal Particle	700 lines	Recorders	Post, Acquisition, Film Transfer	Decks play back D-3
DVCPRO HD (DVC PRO100)	Component Digital/3.3:1	4:2:2	1/4-inch (6mm)	Metal Particle	500 lines	Recorders, Camcorders	Acquisition, Post	
IMX (D-10) MPEG-2 4:2:2 Profile @ ML (Main Level)	Component Digital/ I-frame only compression	4:2:2 8 bit	1/2-inch (12.65mm)	Metal Particle	700 lines	Recorders	Studio production, compositing, computer graphics	IMX Decks play back Digital Betacam, Betacam SP and Betacam SX tapes

D-6

D-6 was the first of the high definition formats, developed by Toshiba and BTS. Using 19mm (3/4-inch) cassettes, it records uncompressed HD signals, while maximum recording time is 64 minutes on a single cassette. At present, Philips appears to be the only active marketers of the product.

MPEG IMX

By rights, it can be said that MPEG IMX is not a format, but a system. Although there are VTRs manufactured by Sony and soon to be available from Philips as well, the MPEG-2 4:2:2 Profile (P) @ ML 50 represents a means for transferring and storing image data on servers as well as VTRs. SDTI-CP (defined by SMPTE 326M) allows for transfer of data from tape, cameras, servers, editors and other equipment without need for decoding and encoding.

As a technology, MPEG IMX provides a direct line from camera acquisition to distribution with products including camcorders, VTRs, digital disk recorders, servers, and non-linear edit systems.

Additionally, the MPEG IMX VTRs have capability of just about every digital and analog format recorded on 1/2-inch Betacam-type cassettes (Digital Betacam, Betacam SX, Betacam SP and Betacam). Whatever the original recording format, the deck will output 50 Mbps MPEG I-frame on SDTI-CP.

HD D-5

Panasonic expanded it's D-5 product line to high definition with the addition of a 4:1 compression add-on that allows D-5 machines to record high definition signals. Originally the processor was a stand-alone unit to be integrated with a standard D-5 deck, but later models incorporated the processor and VTR into a single unit. Whether internal or as an external unit, the processor still allows D5 VTRs to record and playback the uncompressed D-5 signal (in both 720p and 1080i line resolutions). D-3 playback is an option on most of the latter decks.

DVCPROHD (DVCPRO100)

The most recent iteration of the DVCPRO format is DVCPROHD. Originally called DVCPRO100, it uses essentially the same tape transports and mechanics of the other DVCPRO formats, although it records at 100 Mpbs at tape speeds—four times those of DVCPRO and twice the speed of DVCPRO50. The first offerings of DVCPROHD equipment operate in the 1080i standard for high definition.

Initial product offerings for DVCPROHD, expected to reach market late in 1999, are camcorders and a studio deck, targeted for acquisition and postproduction applications.

John Rice is currently Senior Communications Manager for Sony Broadcast & Professional Company. He recently worked as manager of on-air support for WHYY, the PBS station in Philadelphia, PA. He's been involved in the video production and technology industry for over 20 years as a producer, writer, editor, publisher and consultant.

Video Cameras & Lenses in the Digital Era

by Robert M. Goodman

Digital technology has improved image quality and compressed the range of quality available in video cameras. In the recent past, high quality reproduction was restricted to the most expensive broadcast quality cameras. Less expensive industrial grade cameras produced images with less latitude and resolution. The bottom of the scale was home video cameras manufactured for the consumer market. Digital technology has changed that equation.

Inexpensive mini-DV format cameras marketed to consumers and professional videographers for event coverage are capable of producing image quality that rivals the output of broadcast quality analog video cameras. Mini-DV cameras have been used to shoot dozens of documentaries that have then been transferred to 35mm film for theatrical distribution. Fewer dramatic features have been shot this way but there are examples. Thomas Vinterburg's *The Celebration*, was shot with a single CCD, PAL mini-DV camcorder purchased for approximately $1,500. Harmony Korine's *Julien Donkey Boy* and Miguel Arteta's *Chuck & Buck* were shot with three CCD miniDV camcorders.

Is it possible, given these circumstances, to define what is or isn't a professional video camera? In all likelihood, the answer is no. What defines professional is the skill and intent of the user. Digital video cameras represent a new set of tools available for exploitation by talented directors of photography.

It can be difficult for cinematographers working in the photochemical world of film to understand the digital electronic realm because the terminology is different. Concepts, such as, latitude, logarithmic reproduction scales, exposure index, and resolving power are represented in digital video though the words used to describe these concepts rarely coincide. To make this transition easier, the relationship between film and video terms will be pointed out in this chapter about digital video cameras and lenses.

There are long-standing global givens in film production. The shooting standard is 35mm film stock. The normal frame rate is 24 frames per second. Sound is recorded independently of the film and synchronized in post-production. The aspect ratio of the frame is typically 1.33, 1.66, 1.85, or 2.35 to 1. These givens haven't changed in the past 50 years.

Recording images on videotape hasn't reached its fiftieth milestone. Digital video is in its infancy. Hence, the givens in video production are neither long-standing nor universal. There is no standard production stock, though at the moment, Betacam SP is probably the most widely used format. The video frame rate in the United States adheres to the NTSC (National Television Standards Committee) standard of 29.97 frames per second. The frame rate of the PAL (Phase-Alternating Line) standard, used in Europe, Russia, South America and elsewhere, is 25 frames per second. Single system sound is the norm for video production. The only universal given in video is the aspect ratio, which conforms to the 1.33 Academy standard. However, even that is about to change.

New standards for digital television were set by the Advanced Television Standards Committee (ATSC), an industry body formed under the auspices of the Society of Motion Picture and Television Engineers (SMPTE). This committee agreed on eighteen different standards of digital television. A decision, which at first glance, defies common sense. However, the rules cover everything from the way information is displayed on a computer monitor to standards for high-definition television transmission.

The impetus for setting new standards was the development of high-definition television in the 1980s and the growing convergence of computer and video technology in the 1990s. Another factor was the Federal Communications Commissionís (FCC) desire to maximize usage of the increasingly crowded communications airwaves. The FCC recently mandated all U.S. television stations must begin broadcasting a digital signal using the ATSC transmission standard (8-VSB) by the year 2006. The FCC's intention is to end analog television transmission and free up that portion of the communications spectrum for other purposes. The FCC did not specify what ATSC standard broadcasters should use for their programming nor did they mandate high-definition television.

Does any of this concern you? Unfortunately, it does if you plan to use digital video cameras to record and reproduce images. The ATSC standards are clearly defined using pixels, scan lines, scanning frequency, aspect ratio, and frame rate as criteria. There are six ATSC standards suitable for digital television production. An explanation of each standard appears later in this chapter.

Some or all of these standards will become prevalent in video production. As a result, you will need to decide on the video storage (recording) format for example, Digital Betacam or DVCPro, and the ATSC standard, for instance, 480i or 720p, that encodes (records) images on your preferred storage format. Television broadcasters are still deciding which of the six ATSC standards to use to deliver programming to viewers and which to use for program production. Likewise, the camera manufacturers are trying to decide which standards they'll support.

The production community is also facing difficult choices. Producers of studio motion pictures, who are considering digital video as a replacement for 35mm film, have radically different expectations and needs than an independent filmmaker who's only choice may be digital video. There are a lot of options to consider. Digital video encompasses cameras recording in a high-definition 24 frames per second uncompressed format with a wide exposure latitude and less grain than 35mm motion picture film down to home video camcorders recording in the 29.97 frames per second highly compressed mini-DV format. The looks produced by each camera, as expected, will be noticeably different.

Another issue that should be of concern to image creators is permanence. Every time someone

DIGITAL TELEVISION PRODUCTION					
vertical size value (active)	vertical size value (total)	horizontal size value (active)	horizontal size value (total)	aspect ratio information	frame rate and scan
1,080	1,250	1,920	2,376	16:9 (square pixel)	50p, 25i
1,035	1,125	1,920	2,200	16:9 (non-square pixel)	30i
1,080	1,125	1,920	2,640	16:9 (square pixel)	25p, 25i
1,080	1,125	1,920	2,200	16:9 (square pixel)	60p, 59.94p, 30p, 29.97p, 30i, 29.97i
1,080	1,125	1,920	2,750	16:9 (square pixel)	24p, 23.98p
720	750	1,280	1,650	16:9 (square pixel)	60p, 59.94p
483	525	720	858	16:9 (non-square pixel)	59.94p
486	525	720	858	16:9 (non-square pixel)	29.97i
486	525	960	1,144	16:9 (non-square pixel)	29.97i
576	625	720	864	4:3 (non-square pixel)	25i
486	525	948	1,135	4:3 (non-square pixel)	29.97i
576	625	948	1,135	4:3 (non-square pixel)	25i
486	525	768	910	4:3 (non-square pixel)	29.97i

Figure 1 (* i - interlace, p - progressive)

chooses one standard over another for their production, the other options become less viable in the market. Recording formats will disappear as the technology improves and moves forward. It's an inevitable fact of life for those who choose to use these new tools. The only thing you can do is to make your selection — which camera, which recording format, and which ATSC standard — based on the needs of the project because no one can accurately foretell the future.

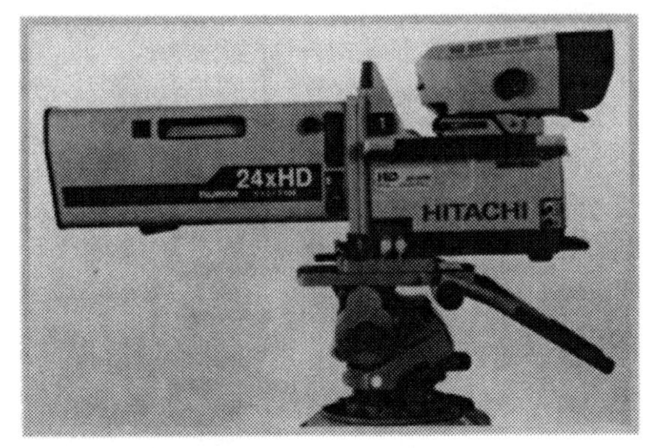

Hitachi Studio Camera

Digital Camera Basics

Camera Types

There are four principal types of cameras: camcorders, dockable cameras, field cameras, and studio cameras. Cameras with built in video recording devices are called *camcorders.* Camcorders are usually smaller and lighter than the other types of cameras because the everything is designed to work as a single unit. The disadvantage is that all the controls over audio and video recording are on the camera. The video recording device is permanently attached so selecting a particular camcorder also forces you to decide about the recording format and ATSC standard.

Camcorders were originally designed for use by one or two-person crews for the purpose of electronic news gathering (ENG). This is the most popular type of video camera on the market.

Sony Dockable

Dockable cameras offer more flexibility because the camera can be attached to a variety of a different recorders. It can be difficult to distinguish between an ENG camcorder and an ENG dockable camera/recorder unit because they look so similar. The disadvantage of having all the controls on the camera remains. However, you can use the same camera head and lenses with different recording formats. In practice, the recorder is rarely switched though it is easy enough to do. Dockable cameras are also very popular.

Organizations that own large number of cameras and need to record in a variety of formats are often the principle buyers. It allows them to standardize on a set of camera electronics for maintenance and service purposes and still have the recording format flexibility they need.Cameras that lack built-in recorders but are portable for use in remote locations are called field cameras. The camera sends the digital picture information over triax cable or via wireless transmitter to recorders in a remote truck or studio. All of the camera's adjustable parameters including color reproduction and contrast can be controlled at recording center.

Field cameras can be equipped for hand-held use or mounted on tripods with rear mounted zoom and focus controls. These cameras are typically used to cover sports and other events.

Cameras designed for studio use make no accommodations for portability. AC power is a necessity. These cameras are designed to mount on hydraulic pedestals that require perfectly level floors for smooth movement. All the lens controls are at the rear of the camera. The viewfinder, typically a 7" or larger monitor, is mounted on the top of the camera. A remote camera control unit, located in the control room, is used to adjust color, contrast, and exposure.

The Imaging Process

The video imaging process converts reflected light into digital information (ones and zeroes) that can be used to record and later reproduce the original image using a video monitor or projector. Lenses whether they are mounted on a film camera or a video camera serve the same purpose--to focus and control light on a specific plane within a specified frame. Thin silicon wafers called Charge Coupled Devices (CCD) replace film in a digital video camera. The CCD (the slang for CCD is "chip") converts the light into digital information. The surface of the CCD is divided into hundreds of thousands of square or rectangular diodes. This grid pattern breaks up the image into pieces called picture elements or pixels. The picture is translated into a series of ones and zeroes that record whether or not light has struck a particular pixel represented by a diode on the CCD.

The RGB additive system of reproducing color information is used for video. Most cameras have a prism that splits the light coming from the lens into a red, blue and green image. Typically, separate CCDs are used to convert each of these three resultant images into digital information. The green channel records the black and white detail present in the image. The prism and CCDs form the imager section of the camera.

Image quality is judged, in film or video, on four elements. *Image sharpness* is a measure of resolution in video terms, or the resolving power of the lens and film combination, in film. *Tonal reproduction* is a measure of the video or film's ability to accurately reproduce the gray scale. *Color reproduction* is judged on two scores: the range of color gamut that can be reproduced and the accuracy of the reproduction of individual colors. *Hue, saturation, and luminance* describe color in the video realm.

The final element, exposure latitude is a measure of the ability to capture detail in both the deep shadow and bright highlight areas of the picture. In film, the characteristics of the stock determines the exposure latitude. In video, the total dynamic range of the camera determines exposure latitude.

CCD Basics

Image quality in a digital video camera is governed by the performance characteristics of the CCDs. Lenses are obviously important and do have an impact on performance. The data from the CCDs can also be enhanced or degraded by the performance of the Digital Signal Processing (DSP) circuits in the camera. However, the single most critical element is the CCD.

The first rule of thumb is that larger CCDs deliver better performance. The physical size of a CCD is expressed as a diameter in inches. The standard diameters are ⅔-inch, ½-inch, ⅓-inch, and ¼-inch. The next rule of thumb is that resolution (in film terms, resolving power) is a factor of the number of pixels physically present on the CCD. More pixels equate to higher resolutions. For example, a typical mini-DV camcorder may have three ¼-inch CCDs, each with 380,000 pixels, whereas a high-definition video camera may have three ⅔-inch CCDs, each with two million pixels. It's sufficient to say that one is vastly superior to the other though it's rare to encounter differences of this magnitude. Usually, the differences are far more subtle. Thus, CCD design is more complex than just squeezing as many pixels as possible in an allotted space.

The total dynamic range of the camera relies on the sensitivity, smear, and signal to noise ratio characteristics of the CCD. The relative sensitivity of a CCD to light is measured in lux--the amount of light needed to make a one-volt video signal. In contrast, a *footcandle*--a measure of illumination--is the brightness level twelve inches from a lit candle. One footcandle equals approximately 10 lux. One of the design considerations is that larger pixels are more sensitive to light. The more pixels there are the higher the resolution and the lower the sensitivity will be.

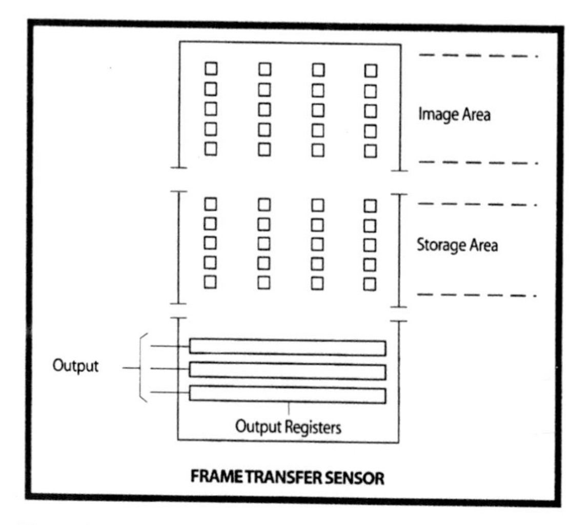

Figure 2

Smear is a result of what happens when too much light strikes the pixels. Normally, light strikes a pixel causing the diode to generate a voltage. The amount of voltage produced by the diode corresponds to the amount of light striking the surface of the pixel. Too much light can cause the diode to overload and transfer excess voltage into nearby pixels. The result of an overload—what is visible in the resulting picture—is a white vertical streak that extends above and below extremely bright areas in the image. Resistance to smear is expressed as a level in minus dB. The lower the level (a camera with a -100dB specification is better than one with a -90dB) the less prone the CCDs and the camera are to smear. Some CCD designs do not exhibit smear.

Signal-to-noise (S/N) ratio is an indicator of how much separation there is between the background noise present in every electronic system

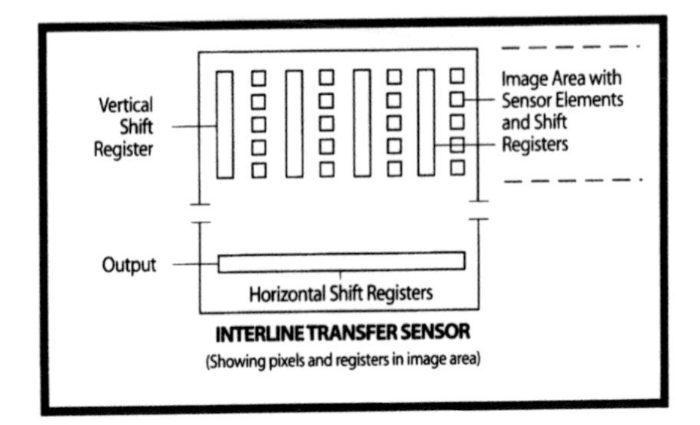

Figure 3

and the information (or signal) being generated. The higher the S/N ratio is, the cleaner the image will be. It's important to have as little noise as possible because digital video signals are usually compressed at some point in either production, post or distribution. Even a tiny bit of noise is likely to be seen as an annoying picture defect after the signal is compressed.

All CCD-based cameras have "electronic shuttering" so they can operate at 1⁄60 of a second for use with interlaced video formats (two fields per frame for an effective rate of 30 frames per second). The shutter (actually a circuit that turns the CCD's pixels on and off) is usually adjustable to higher or lower frame rates. Shutter speed has the same impact in video as it does in film on exposure. There are no variable angle shutters in video cameras because the shutter does not move or rotate.

There are four kinds of CCDs. The most common and the least expensive type is the *Interline Transfer* (IT) CCD which transfers information from the CCD a line at a time (see Figure 3). IT CCDs are sensitive to smear. *Frame Transfer* (FT) CCDs are

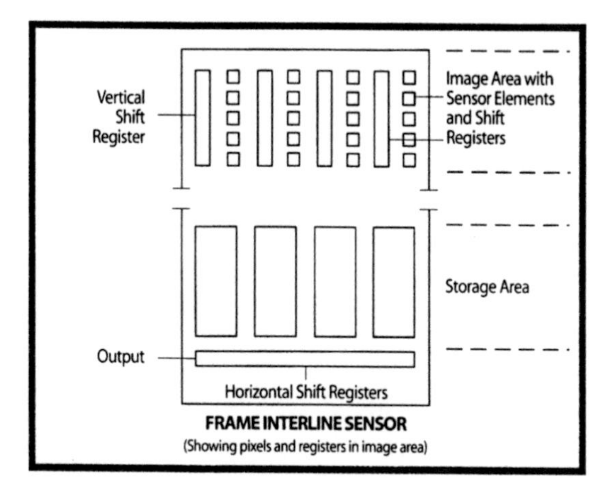

Figure 4

more expensive and less commonly used. FT CCDs do not smear and have exceptional low light performance. Because the signal from a single video field is transferred simultaneously (see Figure 2). This design has very low aliasing and little or no fixed pattern noise.

The designs most often found in high-end cameras are the *Frame Interline Transfer* (FIT) design or *Hole Accumulated Diode* (HAD) CCDs. FIT CCDs have minimal smear, excellent color reproduction and exhibit some lag (see Figure 4). *Lag* is a video term used to describe blurring that occurs when a camera attempts to record fast moving objects. It's called lag because a "ghost" of the image gets stuck in the CCD's memory for a split second before disappearing. HAD CCDs, which are available in either IT or FIT configurations, do not smear and have excellent low light characteristics.

The aspect ratio of the CCD and the image should be identical. Analog NTSC television has a

4:3, or in film terms, a 1.33:1 aspect ratio. Analog cameras all have 4:3 CCDs. The digital high-definition ATSC standard for television uses a 16:9 or a 1.78:1 wide-screen aspect ratio. Cameras designed for HDTV use 16:9 CCDs. However, the market is in transition, so companies have now made "switchable" cameras available.

Switchable cameras can record images in either aspect ratio. The problem is that a 16:9 image has a third more horizontal picture content than a 4:3 image. The least expensive way to record a 16:9 image on a camera with a 4:3 CCD is to electronically squeeze the picture and expand it on playback, which reduces the resolution.

Another method is to limit the height of the picture by limiting the number of active pixels on a 4:3 CCD and thereby, creating the 16:9 aspect ratio. The optimal method is to use a 16:9 CCD and reduce the picture width by limiting the number of active pixels so the resulting image conforms to the 4:3 aspect ratio. Using a 4:3 CCD to record 16:9 images will result in lower resolution and less satisfactory results than using a 16:9 CCD to record a 4:3 image.

Digital Signal Processing

The *digital signal processor* (DSP) in a video camera provides control over every aspect of the image. These specialized computer chips process the output of the CCDs and enable digital cameras to capture images with greater fidelity than analog cameras can deliver. The images are sharper, have less noise, and better color and contrast.

DSP technology simplifies camera setup and makes digital video cameras extremely stable. Stability means that adjustments to the camera are rarely required to maintain the settings that determine the look of the camera. Camera settings can be controlled, precisely, and transferred from camera to camera, which makes consistency easy to achieve.

Tonal reproduction, picture sharpness, exposure latitude and color reproduction are managed by the DSP. By creatively manipulating the camera's DSP controls, it's possible to achieve the looks cinematographers create through film stock selection, or using techniques, such as, fogging, filtering, push and pull processing, or at the answer print phase. DSP settings can be saved for reuse or to match multiple cameras on set. Some camera manufacturers can supply pre-programmed settings, that replicate the look of different film stocks or other visual effects.

The primary function of the digital signal processing is to translate the output of the CCDs, which produces a linear gamma, into a recordable video signal. In video, gamma describes what cinematographers call the characteristic curve or H&D curve. The dynamic range of a high-end CCD may exceed 70dBs — the ability to reproduce a contrast range of 600:1, which is a range from absolute black to two and a half stops beyond the whitest white displayable on a video monitor. It should be self-evident that compression of the highlight information is necessary in order to reproduce the signal.

Many cameras use what's called *pre-knee* processing. The knee, in video, is the same as the shoulder of a characteristic curve. The output from the imager (the prism and three CCD block) in many of today's "digital" cameras is actually an analog signal. The knee is compressed, at a fixed rate, before the signal is sent to the analog to digital converter (A/D converter) that is the first component in many DSPs. The intent is to preserve the widest possible exposure latitude within the limitations of the sampling rate of the A/D converter.

Sampling rates are measured in bits. More bits equals more processing power. More processing power allows for greater latitude, detail, and color accuracy in the picture. The perfect A/D converter, which has yet to be developed, is a 16-bit processor.

In an ideal 16-bit A/D converter, nine bits would be used to process the signal within the normal exposure range for video. Three bits would process the information above video white--the overexposed portion of the signal--for knee control. The end of the characteristic curve in film is commonly called the "shoulder" but video engineers have labeled that portion of the curve, the knee. Gamma correction, which affects the contrast of the image, would use another two bits. In video, gamma correction has a logarithmic impact on the highlight and shadow areas and a linear impact on the midrange. The remaining two bits would be split between white balance control, or in film terms, color temperature adjustment and black gamma correction, which adjusts the level of detail in the shadows.

In the real world, a 12-bit A/D converter is the current state-of-the-art and compromises must be made. The sections of the DSP that process the output of the converter correct the compromises introduced by analog to digital conversion. The processing power of a DSP is also measured in bits.

Camera manufacturers are currently using 10 to 30-bit DSPs.

The names camera manufacturers use to describe the features and capabilities of the DSPs in their cameras vary greatly. Most provide similar features though it may not be easy to discern this from the product information. The most common DSP functions include controls for knee, gamma, black gamma, white balance, iris, gain, matrix, and contour.

The *knee* function manages the highlight compression of the video signal. Some DSPs have separate controls for the knee point and knee slope. The gamma function manages the luminance and contrast of the video signal. This allows the operator to manipulate the characteristic curve of the camera.

The *black gamma* function manages the contrast and detail of the video signal in the shadow areas. Some DSPs split this function into a black stretch function, for more detail, and black press, for greater contrast. The *white balance* function manages the color temperature of the video signal. There are usually presets for 6,700K, 5,600K, 3,200K and a modifiable setting.

The *automatic iris* function manages the aperture to produce properly exposed images. Some DSPs can provide automatic exposure control that coordinates the camera's gain function, which electronically boosts the sensitivity of the CCDs, the camera's variable shutter and the automatic iris to produce pleasing pictures under any lighting condition. The *matrix* function manages the hue and saturation of the video signal data in order to faithfully reproduce colors, at all luminance levels.

The *contour* or *detail enhancement* function manages the edges between areas with differing levels of contrast. This function is often divided up into control over skin detail, soft detail, and diagonal detail. *Skin detail* control reduces the edge sharpness in skin color areas while maintaining sharpness in the rest of the picture. This function gives the talent a smoother complexion and a more youthful appearance. *Soft detail* is used to modify the excessively sharp edges that may occur in areas with great contrast. This function reduces detail enhancement to produce softer gradations and a more natural image. Diagonal detail increases the sharpness in the diagonal parts of the image to create better edges. This function increases the resolution and reduces color moiré.

Some other common DSP features include: *zebra patterns*, that can be set to indicate areas in the picture that exceed a specific brightness level; a SMPTE color bar generator, which provides a color and contrast test pattern for postproduction purposes; and data storage of the DSP settings. Manufacturers use a variety of schemes to store setup information. Every camera can store at least two settings in its internal memory--a factory preset and the last user setting.

Camera settings may also be stored on special IC or memory cards, that can be used to transfer information from camera to camera of the same make and model. Some cameras can store DSP settings on the videotape or send it via a serial port to a laptop computer for archival purposes. This information allows a consistent look and feel to be maintained across time and space. The stored settings can be transferred to a new camera using a memory card or transmitted via email. The setup used for a particular shoot can be recalled at a later date if a reshoot is required.

Some camera remote control panels can store setup information for more than a dozen scenes. Any of which can be recalled with the touch of button. In addition, some DSPs even have the ability to store the first frame of the take, which can be recalled as a transparent image, for matching purposes.

Lenses

Virtually every video camera uses zoom lenses. Prime lenses are rare. Professional video cameras with ⅔-inch or ½-inch CCDs employ the B4 lens mount--a bayonet mounting system. Camcorders with smaller diameter CCDs--the Canon XL1 being the sole exception--are not designed with interchangeable lenses. The XL1 uses a bayonet mounting system compatible with Canon's still photography cameras. See the Canon XL1 entry for more information.

Lenses for video cameras are available in three configurations: Studio/Field, ENG/EFP, and Electronic Cinematography. Studio/Field lenses are completely enclosed in a metal housing, which holds the lens elements, focus and zoom motors, and sensors for the digital servo system. These lenses are used with rear mounted controls or via computer or robotic control. Light-weight ENG/EFP lenses resemble the zooms used in film production. Focus, aperture, and zoom controls are adjustable, manually or using the servo controls mounted on the lens. Nearly all ENG/EFP lenses have a macro feature, which reduces the minimum object distance. Many have built-in 2X tele-extenders.

Fujinon wide-angle ENG Lens.

Electronic Cinematography lenses, available in zooms and primes, have gear rings designed for film lens accessories (follow focus and motorized controls), larger focus, iris, and zoom scales than those found on ENG/EFP lenses and use T-stop markings rather than f-stops.

Electronic and optical image stabilization systems are common on miniDV and DV8 camcorders because the abilities of the intended operators are limited. Professional ENG/EFP lenses are available with built-in optical image stabilization. Image stabilizers which mount in the front of the lens are also available. A variable angle prism compensates for lens movement in optical systems. Electronic systems use a computer algorithm to remove the lens movement. Fluid-dampened lens designs are also available.

Professional image stabilization is intended for use in places where severe vibration is the norm, for example, when shooting from a helicopter or a speed boat.

HDTV cameras require lenses with much higher performance characteristics. The wide screen aspect ratio lowers the CCD's sensitivity by ten percent because the area of active pixels is smaller. HDTV's higher resolution also cuts the radius of the permissible circle of confusion in half and proportionally reduces depth of field. Shallow depth of field means focusing must be done with greater precision. Out of focus images are easier to see when the resolution is higher.

Lenses are evaluated differently for film and video. The imaging performance of a film lens is expressed as its resolving power. A video lens is evaluated by its modulation transfer function (MTF), a measure of the lens' ability to reproduce contrast. MTF is also called *optical transfer function* (OTF).

Resolving power is measured by photographing a resolution chart that has lines of various widths and determining the point at which the lens ceases to reproduce them as separate lines. As the lines become more closely spaced, the contrast of the image goes down until the lines can no longer be resolved. Contrast between black and white is at 100 percent when the lines on a resolution chart are at their widest spacing. At the point at which it's no longer possible to distinguish between the black lines and the white space--when the image is evenly gray--contrast is zero.

A video camera converts images into electrical signals. The maximum bandwidth of the signal path limits the amount of fine detail (expressed as spatial frequency) that can be reproduced. The size of the CCD changes the spatial frequency. In a camera with ⅔-inch CCDs, NTSC video has 30 lines/mm and HDTV 74 lines/mm of spatial frequency. So the performance of the lens must be evaluated taking this into account. MTF is shown as curve on a graph that places spatial frequency on the x-axis (horizontal) and contrast reproducibility on the y-axis (vertical). Lens performance must be evaluated at the spatial frequency limit of the video system. An image that is the least bit out of focus lowers lens performance far more in an HDTV system than it does in a NTSC system.

Diffraction, which wasn't a factor with analog NTSC video, is critical in a digital HDTV environment. The spatial frequency approaches 35mm film and the same rules about the diffraction limit apply. The phenomenon of diffraction or blurring occurs because light has the characteristic of waves despite the fact that it travels in straight lines. Light waves can turn in behind an object like ripples do on water. Diffraction is at its least noticeable when the lens is wide open. The more the lens is stopped down, the more diffraction occurs. More blurring lowers the MTF of the lens. The point at which performance ceases to improve is called the diffraction limit. In practical terms, HDTV lens should be operated at wide apertures and never beyond F5.6

There are other minor differences between film and video lenses. The typical video lens uses an internal focusing system which keeps the front barrel stationary. The gearing on video lenses precludes the use of standard follow focus controls. Most video lenses are marked in F-stops rather than T-stops. T-stops have been less of a concern because lenses are rarely changed and differences in exposure from one lens to another are easy to detect using a high-resolution field monitor. Video lenses don't have markings as large and bold as those on film lenses because the camera operator instead of an assistant cameraman controls the zoom and focus.

The ATSC Formats

The American Television Standards Committee (ATSC) defined standards for digital television transmission (over the air broadcast). There is the misconception that the ATSC defined production standards, which persists in some circles. The ATSC standards will have an impact on production because the option exists to broadcast in the 16:9 wide screen aspect ratio and the different standards reproduce differing levels of detail. It will be more of a production design challenge than an issue for cinematographers.

Seven of the 18 digital standards are relevant. Standard Digital or Definition Television (SDTV, 480i) is a digital version of the current television standard. There are 480 visible vertical lines by 704 horizontal pixels. The signal is interlaced with an aspect ratio of 4:3. ATSC also allows for a progressive scan version (all the lines in a field are scanned at one time) of the SDTV standard, called 480p, and for a 16:9 aspect in either 480i or 480p.

The next step up the resolution scale is the 720p standard, which has the potential to be the "high-enough definition" choice of broadcasters. It's a progressive scan format with 720 visible vertical lines by 1,280 pixels and an aspect ratio of 16:9.

True HDTV is defined as 1080 visible vertical lines by 1,920 pixels with an aspect ratio of 16:9. There are two standards: 1080i is the interlaced version and 1080p is the progressive scan version.

The production community has focused on a third 1080 standard called 1080/24p in its quest for a universal video production standard that can deliver a master in any current ATSC standard, or in NTSC or PAL, or transfer to film for exhibition. The goal is to create video cameras capable of producing image quality that rivals the quality of 35mm motion picture cameras. The 24 frame per second progressive version of 1080 is destined to become the high-definition video production standard for digital cinematography. Digital postproduction and advances in large screen video projection have accelerated the demand for digital origination.

George Lucas has been instrumental in pushing the development of this production equipment forward. The advantage of 1080/24p for producers is that it makes it easy to deliver video masters in all the other standards by down converting the signal.

THE CAMERAS

The cameras in this section are categorized by ATSC format and then by CCD size. There are too many models to fully describe every camera available on the market. Each category includes an overview of the features typically found on cameras within the category and a brief description of the various makes and models. Specialized or single purpose cameras appear in their own category.

480I/480P CAMERAS

Single CCD (1/4") CAMCORDERS

A single CCD camcorder reproduces color by using a filter placed over the CCD. Some manufacturers use complementary color filters — Green, Cyan, and Yellow — and others use Red, Green, and Blue filters. In either case, the pixels on the CCD are divided into triads, effectively lowering the pixel count by a third. As expected, the resolution of these camcorders is much lower than cameras with three CCDs. There are two types of camcorders in this category.

Digital8 camcorders, manufactured by Sony Corporation, record a digital signal on 8mm or Hi-8 cassettes. Representative models include the: DCR-TRV103, TRV310, TRV315, and TRV510. All have an IEEE1394 DV out port for computerized editing. All use the Sony HandyCam design with fold out LCD color viewscreens, rear mounted batteries, and fixed lens. Image stabilization and digital zoom capabilities are standard features.

DV camcorders, manufactured by Canon, JVC, Panasonic, and Sony, record on miniDV cassettes. Representative models include: Canon's Elura2, Ultura, Optura Pi, ZR-10; JVC's GR-DVM80, GR-DVM90, GR-DVL9800, GR-DVF11, GR-DVF21, GR-DVF31, and GR-DLS1U; Panasonic's PV-DV100, PV-DV200, PV-DV400, PV-DV600, PV-DV800; and Sony's DCR-PC5, DCR-TRV11, DCR-TRV20, and PC100.

These camcorders use one of three design approaches: upright audio recorder, HandyCam style, or modified still camera. Canon uses optical image stabilization on all its camcorders; the other manufacturers use either electronic or optical stabilization. All have IEEE1394 DV ports (also know as "iLink or "FireWire") for editing purposes though some are output only. Some models have analog inputs and outputs for dubbing older tape formats to miniDV. Some have a progressive scan mode, which produces video that looks more like film though the manufacturers originally intended this mode to be used for recording still images. The pixel count varies from model to model and from manufacturer to manufacturer.

The image quality of all of these camcorders is very good in medium to close-up shots under brightly lit conditions. In low light, performance drops off considerably. The shadow areas are noisy and in dim light, the colors appear over saturated with minimal accuracy. The gain feature on most of these camcorders increases the noise level as significantly as it brightens the picture. Even under bright conditions, wide shots are minimally acceptable, at best. These cameras can not resolve enough detail. The compression artifacts are particularly noticeable in the sky areas.

Three (1/4", 1/3" or 1/2") CCD CAMCORDERS

The image quality dramatically improves with three CCD camcorders. These units use three tape formats — miniDV, DVCAM, and DVCPRO and three CCD sizes. MiniDV camcorders were designed for consumer use or what manufacturers like to call *prosumer* (Professional/consumer) use. The manufacturers assumed that wedding and event videographers would embrace these cameras; none anticipated these cameras would be used for fiction and nonfiction feature filmmaking. The designs of these camcorders are far more imaginative than either the low-end consumer camcorders or professional ENG/EFP cameras.

All have IEEE1394 DV I/O (input/output) ports for editing, video and audio outputs, and stereo mini inputs for an external microphone. All record drop-frame timecode though none provide user control over timecode. White balance and audio level controls are standard.

There are three ¼-inch CCD designs. Canon employs a 270,000 pixel IT CCD with *pixel shift* in its GL-1 (HandyCam design) model. This design uses larger pixels to improve low light sensitivity and shifts the green CCD vertically and horizontally to increase the resolution. The manufacturer claims that the results are equivalent to a CCD with 410,000 pixels. Color rendition is more accurate but apparent sharpness suffers.

Sony uses 410,000 pixels IT CCDs in its TRV900 (HandyCam design) model. Panasonic's AG-DVC10 uses 270,000 pixel IT CCDs in its shoulder-style design camcorder. Sony's CCD design has more inherent resolution but poorer low light sensitivity. The images produced by Sony's camcorder tend to have hard, distinct edges associated with video. The Canon GL-1's flourite glass lens and CCD design produce a softer, more subtle video image. Panasonic's camera is more likely to produce images similar to Canon's GL-1 than to Sony's models because of the pixel count. All of these models have a digital zoom feature to extend the range of the lens and some form of image stabilization.

All three camcorders are equipped with lenses that use concentric focusing. This system employs a

Canon's XLI Mini DV camcorder.

set of lens elements that float between the front and rear elements to focus the image. There are no beginning and end stops as there are in a geared mechanical system. Rack focus is extremely difficult to do because there is very little range from in-focus to out-of-focus. Concentric focusing is also used in ⅓-inch CCD camera designs.

Panasonic's AG-EZ1 and AG-EZ30 use ⅓-inch 270,000 pixel IT CCDs. The Panasonic EZ models are more tubular and smaller than the squared-off look of the HandyCam style camcorder. The AG-EZ1 has a viewfinder at the rear and the EZ-30 has both a rear viewfinder and a swing out LCD viewscreen. Both offer electronic image stabilization and digital zoom.

Canon's XL1 has its own distinctive design though it also uses ⅓" 270,000 pixel IT CCDs. Pixel shift technology is employed to improve the resolution and sensitivity. More importantly, this camera is one of the few miniDV camcorders designed for use with interchangeable lenses. The bayonet lens mount is based on Canon's EOS still camera mounting system though an adapter is required to mount EF lens.

The difference in image size (CCD versus 35mm film) means that a 35mm still lens will have a focal length 7.2 times greater when mounted on the XL1. The optical image stabilized 16X zoom lens, which is standard, is only a 40mm lens (in 35mm still terms) at its widest. The zoom rocker switch on the lens provides touch sensitive speed control. Canon offers a 3X zoom lens, which is a 28mm lens (in 35mm still terms) at its widest. The 3X zoom does not have built-in image stabilization. Third-party manufacturers have created dozens of accessories for this camera including: Nikon still lens adapters, manual zoom lenses, battery and power adapters, audio gear, and camera support devices. Other unique features are the XL1's dual stereo audio inputs with level and attenuation controls and the ability to record four tracks of audio in the 32 kHz mode.

Sony's VX2000, PD-150A and DSR-250 use ⅓-inch 380,000 pixel (450,000 pixels in the PAL versions) IT CCDs. The VX2000 is a quasi-ENG style camcorder. The PD-150 is a modified VX2000 capable of recording on miniDV or DVCAM tape. The audio capabilities of the camera were enhanced with two XLR audio jacks, which can be set to mic, line, or mic attenuator. Still images can be recorded using camera's memory stick. The images can be printed or used as a key source for in-camera effects.

The DSR-250 is a professional ENG/EFP-style camcorder that records on miniDV or DVCAM. It has a high-resolution black and white viewfinder, optional swing-out color LCD screen, user-settable timecode, switchable XLR audio jacks, and custom presets for color level, sharpness, white balance shift, and audio gain control. The camera's memory stick can record still images for printing or use as a key source for in-camera effects. These cameras can only record on two of the four audio tracks in the 32kHz mode while shooting video.

There are two miniDV cameras that use ½-inch CCDs. The JVC GY-DV500 and GY-550 are professional ENG/EFP style camcorders with bayonet mounts for mechanical servo zoom lenses. Both employ 380,000 pixel IT CCDs and a 14-bit DSP. Gamma, detail, white balance, black stretch/compress are user controllable. Sensitivity is rated at f/11 at 2000 lux. Other significant features include: a variable shutter for shooting computer screens, RS-232 serial port for computer control, two XLR audio inputs with phantom power, IEEE1394 DV I/O, and a professional viewfinder. The GY-DV550 is the same camera with a built-in interface for a remote camera control unit for use in studio environments.

Panasonic's AG-DVC200 is a professional ENG/EFP style camcorder with a bayonet mount for mechanical servo zoom lenses. The camera has ½-inch 410,000-pixel IT CCDs and a 10-bit DSP. However instead of using miniDV cassettes, this camcorder accepts large cassettes that offer 270 minutes of recording time in the miniDV format. Gamma, skin detail, white balance, black stretch/compress, color phase are user controllable. Sensitivity is rated at f/11 at 2000 lux with a S/N ratio of 62dB.

Other signficant features include: three XLR audio inputs with 48-volt phantom power, IEEE 1394 DV I/O, professional viewfinder, +36dB gain, user scene memory storage, a 6-speed shutter with synchro scan for shooting computer screens, and a built-in gold mounting plate for Anton/Bauer batteries.

DVCAM

Sony makes five camcorders with ¼-inch, ⅓-inch, ½-inch or ⅔-inch CCDs, that record in the DVCAM format. The Sony DVCAM camcorders with ⅓" CCDs, the DSR-PD150 and DSR-250, appear in the section above because they can record on miniDV and DVCAM. The DSR-PD100A looks like a HandyCam camcorder. It uses 380,000 pixel ¼-inch IT CCDs. The PD100A has a 12X zoom lens, still image progressive scan mode, electronically generates 16:9 (from 4:3 CCDs), optical image stabilization, an XLR mic input adapter that mounts on the cameraís flash hot shoe, and a memory stick card for JPEG still image storage. An adaptor for transferring the images to a desktop computer (Mac or PC) or laptop is included.

The DSR-300A is a professional ENG/EFP style camcorder with a bayonet lens mount for mechanical servo zoom lenses. The camera has 410,000 pixel ½-inch Power HAD IT CCDs and a 10-bit DSP. Sensitivity is rated at f/11 at 2000 lux and signal to noise ratio of 62dB. Gamma, skin detail, black stretch/compress, color matrix, and

JVC's DY-90 camcorder.

white balance can be controlled. Setup information about the camera is recorded automatically on tape for later recall. The 1.5-inch viewfinder is a high-resolution black and white CRT with an adjustable diopter to compensate for differences in eyesight.

DVCPRO

Panasonic manufacturers three camcorders which record in the DVCPRO format. The AJ-D215 is a professional ENG/EFP style camcorder with a bayonet mount for interchangeable lenses. The camera has 270,000 pixel ⅓-inch IT CCDs with resolution enhancement. Large DVCPRO cassettes, with up to 184 minutes of recording time, can be used in the AJ-D215 which makes this camera well-suited to event production. The AJ-D400 is a professional ENG/EFP camcorder with 410,000 pixel ½-inch FIT CCDs. This camcorder uses standard size DVCPRO cassettes, for up to 66 minutes of recording time, and is intended for corporate and industrial production.

The AJ-D700A is nearly identical to the AJ-D400. The only differences are front and rear headphone jacks, a PC card for storing setup files, and a choice of viewfinders. The AW-F575 is a dockable camera with ½-inch 400,000 pixel FIT CCDs, a 10-bit DSP, a sensitivity rating of f/8 at 2000 lux, 65dB signal to noise ratio, and a maximum gain of +30dB.

D-9

JVC makes three ENG/EFP style cameras for the D-9 (formerly Digital-S) format. The DY-700U (DY designates a camcorder, U indicates NTSC, E represents PAL) and the KY-19U (KY designates dockable cameras) employ 380,000 pixel IT CCDs. Both have B4-style bayonet mounts for interchangeable lens, a variable shutter for shooting computer screens, sensitivity ratings of f/8 at 2000 lux, signal to noise of 62dB, high-resolution black and white viewfinders, XLR connectors, dual SMPTE timecode generators and an RS-232C interface. The DY-70 is a similar camera but with improved versions of the 380,000 pixel IT CCDs, a 14-bit DSP, and sensitivity ratings of f/11 at 2000 lux.

Three 2/3-inch CCD CAMERAS

The vast majority of professional video cameras are those in this category—cameras with ⅔-inch CCDs. All have B4 bayonet mounts for interchangeable lens, high-resolution black and white viewfinders with adjustable diopters, XLR balanced audio connectors, BNC video connectors, SMPTE timecode generators, user selectable IRE ranges for zebra patterns, variable shutters, tone and color bar generators, optional camera remote control units, and dozens of special purpose and power accessories. A wide range of lenses from Angenieux, Canon, and Fujinon are available for these cameras.

All of the camera models a particular manufacturer sells tend to produce images that have what could be called a company look. It reflects the engineering design preferences that exist within every company. This shouldn't be taken to mean that if you like one of the cameras produced by a particular manufacturer, you're bound to like all the others. Even though there are subtle differences that distinguish one manufacturer from another, the setup features on nearly all the cameras in this category offer enough control to make the look suit your preferences.

The dozens of models, from seven manufacturers, include: camcorders for miniDV, D-9, DVCPRO, DVCPRO50, DVCPROHD, DVCAM, BetacamSX, EDITCAM, and HDCAM formats, dockable cameras for format flexibility, and field and studio configurations. The highlights presented below are intended to help you narrow the choices. You should review all of the specifications before making a decision about which camera will meet your production needs. And ideally, you should test the camera under production conditions before making a final decision. The Internet addresses of camera and lens manufacturers appear at the end of this chapter.

MiniDV

JVC's GY-DV700W has 760,000 pixel (16:9) IT CCDs with a 14-bit DSP, a sensitivity rating of f/11 at 2000 lux, black stretch/compression controls, and manual and automatic shooting modes.

D-9

JVC makes three models: the DY-90 uses 380,000 pixel IT CCDs; and the KY-D29U and D29UW (16:9 version) use 760,000 pixel IT CCDs. All of them have a 14-bit DSP, a sensitivity rating of f/11 at 2000 lux and storage for two scene files.

DVCPRO/DVCPRO50

Panasonic and Ikegami manufacture DVCPRO and DCVPRO50 cameras. Panasonic's AJ-D610WA has 520,000 pixel 16:9 IT CCDs, a 10-bit DSP, maximum gain of +36dB, PC card memory storage for camera setup, a six-speed variable shutter for shooting computer displays and a gold mounting plate for Anton/Bauer digital batteries. The AJ-810 has 410,000 pixel IT CCDs, a 10-bit A/D convertor, 16-bit DSP, a sensitivity rating of f/11 at 2000 lux, 62dB signal to noise ratio, +46dB maximum gain and PC card memory storage for camera setups.

The AJ-D910WA has 520,000 pixel 16:9 IT CCDs, a 10-bit A/D converter, 16-bit DSP, PC card memory storage for camera setup, a maximum gain of +30dB and is available in either DVCPRO or DVCPRO50 versions. The AJ-D900WA has 520,000 pixel 16:9 FIT CCDs, a 10-bit A/D converter, 16-bit DSP, a sensitivity rating of f/9 at 2000 lux, 63dB signal to noise ratio, maximum gain of +36db, and a PC card to store camera setups.

Panasonic's AJ-PD900WA is the progressive scan version of the AJ-D900WA. It has 520,000 pixel 16:9 FIT CCDs, a 10-bit A/D converter, 16-bit DSP, a sensitivity rating of f/9 at 2000 lux, 63dB signal to noise ratio, maximum gain of +36db, PC card to store camera setups and outputs a 480p signal for recording in the DVCPRO50 format.

Ikegami offers two 16:9 switchable DVCPRO50 camcorders. The HL-V79W uses 520,000 pixel 16:9 FIT CCDs with a 10-bit A/D converter, 28-bit DSP and maximum gain of +48dB. The HL-V75W is the IT CCD version. Ikegami also offers four DVCPRO camcorders in either 4:3 or 16:9 switchable versions: the HL-V77 and HL77W (16:9 version) have 520,000 pixel FIT CCDs; HL-V73W (16:9 version) has 520,000 pixel IT CCDs and the HL-V73 (4:3 version) has 400,000 pixel IT CCDs. The DSPs are identical to the HL-V79W.

DVCAM

Sony's DVCAM camcorder, the DSR-500WS has 520,000 pixel HAD IT 16:9 CCDs, a 10-bit A/D converter, a sensitivity rating of f/11 at 2000 lux, 63dB S/N rating, user setup files, and automatically records setup information on tape. Ikegami's HL-DV7W has 520,000 pixel IT 16:9 CCDs, a 10-bit A/D converter, a sensitivity rating of f/11 at 2000 lux, 64dB S/N rating, and a maximum gain of +48dB. A 4:3 version of this camera, the HL-DV5 with 400,000 pixel IT CCDs is also available.

Ikegami's HL-DV7W DVCAM switchable (4:3/16:9) camcorder uses three 520,000 pixel ⅔-inch

Ikegami's Editcam2 Hard Disk Camera

IT CCDs and 10-bit DSP. Sensitivity is rated at f/11 at 2000 lux and a S/N rating of 64 dB. It comes with a standard iLink terminal and can be connected to any VTR equipped with a DV interface.

BETACAM SX

Sony's BetacamSX camcorder, the DNW-9WS has 520,000 pixel HAD IT 16:9 CCDs, a 10-bit A/D converter, a sensitivity rating of f/9 at 2000 lux, 63dB S/N rating, and one setup file that can be stored on a memory card.

EDITCAM Camcorders

Ikegami manufacturers two camcorders that record on hard drives instead of tape. The drives can be swapped in and out for use with Avid nonlinear editing systems. The Editcam system eliminates the need to digitize footage. The DNS-201W model has 520,000

JVC HD D-9 720p camera.

(16:9) pixel IT CCDs with a sensitivity rating of f/11 at 2000 lux and the DNS-21W 520,000 (16:9) FIT CCDs with a sensitivity rating of f/8 at 2000 lux. Both employ a 10-bit DSP.

Dockable Cameras

Hitachi, Ikegami, Philips, Sony and Thomson manufacture dockable cameras for use with a variety of recording formats. Hitachi's Z3000W uses 640,000 pixel IT 16:9 CCDs and has a 10-bit A/D converter, 18-bit DSP, a sensitivity rating of f/11at 2000 lux, a maximum gain of +36dB, a sensitivity rating of 65dB, and memory card storage for one file and four scenes. Ikegami's HL-45 and HL-45W (16:9 version) use 520,000 pixel IT CCDs, with sensitivity ratings of f/10 and f/11 respectively, at 2000 lux, a maximum gain of +36dB, three black stretch and three black compress settings, and

Philips LDK-6000HD dockable camera.

memory card storage for camera setup. The HC-400 model uses 410,000 pixel IT CCDs and the HC-400W uses 520,000 pixel 16:9 IT CCDs. Both HC-400 models have memory card storage for one file and four scenes.

Philips LDK 100 series is available in four versions: the 100 IT (4:3 version) and 100 ITW (16:9), which use 510,000 pixel IT CCDs; the 100 FT (16:9) with 594,000 pixel FT CCDs (available in 4:3 or 16:9 versions); and the 100 DPM (16:9 switchable) with 594,000 DPM FT CCDs. DPM FT CCDs use a frame transfer design with a proprietary Dynamic Pixel Management system that allows the pixels to be remapped on the CCD whenever the camera switches between 4:3 and 16:9. The IT versions have a sensitivity rating of f/11 at 2000 lux and the FT and DPM versions have a sensitivity rating of f/9 at 2000 lux. All of them have 12-bit A-to-D conversion, a 22-bit dual sensor DSP, a maximum gain of +42dB, dual skin contour

Panasonic AJ-HDC20 DVCPRO HD camcorder.

controls, and memory card storage for two files and four scenes. Each camera head includes four scene files, one factory scene file and one customizable scene file. This is in addition to the scene file memory card system.

The Philips LDK 200 series uses 594,000 pixel (16:9 switchable) DPM FT CCDs, 12-bit A/D conversion with 22-bit DSPs and has three remotely controllable filters sets for neutral density, color correction, and special effects; a five channel intercom and a link to personal computers for camera setup information storage. The DSP includes two skin detail settings, six-vector variable matrix, matrix position, gamma, gamma curve, highlight handling, horizontal and vertical aperture correction, extended knee contour, leaking pixel concealment, and digital shading and contrast correction. The LDK 200 series can be configured as a DVCPRO or DVCPRO50 camcorder or as field camera with rotary triax connectors and dual

Sony's 1080/24p Cinealta HD camcorder.

channels of video return. Both power and signal are provided for teleprompter use. The camera also has an (optional) zoom grip that allows the operator to use the camera from a low shooting angle position, while also providing a trigger button for Stop, Play and Record functions.

Sony's DXC-D35/D35WS (16:9 version) uses 520,000 pixel HAD IT CCDs, with sensitivity ratings of f/11 at 2000 lux, a maximum gain of +42dB, digital controls for skin detail, black stretch and compress, vertical and horizontal detail, and user files for camera setup.

Thomson's 1657D series of cameras are available in IT or FIT versions with either 4:3 or 16:9 CCDs. All of Thomson's cameras use a 12-bit A/D converter with 20-bit DSP, have a sensitivity rating of f/8 at 2000 lux, 63dB signal to noise rating, and controls over master gamma, fine gamma, black stretch, six different contour levels, detail, contrast compression, and two skin detail levels.

FIELD CAMERAS

Hitachi, Ikegami, Philips, and Thomson manufacture field cameras. Hitachi's SK-2700 series is available in a switchable 16:9/4:3 version, the SK-2700PWA (SK-2700W studio) or in a standard 4:3 version, the SK-2700PA (SK-2700 studio). The SK-2700PWA has 640,000 pixel IT CCDs and the SK-2700PA uses 600,000 pixel IT CCDs. All of Hitachi's SK-2700 cameras have 12-bit A/D conversion, 30-bit DSP, a sensitivity rating of f/8 at 2000 lux, 62dB signal to noise rating, and plug-in filter wheels. The DSP includes two skin detail settings, high chroma detail, soft detail, six-vector color correction, saturation, knee saturation, knee aperture, 14-segment adjustable gamma, and digital shading correction. Hitachi's SK-777 has 640,000 pixel (16:9 switchable) FIT CCDs, a 12bit A/D convertor, sensitivity rating of f/11 at 2000 lux, and a memory card for storing settings. Ikegami's HL-59/59W use 520,000 pixel FIT CCDs with a 10-bit DSP. This model also has a three-position black stretch/black press control and storage for eight scene files.

The HK-387PW uses 640,000 pixel 16:9 IT CCDs with 12-bit A/D conversion and 16-bit DSP. This model has a sensitivity rating of f/8 at 2000 lux, 62dB signal to noise rating, and memory card storage for twenty camera setup files and 240 scene files. Ikegami's HK-388 is available in a studio or portable version with three choices of imagers.

The HK 388/388P ("p" indicates portable version) uses 520,000 pixel FIT CCDs. The HK-388PH/388PH uses 640,000 pixel FIT CCDs. The HK-388W/388PW uses 640,000 pixel (16:9 switchable) FIT CCDs. All the HK-388 models have

12-bit A/D conversion, 16-bit DSP, a sensitivity rating of f/8 at 2000 lux, a S/N rating of 62dB.

Philips' LDK 23 is a slow motion camera (running at triple speed) with 594,000 pixel (16:9 switchable) DPM FT CCDs and a sensitivity rating of f4 at 2000 lux. The LDK-2000 is a 480p camera using 594,000 pixel (16:9 switchable) DPM FT CCDs, with 12-bit A/D conversion, a 24-bit DSP, a sensitivity rating of f/8 at 2000 lux, and a S/N rating of 63dB. The DSP includes two skin detail settings, six-vector variable matrix, matrix position, gamma, gamma curve, highlight handling, horizontal and vertical aperture correction, extended knee contour, and digital shading and contrast correction. Thomson's 1707 camera is available with the same CCDs as the LDK 20 and uses 12-bit A/D conversion with 20-bit DSPs. The 1707's DSP controls are identical to those in Thomson's 1657 camera.

720p/1080i Cameras

Hitachi, Ikegami, JVC, Panasonic, Philips, and Sony currently manufacture HDTV cameras, in field or studio configurations, capable of producing images in the 1080i or 720p HDTV formats. These cameras are expensive and include every possible feature one could want. All offer the most extensive user controls possible over video gamma, contour, matrix, black gamma, and detail. Variable speed shutters for shooting computer screens are standard.

Every camera offers some way of storing camera setup information and scene information. The signal to noise ratings for HDTV cameras are typically in the mid 50dB range and should not be directly compared to

SDTV cameras. Most of these cameras can be purchased in studio or field configurations; some are convertible.

Hitachi's SK-3000 (the studio version) or the SK-3000P (field version) use 2.2 million pixel FIT CCDs with 12-bit A/D conversion, 30-bit DSP, a sensitivity rating of f/8 at 2000 lux and a 54dB signal to noise ratio. Both versions can simultaneously output signals in 480i (16:9 or 4:3) and 1080i. Plug-in modules for the camera control units are available to output signals in 480p or 720p.

Ikegami's HDK-790D (the studio version) or the HDK-79D (field version) use 2.2 million pixel FIT CCDs with 10-bit A/D conversion and a 28-bit DSP. It has a memory card that can store 20 complete camera setup files and 240 scene files. Ikegami's camera can output a signal in the 1080i, 720p, 480p, or 480i formats. Ikegami's native 720/60p HD camera uses 1 million pixel (720p) FIT CCDs and is available in studio and field configurations. It has a 12-bit A/D converter, 30-bit DSP, a sensitivity rating of f/8 at 2000 lux, 54dB signal to noise ratio, and provides 720p, 480p, and 480i output. The HDL-V90 is a DVCPROHD camcorder with 2.2 million pixel (1080i) FIT CCDs, a 12-bit A/D convertor, 30-bit DSP, a sensitivity rating of f/8 at 2000 lux, 54dB signal to noise ratio, and a 8MB memory card for storing setup files and scenes.

The HDL-V90 outputs a 1080i signal. JVC's KH-100U is a 1080i camera. It has 1 million pixel IT CCDs, a sensitivity rating of F7 at 2000 lux and a signal to noise ratio of 52dB. Panasonic's AK-HC880 (studio version) or the AK-HC830 (field version) use 2.2 million pixel FIT CCDs and output in 1080i.

Philips's LDK 6000HD series of dockable cameras comes in three versions: 1080i, 720p, or a

1080i/720p switchable version which has the company's exclusive Dynamic Pixel Management (DPM) frame transfer (FT) CCDs. All use 9.2 million pixel FT CCDs with 12-bit A/D conversion, dual 22-bit DSPs, a sensitivity rating of F8 at 2000 lux, 54dB signal to noise ratio, maximum gain of +12dB, no vertical smear, and memory storage for two operator files and four scenes. The DPM circuitry remaps the CCD at the push of a button to permit switch between native 1080i or native 720p.

Sony's HDC-700A (the studio version) or the HDC-750A (field version) use 2 million pixel HAD FIT CCDs with 10-bit A/D conversion. These cameras output in 1080i and 480i/480p. The signal to noise rating is 54dB in the HDTV mode and 60dB in SDTV mode.

Sony and Panasonic also manufacture camcorders that use the HDTV recording formats each company champions. Sony's HDW-700A uses an HDCAM format recorder. The camera section is identical to the HDC-700A/HDC-750A versions mentioned above. Panasonic's camcorders use 10-bit A/D conversion, a 16-bit DSP, have DVCPROHD format recorders, and output signals in 1080i and in SDI for monitoring and playback.

The AJ-HDC20A 1080i camcorder uses 2.2 million pixel FIT CCDs and the AJ-HDC10A uses 1 million pixel IT CCDs. The HDC20A model has a sensitivity rating of f/8 at 2000 lux, 54dB signal to noise ratio, maximum gain of +18dB, and shutter speeds from 1/30 to 1/2000 of a second. The HDC10A has shutter speeds from 1/100 to 1/2000 of a second. Panasonic has also developed the AJ-HDC27A 720p/60 camcorder, that is now available.

1080/24p CAMERAS

Panasonic, Philips, and Sony have announced or are delivering cameras capable of outputting in native 1080/24p. Panasonic's AK-HC900 series of cameras will output native 1080/24p, 1080/60i, 720/60p, and 480/60i signals. Philips LDK 7000HD camera series outputs native 1080/24p, 1080/30p, 1080/60i, 720/24p, and 720/60p. All use 9.2 million pixel DPM FT CCDs with 12-bit A/D conversion, a 22-bit DSP, no vertical smear, frame rates of 24, 30, 60, 72 fps, and memory storage for two operator files and four scenes. These cameras are 16:9 or 2:37:1 switchable in 1080 mode and 16:9 or 2.67:1 switchable in 720 mode. Sony's HDC900 (studio), HDC950 (field) and HDW-F900 (HDCAM 24p CineAlta camcorder) series of cameras output native 1080/24p, 1080/60i, 1080/50i, 1080/30p 1080/25p, 720/60p, 720/30p, 720/24p signals. All use 2.2 million pixel (1080) FIT CCDs with 12-bit A/D conversion, a sensitivity rating of f/10 at 2000 lux, 54dB S/N ratio, +36db maximum gain, and a memory stick for storing camera setup and scene files.

Specialized Cameras

If you consider that a high-quality CCD can be as small as ¼-inch, it's easy to imagine cameras that come in every imaginable size and shape. It's just as easy to see that manufacturers can create speciality cameras to meet the needs of the scientific, medical, and sports communities. Miniaturized self-contained packages that consist of a lens and a CCD imager, capable of outputting standard definition or HDTV video are commonly called lipstick cameras or microcams. Ikegami's HDL-10 HDTV camera is one example.

Ikegami HDL-10 Specialty camera.

Detectives, investigative journalists, and law enforcement agencies have all found uses for lipstick cameras. Probe cameras, developed for medical use, are even smaller. Typically, they consist of a tiny lens and CCD mounted on the end of a fiber optic cable that sends images to the processing electronics at other end. Box or minicam cameras are generally low-resolution cameras designed for security use in buildings. They are often completely self-contained though some do use interchangeable lens.

It's rare to find cameras that have been specially modified for underwater use though some are available. Housings for professional video cameras are readily available should you need to shoot underwater or inclement conditions. Video cameras have been developed for scientific use that are sensitive to specific portions of the spectrum, such as the infrared range. Night vision adapters, readily available for any professional camera, also reproduce a portion of the spectrum infrared. High-speed video cameras are also available. These cameras are capable of recording images at up to180 fields per second and can be found on any Sunday at professional football games for slow motion shots.

Manufacturers Websites

Angenieux Lens—www.angenieux.com
Canon Cameras—www.canondv.com
Canon Broadcast Lens—www.usa.canon.com
Fujinon Broadcast Lens—www.fujinon.co.jp
Hitachi Denshi America—www.hdal.com
Ikegami Electronics—www.ikegami.com
JVC Professional Products—www.jvc.com/pro
Panasonic Broadcast & Digital Systems—
www.panasonic.com/broadcast
Panasonic Consumer Electronics—
www.panasonic.com
Philips Digital Networks—
www.broadcast.philips.com
Thomson Broadcast—
www.thomsonbroadcast.com
Sony Broadcast & Professional Company—
www.sony.com/professional

***Robert M. Goodman** is an award-winning writer and Emmy nominated director. His credits include* Going Digital, The Road Taken, America's Dream Highway, *and* Gifts in the Mail. *He's currently developing projects for film and television. Goodman was one of 20 nonfiction producers in North America selected for IFFCON '98 and he's been featured on John Pierson's* Split Screen, *which airs on Bravo and the Independent Film Channel. Goodman is also a contributing editor for* Digital Cinema, The Independent Film & Video Monthly, DigitalTV *and* Videography *magazines and one of the authors of* A Guide to Digital Television.

Camera Filters

by Ira Tiffen, ASC Associate Member

Camera filters are transparent or translucent optical elements that alter the properties of light entering the camera lens, thus improving the image being recorded. Filters can affect contrast, sharpness, highlight flare, color, and light intensity, either individually, or in various combinations. They can also create a variety of "special effects." It is important to recognize that, even though there are many possibly confusing variations and applications, all filters behave in a reasonably predictable way when their properties are understood and experienced. The following will explain the basic optical characteristics of camera filters, as well as their applications.

In their most successful applications, filter effects blend in with the rest of the image to help tell the story more effectively. Subtle softening can remove years from an actor's face. A candlelight glow sets the stage for romance. The sinister gleam from a knife in the shadows can glint most menacingly. A colorless sky can be infused with the most dramatic tones of amber sunset. There are many more uses for filters than there are different types. Use caution when using a filter in a way that draws attention to itself as an effect. Combined with all the other elements of image-making, filters make visual statements, manipulate emotions and thought, and make believable what otherwise would not be. They get the viewer involved.

Filter Planning

Filter effects can become a key part of the "look" of a production, if considered in the planning stages. They can also provide a crucial last-minute fix to unexpected problems, if you have them readily available. Where possible, it is best to run advance tests for pre-conceived situations when time allows.

Filter Source References

There are several filter manufacturers who should be contacted regarding available types and model numbers. Filters of the same name, from different manufacturers, may not have the same characteristics. For color filters, the one industry standard is the Wratten system. This is used by virtually every manufacturer for assigning numerical designations to filters of known color characteristics. Wratten-numbered filters have defined transmission properties that are at least cross-referenced by the various key suppliers.

Media Performance Variations

Filters will function similarly in different formats, but especially as relates to their individual characteristics. Differences in media, as in film vs. video, or SDTV vs. HDTV, will be incorporated into the final result in a generally logical way. Where the format has lesser contrast range, it may require more help with a stronger contrast-control filter; where it has less inherent resolution, it may take a stronger image-softening filter to leave its mark.

One of the more important benefits filters impart to video, oddly enough, is the "film look." This generally refers to film's greater contrast range and higher resolution. This is often addressed through the use of contrast control filters that can allow more detail to show at the ends of the brightness scale, thus giving the appearance of greater range.

Some "special effect" filters, such as stars and nets, have discrete patterns, such as a series of lines on their surface. As the size of the recording element (for example, CCD chip vs. film formats) gets smaller, the depth-of-field increases for any given field-of-view. This means that the smaller video formats run a greater risk of allowing the filter pattern to appear in focus in the image. For this reason, as well as a matter of convenience, many video cameras have filters mounted behind the lens in a filter wheel located within the camera body. This will reduce the likelihood that a filter's pattern will appear in the image.

In turn, locating the filter behind the lens may also produce some variation in a filter's effect from the traditional front-of-the-lens mounted position. Generally, though, both positions work in similar ways; for critical applications, testing is recommended.

Typically, the filter wheel, as supplied by the camera manufacturer, has four to five filters, primarily for basic exposure-improvement. The wheel can often be removed to allow user-replacement with filters for other purposes.

Sizes, Shapes, and On-Lens Mounting Techniques

Lens-mounted filters are available in round and rectangular shapes in many sizes. Round filters generally come supplied with metal rings that mount directly to the lens. Round filters also can be supplied with self-rotating mounts, where needed, as for polarizers. They can be readily stacked in combination.

Rectangular filters require the use of a special filter holder, or matte box. They offer the additional benefit of allowing slidability, for effects that must be precisely aligned within an image, such as graduated filters. In all cases, it is advisable to use a mounting system that allows for sturdy support and ready manipulation. In addition, the use of a lens shade at the outermost mounting position (from the lens) will minimize the effect of stray off-axis reflection and lens flare.

The trend in lens design has been toward "internal-focus" operation, meaning that only internal components move during focus or zoom operation. This simplifies filter use, as a filter that needs rotational orientation won't move with the front of the lens barrel. With "external-focus" lenses, the front of the lens rotates, and a separate means of aligning the filter to a non-moving element, such as the base of the lens barrel mount, must be contrived to maintain filter position as desired.

Filter Factors

Many filter types absorb light that must be compensated for when calculating exposure. Video cameras generally are capable of determining proper exposure through-the-lens. When used in this manner, any filter in the optical path will automatically be compensated for. For a variety of reasons, however, such as planning lighting requirements, it may be useful to know how to work with their light-reducing qualities.

Filters are supplied with either a recommended "filter factor" or a "stop value." Filter factors are multiples of the unfiltered exposure. Stop values are added to the stop to be set without the filter. Multiple filters will add stop values. Since each stop added is a doubling of the exposure, a filter factor of 2 is equal to a one stop increase. (For example: three filters of one stop each will need three additional stops, or a filter factor of 2 x 2 x 2= 8 times the unfiltered exposure.)

When in doubt in the field about compensation needed for a filter that you have no information on, you might use your light meter with the incident bulb removed. If you have a flat diffuser, use it, otherwise just leave the sensor bare. Aim it at an unchanging light source of sufficient intensity.

On the ground, face up at a blank sky can be a good field situation. Make a reading without the filter. Watch out for your own shadow. Make a reading with the filter covering the entire sensor. No light should enter from the sides. The difference in the readings is the compensation needed for that filter. You could also use a spot meter, reading the same bright patch, with similar results.

There are some exceptions to this, depending on the intensity of the filter color, the meter sensitivity (color and calibration), and the target color (which should be as close to gray as possible), but this is often better than taking a guess.

Filter Grades

Many filter types are available in a range of "grades" of differing strengths. This allows the extent of the effect to be tailored to suit various situations. The grade numbering range can vary with the effect type, and generally, the higher the number, the stronger the effect. Unless otherwise stated, there is no mathematical relationship between the numbers and the strengths. A grade 4 is not twice the strength of a grade 2. A grade 1 plus a grade 4 doesn't add up to a grade 5.

A Note About Electronic Image Manipulation

Video camera technology incorporates a variety of electronic means of improving the recorded image. Use them whenever they present an effective, expedient response to imaging issues. Think of filters as a way of making it easier for the camera to give you the results you want.

For instance, instead of increasing the electronic gain in dim-lit situations, you might find a contrast control filter can give shadow detail that might otherwise go missing. Fluorescent lighting can often be color-corrected electronically, yet you may also discover that by white-balancing through a fluorescent correction filter the results are more satisfying.

Sometimes, it may just be easier to use an optical filter color or effect without changing the base camera settings, both for convenience and consistency.

In addition, computer-aided post-enhancements are getting increasingly better and easier to use, making them more prevalent in daily production. They function best, and most cost-effectively, if the original images capture all necessary detail, in as close to the final version as possible. Optical filters are an effective way of providing the best material to start with.

Camera Filters for Both Color and Black-and-White

General Protection

Clear filters on the front of the lens do a great job of minimizing damage to the front lens element. They are cheaper, much faster and easier to replace than that lens element as well. Clear filters can be obtained with high efficiency anti-reflection coatings. This will minimize light lost due to reflection, as well as reduce the chance of internal reflection problems.

Ultraviolet Filters

Video cameras often exhibit a greater sensitivity to what is to the human eye invisible, ultraviolet light. This is most often outdoors, especially at high altitudes, where the UV-absorbing atmosphere is thinner; and over long distances, such as marine scenes. It can show up as a bluish color cast, or it can cause a low-contrast haze that diminishes details, especially when viewing far-away objects. Ultraviolet filters absorb UV light generally without affecting light in the visible region.

It is important to distinguish between UV-generated haze and that of air-borne particles, such as smog. The latter is made up of opaque matter that absorbs visible light as well as UV, and will not be appreciably removed by a UV filter.

Ultraviolet filters come in a variety of absorption levels, usually measured by their percent transmission at 400 nanometers (nm), the visible-UV wavelength boundary. Use a filter that transmits zero percent at 400 nm for aerial and far-distant scenes; one that transmits in the 10-to-30 percent range is fine for average situations.

Infra-Red Filters

Certain special situations call for the use of cameras with infra-red sensitivity. For aerial haze penetration, recording heat effects, and other purposes they are invaluable. Their color and tonal renditions are very different, however, from standard cameras. Various filters are used to reduce unwanted visible light.

Red, orange and yellow filters, as used for panchromatic black and white film—such as a Wratten #25 Red—can enhance contrast and alter color. Filters that absorb all visible light, transmitting only infra-red—as with the Wratten #87 or #89 series of filters—can be useful. Bear in mind that you can not see through these filters, making their use more complicated. The results will vary with camera characteristics and other factors.

Since most lenses focus infra-red light wavelengths slightly differently than other colors, you may need to use a different focusing scale on your lens for infra-red use. Prior testing for most situations is a must.

Neutral Density Filters

When it is desirable to maintain a particular lens opening for sharpness or depth-of-field purposes, or simply to obtain proper exposure when confronted with too much light intensity, use a neutral density (ND) filter. This will absorb light evenly throughout the visible spectrum, effectively altering exposure without requiring a change in lens opening and without introducing a color shift.

Neutral density filters are denoted by (Optical) Density value. Density is defined as the log, to base 10, of the Opacitance. The Opacitance (degree of absorption) of a filter is the reciprocal of (and inversely proportional to) its Transmittance. As an example, a filter with a compensation of one stop has a Transmittance of 50 percent, or 0.5 times the original light intensity.

The reciprocal of the Transmittance, 0.5, is 2. The log, base 10, of 2 is approximately 0.3, which is the nominal density value. The benefit of using density values is that they can be added when combined. Thus two ND .3 filters have a density value of 0.6. However, their combined transmittance would be found by multiplying 0.5 x 0.5 = 0.25, or 25% of the original light intensity.

Neutral density filters are also available in combination with other filters. Since it is preferable to minimize the number of filters used (see section on multiple filters), common combinations such as a Wratten 85 (daylight conversion filter for tungsten-corrected media) with a ND filter are available as one filter, as in the 85N6. In this case, the two stop ND .6 value is in addition to the exposure compensation needed for the base 85 filter.

There are two types of neutral density filters in general use. The most prevalent type uses organic dyes to attenuate light. For situations where it is necessary to obtain the most even control from near-ultraviolet, through the visible spectrum, into the near infra-red, a metallic vacuum-deposition coating (often a nickel-alloy) is ideal. For most situations, though, the silvered-mirror appearance of these filters imparts internal reflection problems that need to be addressed in use.

Special metallic coatings can also be employed for recording extremely bright-light situations, such as the sun during an eclipse. These filters are very dense, to reduce the potentially blinding level of light. The best have a density value of about 5.7, which allows less than 0.001% of the overall light through.

Graduated ND Filters

Often it is necessary or desirable to balance light intensity in one part of a scene with another in situations where you don't have total light control, as in bright exteriors. Exposing for the foreground will produce a washed-out, over-exposed sky. Exposing for the sky will leave the foreground dark and under-exposed.

Graduated ND filters are part clear, part neutral density, with a smoothly graded transition between. This allows the transition to be blended into the scene, often imperceptibly. A ND .6-to-clear, with a two-stop differential, will most often compensate the average bright sky-to-foreground situation.

These filters are also available in combination colors, as where the entire filter is, for example a Wratten 85, while one half also combines a graded-transition neutral density, as in the 85-to-85N6. This allows the one filter to replace the need for two.

Graduated filters generally come in three transition types. The most commonly used is the "soft edge." It has a wide enough transition area on the filter to blend smoothly into most scenes, even with a wide angle lens (which tends to narrow the transition within the image). A long focal length, however, might only image in the center of such a transition. In this case, or where the blend must take place in a narrow, straight area, use a "hard edge" gradation. This is ideal for featureless marine horizons. For situations where an extremely gradual blend is required, an attenuator is used. It changes density almost throughout its length. It is important to photograph as much of the filter as possible to achieve the best results.

The key to getting good results with a graduated filter is to help the effect blend in as naturally as possible. Keep it close to the lens in order to maximize transition softness. Avoid having objects in the image that extend across the transition in a way that would highlight the existence of the filter. Don't move the camera unless the transition can be maintained in proper alignment with the image throughout the move. Make all positioning judgments through a reflex viewfinder at the actual shooting aperture, as the apparent width of the gradation is affected by a change in aperture.

Graduated filters are best used in a square, or rectangular format, in a rotating, slidable position in a matte box. This will allow proper location of the transition within the image. They can be used in tandem, for example, with one affecting the upper half and the second the lower half of the image. The center area can also be allowed to overlap, creating a stripe of the combination of effects in the middle, most effectively with graduated filters in colors.

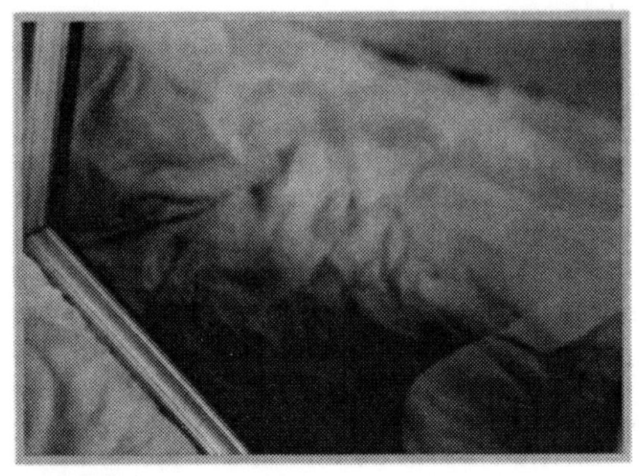
(no filter)

Polarizing Filters

Polarizers allow color and contrast enhancement, as well as reflection control, using optical principles different from any other filter types. Most light that we record is reflected light that takes on its color and intensity from the objects we are looking at. White light, as from the sun reflecting off a blue object, appears blue because all other colors are absorbed by that object.

A small portion of the reflected light bounces off the object without being absorbed and colored, retaining the original (often white) color of its source. With sufficient light intensity, such as outdoor sunlight, this reflected "glare" has the effect of washing out the color saturation of the object. It happens that, for many surfaces, the reflected glare we don't want is polarized while the colored reflection we do want isn't.

The waveform description of light defines non-polarized light as vibrating in a full 360 degree

(with polarizer)

range of directions around its travel path. Polarized light is defined as vibrating in only one such direction. A polarizing filter passes light through in only one vibratory direction. It is generally used in a rotating mount to allow for alignment as needed.

In our example above, if it is aligned perpendicularly to the plane of vibration of the polarized reflected glare, the glare will be absorbed. The rest of the light, the true-colored reflection, vibrating in all directions, will pass through no matter how the polarizing filter is turned. The result is that colors will be more strongly saturated, or darker. This effect varies as you rotate the polarizer through a quarter-turn, producing the complete variation of effect, from full to none.

Polarizers are most useful for increasing general outdoor color saturation and contrast. Polarizers can darken a blue sky—a key application—on color as well as in black-and-

(no filter)

white, but there are several factors to remember when doing this. To deepen a blue sky, it must be blue to start with, not white or hazy. Polarization is also angle-dependent.

A blue sky will not be equally affected in all directions. The areas of deepest blue are determined by the following "rule of thumb." When setting up an exterior shot, make a right angle between thumb and forefinger. Point your forefinger at the sun. The area of deepest blue will be the band outlined by your thumb as it rotates around the pointing axis of your forefinger, directing the thumb from horizon to horizon.

Generally, as you aim your camera either more into or away from the sun, the effect will gradually diminish. There is no effect directly at or away from the sun. Do not pan with a polarizer, without checking to see that the change in camera angle doesn't create undesirable, noticeable changes in color or saturation.

(with polarizer)

Also, with an extra-wide-angle view, the area of deepest blue may appear as a distinctly darker band in the sky. Both situations are best avoided. In all cases, the effect of the polarizer will be visible when viewing through it.

Polarizers need approximately 1-1/2 to 2 stops exposure compensation, generally without regard to rotational orientation or subject matter. They are also available in combination with certain standard conversion filters, such as the 85BPOL. In this case, add the polarizer's compensation to that of the second filter.

Certain camera optical systems employ internal surfaces that themselves polarize light. Using a standard (linear) polarizer will cause the light to be further absorbed by the internal optics, depending on the relative orientation. A circular polarizer is a linear one to which a clear quarter wave retarder has been added on the side facing the camera. This "corkscrews" the plane of polarization, effectively depolarizing it and eliminating the problem. The circular polarizer otherwise functions in the same manner.

Polarizers can also control unwanted reflections from surfaces such as glass and water. For best results, be at an angle of 33 degrees off the plane of the reflecting surface. Viewing through while rotating the polarizer will show the effect. It may not always be advisable to remove all reflections. Leaving some minimal reflection will preserve a sense of context to a close-up image through the reflecting surface. A close-up of a frog in water will appear as a frog out of water without some tell-tale reflections.

For relatively close imaging of documents, pictures, oil paintings, cel animation and small three-dimensional objects in a lighting-controlled environment—as on a copy stand—use plastic polarizing sheets mounted on lights aimed at 45 degrees to the subject (from both sides of the camera). This will maximize the glare-reducing efficiency of a polarizer on the camera lens. The camera, in this case, is aimed straight at the subject surface, not at an angle. The lighting polarizers should both be in the same, perpendicular orientation to the one on the lens. Again, you can judge the effect through the polarizer.

Special Effect Filters

General Information

The following filter types are available in a wide range of grades useful in both color and black-and-white imaging. They have no recommended filter factors, but may require exposure compensation based on several factors. Filters that lower contrast or create flare will have a greater effect where contrast and/or light intensity is higher.

Working with light, the more light they have, the more they can do. The same filter, in two different lighting conditions, may produce two different effects. With diffusion, or image softening filters, higher contrast scenes appear sharper, needing more diffusion than scenes of lower contrast. Diffusion requirements will also vary with other conditions. Smaller recording chip sizes will allow less diffusion, as will large-screen projection. In addition, color may allow less diffusion than black and white. These relationships should cause you to choose exposure and filter grade based on the situation and personal experience. Prior testing is always recommended, when possible.

Diffusion Filters

Many different techniques have been developed to diffuse image-forming light. Stronger versions can blur reality for a dream-like effect. In more subtle forms, diffusion can soften wrinkles to remove years from a face. The optical effects all involve bending a percentage of the image-forming light from its original path to defocus it.

Some of the earliest portrait diffusion filters still in use today are "nets." Fine mesh, like a stocking, stretched across the lens, has made many a face appear youthful and flawless. More recently, these can be obtained as standard-sized optical glass filters, with the mesh laminated within. These function through selective diffusion.

Diffusion filters also have a greater effect on small details, such as wrinkles and skin blemishes, than on the rest of the image. The clear spaces in the mesh transmit light unchanged, preserving the overall sharp appearance of the image. Light striking the flat surface of the net lines, however, is reflected or absorbed.

A light-colored mesh will reflect enough to tint shadows, either lighter (which lowers contrast), or also adding its color while leaving highlight areas alone. The effect of diffusion, however, is produced by the diffraction of light that just strikes the edges of the mesh lines. This is bent at a different angle, changing its distance to the focal plane, putting it out of focus. It happens that this has a proportionately greater effect on finer details than on larger image elements. The result is that fewer wrinkles or blemishes are visible on a face that otherwise retains an overall, relatively sharp appearance.

The finer the mesh, the more the image area covered by mesh lines, and the greater the effect. Sometimes, multiple filters are used to produce even stronger results.

Mesh with a square pattern can produce small four-pointed stars from lights in the scene. Most of the time, this is not desirable. Most mesh patterns used have a hexagonal pattern to minimize this effect.

As with any filter that has a discrete pattern, be sure that depth of-field doesn't cause the net filter lines to become visible in the image. Using small apertures, or short focal length lenses often make this more likely—as will using a smaller recording format, given an equal field of view.

Generally, mid-range or larger apertures are suitable, but test before critical situations.

When diffusing to improve an actor's facial appearance, it is important not to draw attention to the presence of the filter, especially with stronger grades, when diffusion is not required elsewhere. It may be desirable to lightly diffuse adjacent scenes or subjects, not otherwise needing it, to ensure that the stronger filtration, where needed, is not made obvious.

In diffusing faces, it is especially important that the eyes do not get overly soft and dull. This is the theory behind what might be called circular diffusion filters. A series of concentric circles, sometimes also having additional radial lines, are etched or cast into the surface of a clear filter. These patterns have the effect of selectively bending light in a somewhat more efficient way than nets, but in a more radial orientation. This requires that the center of the circular pattern is aligned with one of the subject's eyes; not always an easy, or possible, task, to keep it sharp. The rest of the image will exhibit the diffusion effect.

A variation on the clear-center concept is the Center-Spot filter. This is a special application filter that has a moderate degree of diffusion surrounding a clear central area that is generally larger than that of the circular diffusion filter. Use it to help isolate the main subject, held sharp in the clear center, while diffusing a distracting background, especially in situations where a long lens and depth-of-field differentiation aren't possible.

Another portrait diffusion type involves the use of small dimples, or clear refracting shapes dispersed on an otherwise clear optical surface.

(double fog filter)

They can be round or diamond-shaped and are capable of more efficient selective diffusion than the net type. They also have no requirement to be aligned with the subject's eye. They don't lower contrast, as by tinting shadows, as light-colored nets do. These dimples refract light throughout their surface, not just at the edges.

For any given amount of clear space through the filter, which is relative to overall sharpness, they can more efficiently hide fine details than net filters. One variation of this concept involves a minutely detailed series of patterns, made up of tiny lenslets. Each has a greater degree of curvature, with more optical power, than that developed by the dimples. This produces a maximum of selective diffusion efficiency for any given amount of overall sharpness.

The above types of filters, though most often used for "portrait" applications, also find uses wherever general sharpness is too great, and must be subtly altered.

(no filter)

Sliding Diffusion Filters

When attempting to fine-tune the application of diffusion within a sequence, it can be invaluable to be able to vary the strength of the effect while recording. This can be accomplished by employing an oversized filter that has a graduated diffusion effect throughout its length. It is mounted to allow sliding the proper grade area in front of the lens, that can be changed "on-camera." When even more subtle changes are required, maintaining consistent diffusion throughout the image while varying the overall strength, a dual opposing gradient filter arrangement can be used.

Fog, Double Fog, and Mist Filters

A natural fog causes lights to glow and flare. Contrast is generally lower, and sharpness may be affected as well. Fog filters mimic this effect of

(mist filter)

atomized water droplets in the air. The soft glow can be used to make lighting more visible and make it more dramatic for the viewer. The effect of humidity in, for example, a tropical scene can be created or enhanced. In lighter grades, these filters can take the edge off excess contrast and sharpness. Heavier grades can create unnatural effects, as for fantasy sequences. In general, however, the effect of a strong natural fog is not produced accurately by Fog filters in their stronger grades. This is because they are too fuzzy, with too much contrast, to faithfully reproduce the effect of a thick natural fog. For that, Double Fog filters are recommended.

Graduated Fog filters, sometimes called "scenic," are part clear or light fog, and part denser fog effect. Aligning the clear or weaker half with the foreground and the stronger half with the background will render an effect more like that of a natural fog, accumulating strength with distance.

(no filter)

Double Fog filters have milder flare and softening characteristics than standard Fog filters while exhibiting a much greater effect on contrast (especially in the stronger grades). A very thick natural fog will still allow close-up objects to appear sharp. So will a Double Fog filter. The key to the effect is the much lower contrast combined with a modest amount of highlight flare.

Mist filters generally produce highlight flare that, by staying closer to the source, appears more as a "halo" than will the more outwardly extended flare of a Fog filter. They create an almost pearlescent glow to highlights. The lighter grades are also used to tone down the excessive sharpness and contrast of video and lens combinations without detracting from the image. Black Mist-type filters also create moderate image softening and modest-to-strong highlight flare, but without as much of a lightening effect on shadows.

Contrast Control Filters

There are many situations, such as bright sunlit exteriors, where proper contrast is difficult to maintain. Exposing for either highlights or shadows will leave the other severely under or over exposed. Low Contrast filters create a small amount of "localized" flare near highlight areas within the image. This reduces contrast by lightening nearby shadow areas, which leaves the highlights almost unchanged.

The Soft Contrast series of filters include a light absorbing element in the filter which, without exposure compensation, will reduce contrast by also darkening highlights. Use this latter filter when lighter shadows are not desired. In both cases, the mild flare produced from bright highlights is sometimes used as a lighting effect.

Another type of filter reduces contrast without any localized flare. The Tiffen Ultra Contrast filter series uses the surrounding ambient light, not just light in the image area, to evenly lighten shadows throughout. Use it where contrast control is needed without any other effect on sharpness or highlight flare being apparent.

These filters, as well as the various Fog and Mist types, are the ones most often used to provide video images with the "film look." They can also be used in telecine to interrupt light when transferring film to tape.

Star Effect Filters

Lighting can be enhanced in ways that go beyond what exists in nature. Star filters create points of light, like "stars," streaking outward from

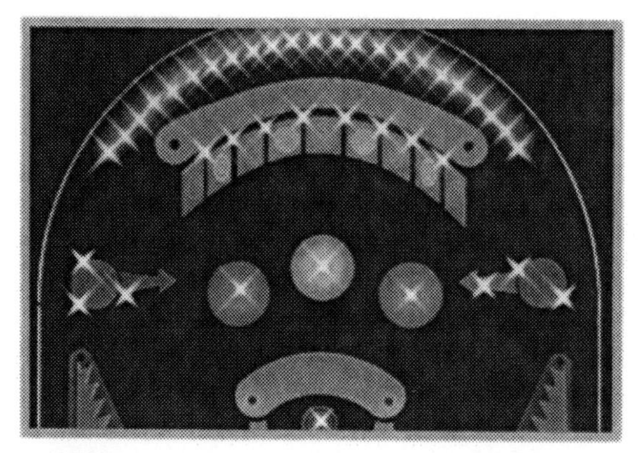

(star filter)

a central light source. This can make lighting within the scene take on a more glittering, glamorous appearance. The effect is produced by a series of thin lines etched into the flat optical surface of a clear filter. These lines act as cylindrical lenses, refracting light points into long thin lines of light running perpendicular to the etched lines. Lines on the filter positioned horizontally produce vertically oriented star lines.

The size and brightness of the star lines produced are first a function of the size, shape, and brightness of the light source. Additional control is gained by choosing a particular spacing between the lines on the filter. Generally this spacing is measured in millimeters. A 1 mm spacing has twice as many lines per unit area as a 2 mm spacing. It will produce a brighter star for any given source. Spacings offered generally range from 1 mm to 4 mm, as well as both narrower and wider for specialty effects.

The number of directions that lines run in determines the number of points produced. Lines in one direction produce a two-pointed star, just a streak through the center of the light. There are 4, 6, 8, 12 and more points available. With an 8 or 12 point filter, the many star lines will tend to overpower the rest of the image, so use them carefully. Although the more common types have a symmetrical arrangement of points, they can also be obtained with asymmetric patterns, which tend to appear more "natural," and less synthetic.

As with any filter that has a discrete pattern, be sure that depth of field doesn't cause the filter lines to become visible in the image. Using small apertures, or short focal length lenses make this more likely, as will using a smaller chip size, given an equal field of view. Generally, mid-range apertures or larger are sufficient, but test before critical situations.

Filters for Black-and-White

Tone Control Filters

Black and white imaging records only tonal differences between colored objects, which appear as black, white, or different shades of gray. Obtaining proper rendition depends on your own desires, and on understanding the differences between the camera's color sensitivity and that of the eye. A blue sky may appear a similar shade of light gray as the clouds that are in it, making the clouds "disappear."

A more "correct" cloud presence is obtained through the use of a yellow filter, such as a Wratten #8, that can absorb blue light. This darkens the sky to more closely match what the eye would see. The

#8 also acts as a general compensator for most subjects, giving a tonal rendition similar to that of the eye. Deeper colors, further to the red end of the spectrum, such as Wratten #15 deep yellow, #16 orange, and #25 and #29 red filters will produce progressively deeper and artificially more dramatic renditions of blue sky.

Remember that, since these filters act on color differences to produce tonal differences, the required colors must be present. The part of the sky you are recording must be blue to be affected as above. Sky sections closer to the sun, or nearer the horizon, are generally less blue than elsewhere. Use of a graduated neutral density filter can darken a sky relative to the foreground, but will not increase contrast between a blue sky and the clouds.

Using filters for contrast control can be a matter of artistic preference, or of necessity. It is possible for two disparate colors, say a certain orange and blue, to record as the identical tone, eliminating any visible difference between them. Filters will lighten objects of their own color and darken those of their complement. Complementary color pairs are: green-red; orange-blue; violet-yellow. An orange filter in the above case will darken the blue, and lighten the orange; a blue filter will perform the reverse.

A green filter, such as Wratten #11, can be used to lighten green foliage and to show more detail. It may also be used to provide more pleasing male skin tones outdoors, especially against blue sky.

Any filter used for the above purposes will have a greater effect if slightly underexposed. Its function depends on absorbing the light of its complementary colors, which increases the proportion of light for colors similar to itself. Exposure compensation is often needed to allow proper image density, but the relative difference is reduced by the addition of light at the absorbed wavelengths through additional exposure.

Filters for Color

General Information

Recording color involves knowing more about light sources than is necessary for black-and-white imaging. Sunlight, daylight, exterior lighting at different times of day, incandescent, fluorescent, as well as other artificial sources, all have color characteristics that vary significantly. We see images through our eyes only after they are processed by our brain, which has the ability to make certain adjustments to the way we see color. White will still appear white to the eye in various lighting, so long as we don't have more than one type visible at a time.

Typically, video cameras are designed to see only a certain type of light as white. All other colors will appear different to the extent of their difference. Filters can be used to provide the necessary fine-tuning.

Unlike film recording, however, filters aren't the only way to effectively control color in the camera. Electronic white balance, cards that incorporate pre-defined corrections, and other electronic means exist for making adjustments. Filters are an aid in bringing light closer to the capabilities of the camera, or for incorporating certain particular color effects.

Knowing that light is a form of energy, we can theoretically view it as energy emitted from a hot object, usually termed a black body, that gives off light as a function of its temperature. The color of that light can be measured in degrees Kelvin. The most common types of light can be categorized by certain anticipated color temperatures, or can be measured with a color temperature meter.

The following discussion of filters for color control will be enhanced by seeking additional information on color temperature and light-source characteristics.

Color Conversion Filters

Color Conversion filters are used to correct for sizable differences in color temperature between the internal video correction and the light source. These are comprised of both the Wratten #80 (blue) and the Wratten #85 (amber) series of filters. Since they see frequent outdoor use in bright sunlight, the #85 series—especially the #85 and #85B—are also available in combination with various neutral density filters for exposure control.

Light Balancing Filters

Light Balancing filters are used to make minor corrections in color temperature. These are comprised of both the Wratten #81 (yellowish) and the Wratten #82 (bluish) series of filters. They are also often used in combination with Color Conversion filters. Certain #81 series filters may also be available in combination with various neutral density filters for exposure control.

Color Compensating (CC) Filters

Color Compensating (CC) filters are used to make adjustments to the red, blue or green characteristics of light. These find applications in correcting for color balance, light source variations, and other color effects. They are available in density variations of Cyan, Magenta, Yellow, as well as Red, Blue, and Green filters.

Decamired® Filters

Decamired filters are designed to more easily handle unusual color temperature variations than the previously mentioned filters. Available in increments of both a red and a blue series, Decamired filters can be readily combined to create almost any required correction. In measuring the color temperature of the light source, and comparing it to that for which the film was designed, we can predict the required filtration fairly well.

A filter that produces a color temperature change of 100°K at 3400°K will produce a change of 1000°K at 10,000°K. This is because the filter relates to a visual scale of color. It will always produce the same visible difference. A color change of 100°K at the higher temperature would hardly be noticed.

To allow simple calculation of such differences, we convert the color temperature into its reciprocal, that is, to divide it into "1." Then, since this is usually a number with six or more decimal places, we multiply it by 10 (super)6, or one million, for convenience. This is then termed the micro reciprocal degrees (mired) value. It identifies the specific change introduced by the filter in a way that is unrelated to the actual temperature range involved.

To see this more clearly, let's look at the following changes in color temperature from both the degree and mired differences. Numbers are degrees Kelvin, those in parentheses are mireds:

9100 (110) to 5900 (170) = difference of 3200 (60)
4350 (230) to 3450 (290) = difference of 900 (60)
4000 (250) to 3200 (310) = difference of 800 (60)

From this, you can see that, although the degree differential varies as the range changes, the actual filtration difference for these examples, in mireds, is the same.

To use this concept, subtract the mired value of the light source from that of the camera setting. If the answer is positive, you need a reddish filter; if negative, use a bluish filter. Mired-coordinated filters are termed as Decamireds. Mired value divided by ten yields Decamireds. The 60 mired shifts, above, would be produced by an R6 filter, where the higher values were that of the lighting.

Sets of such filters generally come in values of 1.5, 3, 6, and 12 Decamireds in both B (bluish) and R (reddish) colors. These numbers are additive; that is, a pair of R3's produces an R6. An R6 plus a B6 cancel each other out to produce a neutral gray.

(no filter)

Fluorescent and Other Discontinuous Spectra Lighting Correction

Since filters never actually add color, but only absorb certain wavelengths to increase the relative proportion of others, the original light source must have the colors you want in it to start with. Some sources are totally deficient in certain wavelengths and they cannot be added back using only filters. This is particularly true of many types of metal halide lighting.

With other lighting types, such as fluorescent, color temperature measurements may not provide the correct filter requirements since color temperature theory is based on having a continuous spectrum (light at all wavelengths). It is possible for a light source to have a sufficient spectral distribution to emulate a correctable color temperature when so measured, but its effect when recorded can be very different. (See chapter on Lighting for further details.)

(with blue filter)

Fluorescent lighting generally produces a greenish color overcast. Each of the many lamp types varies in color, and it can be difficult to get the precise correction even with the white balance function. There are special filters available, however, that are designed as an average correction for the most commonly encountered fluorescent lamps.

Mixed Lighting Situations

A question often arises of what to do when there is more than one type of lighting used in a scene. The key to this is to first try to make all the light sources behave the same. That is, to choose one that predominates, correct the camera for that, and correct the other lighting with gel filters made for them.

You can convert daylight coming through a window with a gel placed over the window. This will make it a similar color temperature to the predominant tungsten, or even fluorescent, lighting inside. Then correct the camera for that type of light.

There are many such combinations that will work, and which one to choose is often a matter of economics. Filtering a factory of fluorescents with gels or filter tubes may cost far more than just gelling up the occasional window.

If there is no way to correct all the lights for one color temperature, try to minimize the intrusion of those for which you cannot correct to the camera. Sometimes this can be used to advantage. The cool blue light from outdoors shining through a window can make the tungsten-lit interior seem that much warmer, and cozier. Once "normal" color is within reach, a variation can often be even better. It all depends on your purpose, and the story you are telling.

Graduated Color Filters

Similar to graduated ND filters, graduated color filters are also produced in a wide range of standard and custom colors, densities, and proportions for many applications. A Blue-to-Clear filter can add blue to a white, hazy sky without affecting the foreground. An Orange-to-Clear filter can enliven a tepid sunset. Color can be added to the bottom of the scene, as with a Green-to-Clear filter used to enrich the appearance of a lawn.

Stripe filters are another type of graduated filter, having a thin stripe of color or neutral density running through the center of the filter, gradating to clear on either side. These are often used to horizontally paint various colors in layers into a sky, as well as for narrow-area light balancing.

Coral Filters

As the sun moves through the sky, the color temperature of its light changes. It is often necessary to compensate for this in a variety of small steps as the day progresses to match the appearance of different adjacent sequences so that they'll look as if they all took place at the same time. Coral filters are a range of graded filters of a color similar to an 85 conversion filter. From light to heavy, any effect from basic correction to warmer or cooler than "normal" is possible. Corals can also compensate for the overly cool blue effect of outdoor shade.

Sepia Filters

People often associate sepia-toned images with "early times." This makes Sepia filters useful tools for producing believable flashbacks and for period effects with color imaging. Other colors are still visible, which is different from original sepia-toned photography, but appear infused with an overall sepia tint.

Didymium Filters

The Didymium filter is a combination of rare earth elements in glass. It completely removes a portion of the spectrum in the orange region. The idea is to increase the color saturation intensity of certain brown, orange, and reddish objects by eliminating the muddy tones and maximizing the crimson and scarlet components. Its most frequent use is for obtaining strongly saturated fall foliage.

The effect is minimal on objects of other colors. Skin tones might be overly warm. Even after subsequent color correction to balance out any unwanted bias in these other areas, the effect on reddish objects will still be apparent. Prior testing should be done, where possible, since color sensitivity of cameras varies.

Underwater Color Correction Filters

When shooting underwater, the light you are recording is filtered by the water it passes through. Longer wavelength reds and oranges are absorbed until only blue is left. The actual effect is determined by numerous factors, such as light source (sun or artificial), water quality, and the water path. The latter is the distance the light travels through the water. In natural (sun)light, this is the depth of the subject from the surface plus the subject-to-camera distance. For artificial lighting, it is the light-to-subject-to-camera distance. The longer the water path, the greater the filtering effect of the water.

In many cases, certain color correcting filters can absorb enough shorter wavelengths to restore better color balance. Aquacolor®, a patented system of filters that precisely compensates for the light-filtering effects of water, comes in densities that match different water-paths. The difference between corrected and uncorrected color can be dramatic.

Special Application Filters

Contrast Viewing Filters

Balancing lighting by eye is a matter of experience. Decisions can be aided, however, through the use of contrast viewing filters. These are designed to handicap the eye, with its much greater range of apparent densities, to resemble the range of the recording medium. Use contrast viewers to judge relative highlight and shadow densities. There are viewers for black-and-white imaging, as well as various viewer densities for color.

Day-For-Night

Day-for-night imaging is an effect that makes a scene recorded in daylight appear as if it were at twilight or night. This is usually accomplished by the use of a filter that both underexposes by about two stops, and can also produce a bluish color overcast. Lighting, contrast, control of the sky and other factors contribute to the reality of this effect.

Close-up and Split-Field Diopter Lenses

Close-up lenses allow for closer focusing than would otherwise be available with the unaided camera lens. These are especially ideal for nature subjects. Cutting such a lens in half produces the Split-Field lens. This can be used to have two fields of focus, one very near, the other very far, in one scene.

Other Filter Considerations

Effect of Depth of Field and Focal Length Changes

Standard color filters generally function without change through variations in depth of field and focal length. This may not be true of many of the "special effect" filter types. There are no solid rules for predicting the variation in filter effect due to depth-of-field or focal length changes. There are some things we can expect, however.

Let's look at a fog/mist type filter that causes a light to glow, or flare. Take the example of a certain grade filter where we can see that the ratio of light diameter to glow diameter is 1:3. As we view this through a changing focal length, we will see that the ratio remains the same, although the magnification will vary accordingly. So the decision to use a filter of a different grade to maintain a certain appearance at different focal lengths will be based on wanting to change the ratio, as opposed to any otherwise corresponding relationship. Some camera operators use stronger effect filters on wide angle lenses than they do on telephoto or zoom lenses to maintain a continuity of look. Tests are advisable for critical applications.

Multiple Filter Use

When any single filter is not enough to produce the desired results, use combinations. Choose carefully, to minimize the number required. Usually the job can be done with no more than three filters. Use filters that individually add to the final effect, without canceling each other out.

For example, don't use a polarizer, which can increase color saturation, in combination with a low contrast filter which reduces saturation, unless it works for some other reason (the polarizer could also be reducing reflections, for instance). Generally, the order they are mounted in is not important. Some popular filter combinations may also be available in one filter, to simplify their use.

Secondary Reflections

Lighting can cause flare problems, especially when using more than one filter. Lights in the image pose the greatest difficulties. They can reflect between filter surfaces and cause unwanted secondary reflections. Maintaining parallelism between filters, and further aligning the lights in the image with their secondary reflections where possible, can minimize this problem. In critical situations, it may be best to make use of a matte box with a tilting filter stage.

Tilting filter(s) of good optical quality only a few degrees in such a unit can divert the secondary reflections out of the lens axis (out of the image) without introducing any unwanted distortion or noticeable changes in the filter's effect.

Internal reflections may also be reduced through the special-ordering of filters with high-efficiency anti-reflection coatings on both sides. These can reduce reflection by over 90 percent and result in much-diminished reflection problems. The downside is that, although offered by some of the filter manufacturers, they add considerable expense, need advance planning (to order), and there are existing techniques (like the tilting matte stage) that seem to be used successfully, even when quite a number of filters are used together.

Another option is that filters can be constructed from what is known as "water white" glass. Although also more costly, these do not have the faint green tint that may be noticed in filters made from the more traditional soda-lime glass. Some may find that, when stacking several (especially colorless) filters together, this may be a preferable alternative.

Custom (Homemade and Field-Ready) Filters

There will be times when you need an effect and don't have time to obtain one ready-made. Certain effects can be produced that, although different from factory filters, can be useful in a pinch, or for unusual custom situations. Net diffusion effects can be produced as they were originally, by stretching and affixing one or more layers of stocking material to the lens end, held in place with a rubber band.

There are also numerous things you can do if you have a clear filter (or several) available. Petroleum jelly can cause flare or diffusion, or even some star-like streaks, depending on its application, to a clear filter, spread with a finger or cloth. The chief benefit here is that the effect can also be applied only to selected portions of the scene. Using clear nail polish produces a similar, but longer lasting effect.

Breathing on a clear filter can produce interesting but temporary fog-like results. Using cut gels can simulate certain graduated filter effects. When doing this, be sure to keep the filter close to the lens and use larger lens openings to keep the visible edge as soft as possible.

COMPARISON OF PHOTOGRAPHIC LIGHT SOURCES

Description	Correlated Color Temperatures (at rated voltage)	Mired Value	Efficacy (Lumens/Watt)
Incandescent			
Standard and tungsten/ halogen	3200K	313	26
CP gas filled	3350K	299	32
Photoflood	3400K	294	34
Daylight blue photoflood	4800K	208	
Carbon arc (225 Brute)			
White flame, Y-1 filter	5100K	196	24
White flame, no filter	5800K	172	
Yellow flame YF 101 filter	3350K	299	
*Xenon, high pressure			
DC short arc	6000K	167	35-50
*Metal halide additive AC arc			
HMI	5600K	179	80-102
CID	5600K	179	80
CSI	4200K	238	85

COMPARISON OF SOME TYPICAL COMMERCIAL/INDUSTRIAL LIGHT SOURCE CHARACTERISTICS

Description	Correlated Color Temperatures (°Kelvin)	Color Rendering Index	Efficacy (Lumens/Watt)
Flourescent Types			
Daylight	6500	79	60
Design White	5200	82	50
Cool White	4300	67	70
Deluxe Cool White	4100	86	50
Natural White	3700	81	45
White	3500	62	70
Warm White	3050	55	70
Deluxe Warm White	2950	73	45
Incandescent	2700	90	35
Mercury Vapor Types			
Clear Mercury	5900	17	50
White Mercury	4000	45	55
Warm Deluxe	3500	62	70
Metal Halide Additive Types			
Multi-arc™; Metal Vapor™	5900	65	80-115
Metalarc C™	3800	70	80-115
High Pressure Sodium			
Lucalox™	2100	25	80-140
Lumalux™			

CORRELATED COLOR TEMPERATURE OF TYPICAL LIGHT SOURCES

Artificial Light

Source			**Mireds**
Match flame	1700K		588
Candle flame	1850K		541
Tungsten-gas filled lamps:		Camera filter	
40-100W	2650-2900K	82B (100W)	317-345
200-500W	2980K	82A	336
1000W	2990K	82A	334

Daylight

Sunlight			
Sunrise or sunset	2000K		500
One hour after sunrise	3500K		286
Early Morning, late Afternoon	4300K		233
Average noon, (Wash. D.C.)	5400K		185
Midsummer	5800K		172
Overcast sky	6000K		167
Average Summer daylight	6500K		154
Light Summer Shade	7100K		141
Average Summer Shade	8000K		125
Partly cloudy sky	8000 -10000K		125-100
Summer skylight	9500 -30000K		105-33

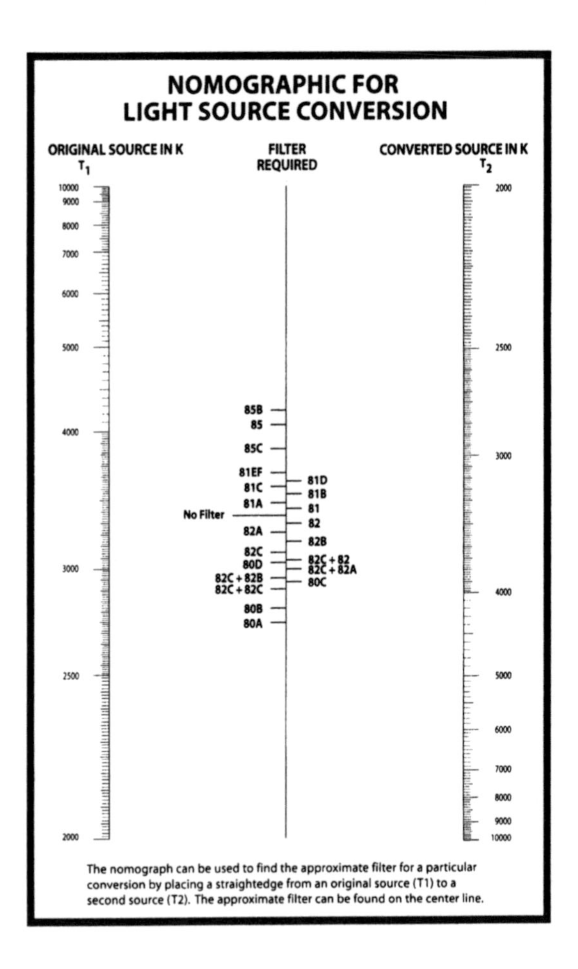

***Ira Tiffen** is an associate member of the American Society of Cinematographers and Vice President of Tiffen Manufacturing.*

Test Equipment In Digital Video Operations

by Gerald McGinty

Early in the application of end-to-end digital operations, 4:2:2 serial digital interface (SDI) in all aspects of video operations from acquisition to post production, people thought that there wasn't a need for monitoring in the familiar sense. After all, except for errors in the transmission of data, there aren't the problems of distortion that have existed in analog operations. That is, levels cannot be in error (even when you fail to terminate), and there is no such thing as problems with linearity, differential gain, group delay, and on and on.

Yet experience has shown that monitoring a digital video signal may be more important than ever. The digital system won't alter prescribed levels, but people do, in many cases because system parameters are new and old habits acquired in analog die hard.

Although many aspects of monitoring seem to disappear, a whole new set of monitoring requirements have emerged. We are now dealing with the serial data stream at the astonishing data rates of 270, 360 Mbps and 1.5 Gbps—and we're only getting started. This requires a totally new approach to signal transmission, and the paramount monitoring problem of detecting and preventing errors in the data from which video display and sound are ultimately derived.

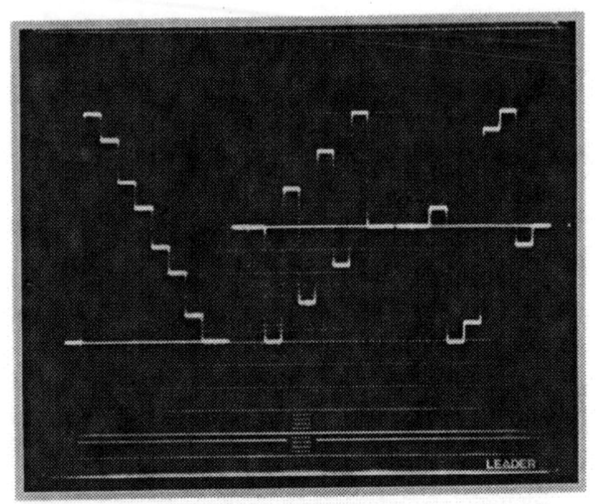

Figure 1. Parade waveform of 100% color bars shows Y, Cb, Cr from left to right.

Waveform and Vector Monitoring

Waveform Display

Let's take a look at test-signal waveforms as they appear on the screen of a digital waveform monitor. We'll look at standard definition television (SDTV) first. In Figure 1, the signal is 100 percent color bars of component video in the form of Y, Cb and Cr. It has been digitized in the 4:2:2 format, which refers to the ratio of sample frequencies applied to Y and the two color-difference signals (13.5 Mbs for Y and 6.75 Mbs for B-Y and R-Y).

Some words about component symbols: Video components have long been known as the primary components GBR, green-red-blue, (RGB in antiquity). These derived signals are used most often in transmission and recording: Y and the color-difference signals B-Y and R-Y. The latter is now referred to as Y Pb Pr for analog components and Y Cb Cr for digital components. The missing color-difference signal, G-Y, is not transmitted as it can be derived from the other two.

Getting back to Figure 1, the waveform monitor has been set to the parade mode. This means that one line of video (1H) is shown for Y, Cb and Cr in that sequence from left to right. What you are looking at is a set of analog waveforms that have been decoded in the waveform monitor from the serial data stream.

The one element that appears to be missing is sync. There is no "sync pulse" as such in the data stream. Instead sync takes the form of four data words that are part of the data stream. But we'll look at an analog representation of digital sync on the waveform shortly, and we can also look directly at the data itself to see how the sync words show up in numbers.

Levels: When 75 Percent Means 75 Percent

Signal levels in digital operations are somehat simpler than in the analog operations to which we have grown accustomed. The 100 percent bars shown in Figure 1 are just as you might expect. The Y signal, at the left spans 100 units on the graticule, and the peak-to-peak swings of the Cb and Cr signals to the right span the same 100 units.

Actually, Cb and Cr start out much larger, but are scaled down to fit 100 units. Figure 2 shows the same waveform display for 75 percent color bars. The first Y bar, white, remains at 100 percent to serve as a calibration level, but the luminance values for the yellow, cyan, green, magenta, red and blue bars

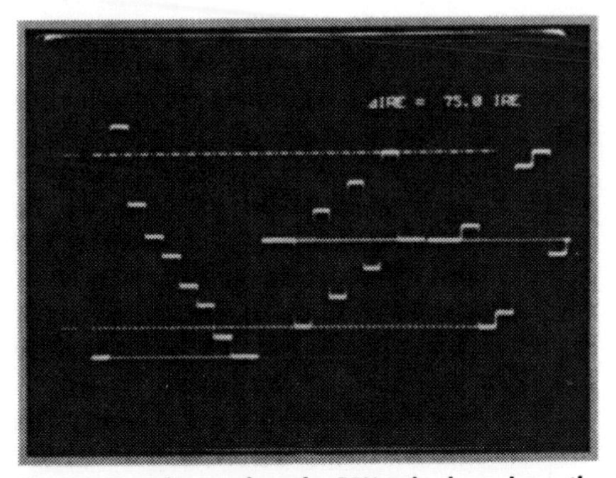

Figure 2. Parade waveform for 75% color bars shows the first Y bar at 100% for calibration purposes. The remaining Y bars, as well as Cb and Cr are at 75%.

have been dropped to 75. And the peak-to-peak swings for Cb and Cr now span 75 percent. To point up the latter, the level cursors on the waveform monitor have been preset to 75 units.

The previous discussion of levels might seem like an elaboration of the obvious, but it is very different from past experience. For example, the standard test signal for decades has been SMPTE and EIA color bars. These are 75 percent bars, but we have been looking at them for years as spanning 100 IRE units. A similar situation occurs for Betacam analog components where the Pb Pr signals for 75 percent bars are scaled to span 100 IRE units. (See Figure 3.)

The Pb and Pr signals in Figure 3 span 0.7 volts, which is equivalent to 100 percent. The use of the voltage scale is standard in component operations. But the waveform monitor used for the

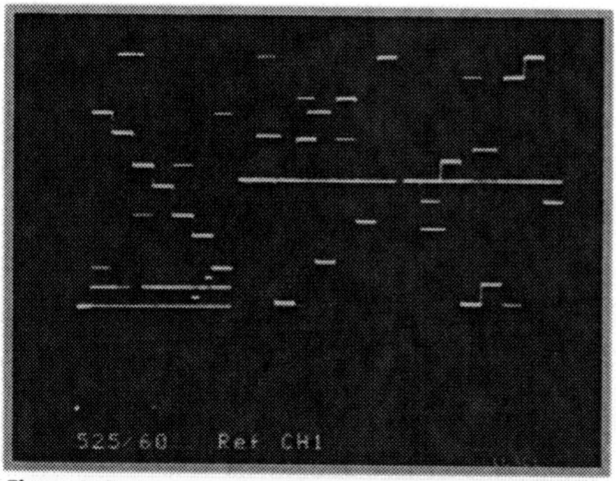

Figure 3. Betacam analog SMPTE color bars that are 75% bars shows that the P-P Cb/Cr bars span 0.7 volts (100%). SMPTE bars also employ 7.5% setup as noted by the black level at the bottom of the pattern. the ± 4 IRE Pluge signal rides on the setup level.

figure has the option of adding cursors using either volts or "%." The "%" cursors, similar in use to IRE units, are shown. But the point is that the Pb/Pr span for 75 percent bars in analog Betacam is 100 units, but converted into digital the swings will span 75 units. A probability for error in level settings is lurking. The important thing to remember is that 75 percent in digital means 75 percent, and the operator must ascertain the status of the test color bars used as the test reference (recorded on the leader).

What happened to setup? Look back at Figures 1 and 2 and you will see that the lowest step in the Y waveforms is at the black (blanking) level. There is no elevation of the black floor called "setup," at least in test color bars, in the standards. Compare this with the analog component signal of SMPTE bars in Figure 3, which shows black (the long line with the

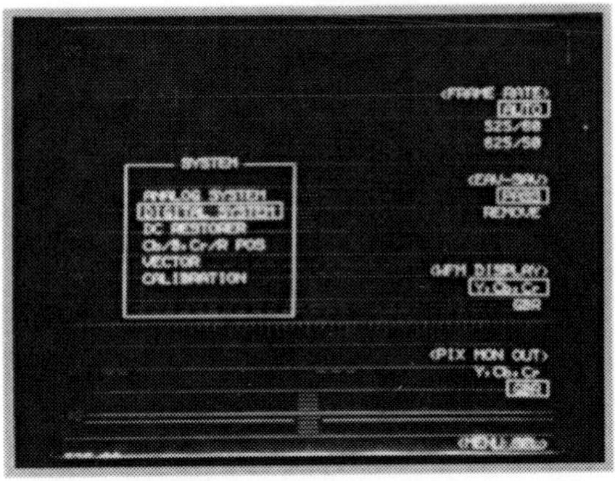

Figure 4. Digital System menu on the waveform monitor permits selection of scan systems, EAV/SAV pass/remove, and the choice of YCvCr or GBR for both waveform display and decoded picture-monitor outputs.

± 4 IRE "Pluge" signal sitting on it) at the customary + 7.5 IRE.

The standards make no mention of setup, and do not show setup on test signals. However, the use of setup appears to remain the standard practice for camera settings. (Hence, the two dashed lines just above the blanking level of the graticule shown in Figures 1 and 2.) The upper dashed line is at 7.5 percent. The lower line at 5 percent is in use in other parts of the world. Setup was never used in Europe and has been dropped in many parts of the world.

An important adjustment of the waveform monitor, in order to make any sense of the scale markings, is to adjust the vertical position control to put the black step on the Y waveform on the zero percent line (the graticule line marked with the time-tick marks).

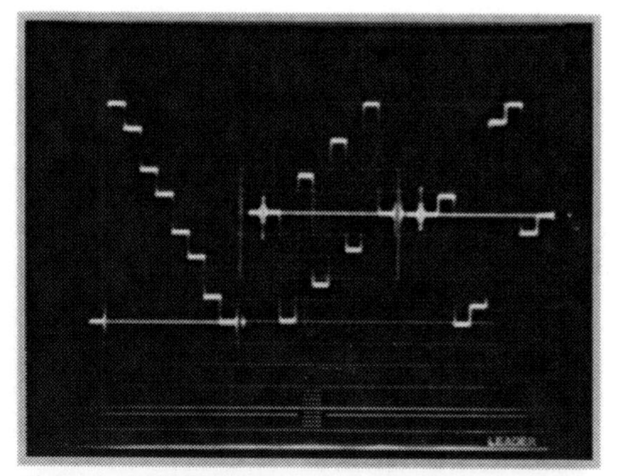

Figure 5. EAV/SAV PASS removes the effect of blanking. EAV and SAV appear as spikes at the beginning and end of all three waveforms. EAV appears smeared to the right as the result of embedded audio in the signal.

Looking at Sync

The parade waveforms shown in Figures 1 and 2 cover active video; that is, the parts of the signal that occur outside the blanking intervals. Those four-word sync signals occur during the blanking intervals, and are called SAV (start of active video) and EAV (end of active video). The waveform monitor lets us look at the analog result of decoding the four word sequence, by opening the display to show the normally blanked areas.

To do this the digital system menu is called up as shown in Figure 4, and the PASS option of EAV/SAV PASS—REMOVE is selected. This results in the waveform display shown in Figure 5.

A sort of ringing spike, similar in appearance to the sinx/x signal, appears to mark the timing locations of SAV and EAV on all three waveforms.

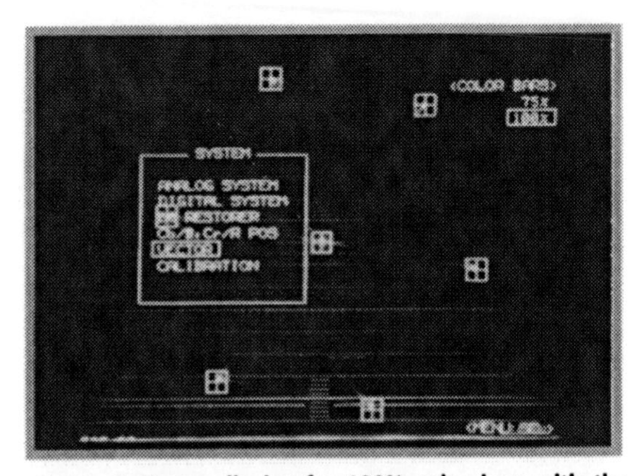

Figure 6. Vector display for 100% color bars with the vector system menu superimposed to show the 75, 100% choice for calibration.

The reason it looks like this is that there is insufficient bandwidth to show the signal as data levels The first two words of the four-word sequence is 3FF (all ones) and 000 (all zeros). This represents a voltage transition that is far too fast to be shown as video.

The low-pass filters that normally follow D/A conversion cannot handle such a transition and the ringing spike that results appears. This is a perfectly normal effect and does not infer insufficient bandwidth of the waveform monitor. The EAV spike forms a useful reference point for timing adjustments between digital feeds, wherein the waveform monitor is synchronized by an external reference.

In ITU-R601 serial digital (525/59.94) operations the timing reference remains black burst. Timing adjustments are not critical in digital operations as the receivers are capable of aligning sets of signals that are within a half line of correct timing.

Vector Display

The vector display is brought up by a touch on the "Vector" key in the "Mode" group (See Figure 6.) This is simply a plot of the component signals Cr vertically and Cb horizontally. Unlike the familiar NTSC vector display, there is no phase adjustment (as a subcarrier plays no part in the location of the vectors). The electronically-generated targets represent considerable precision, as the targets themselves are affected in the same way as the vectors by any non-linearity in the CRT deflection system.

The vector targets give quick view of the accuracy of Cb and Cr, and tell at a glance which or both are within limits. Before the vector display is used it should be set up to match the characteristics of color bars in use. That is either 75 or 100 percent. Figure 6 shows the Vector readout from the "System" menu superimposed over the vector display. Note the choice of 100 or 75 percent in the top-right corner.

[A word about the meaning of 75 and 100 percent. Those percentages do not refer to saturation (a common misunderstanding). The numbers refer to the amplitude of GBR into the encoder.]

The targets apply to test signals from color-bar generators only. But the color space formed by connecting the target centers provides a rough idea of signals within the allowable gamut of Cb and Cr. Similar displays like the "Diamond" make it easier to spot so called "illegal" values of Y Cb Cr that will not transcode back into the allowable gamut for the GBR primaries.

Monitoring Data

What we have been looking at is decoded analog signals reclaimed from the stream of numbers in the

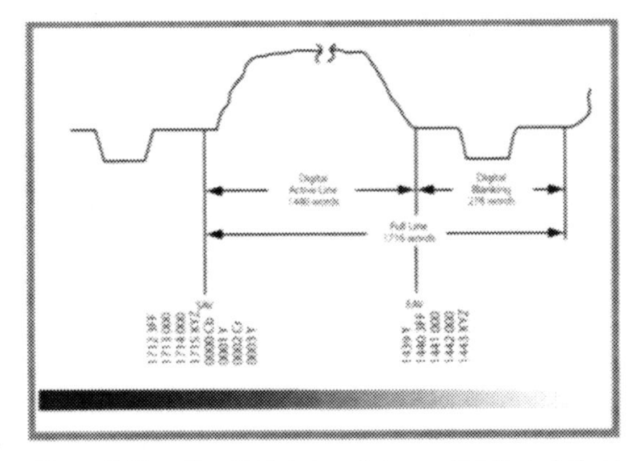

Figure 7. How the 1716 data points are distributed along the raster lines. SAV and EAV data words take the place of sync.

SDI. Now let's look at the numbers themselves.

First, a quick review of how the data is sampled and arranged might be in order. The components Y Cb Cr are sampled at rates in the 4:2:2 ratio. But these factors are applied to some common number. In digital composite NTSC operations (the earliest of which was in time-base correctors), the sample frequency was always chosen to be a multiple of the subcarrier frequency—such as 3fc or 4fc.

The "magic number" chosen for component operations is 3.375 MHz. This number works out well for both 525/60 and 625/50 systems. Hence the sample rate for Y is 4 x 3.375 MHz = 13.5 MHz, and for Cb and Cr the sample rate is 2 x 3.375 MHz = 6.75 MHz. (Note that there are twice as many Y samples as color samples.)

The samples could have been transmitted in YCbCr parallel form using eight wires for 8-bit systems or 10 wires for 10-bit systems. This would require a very stiff bundle of 30 wires for 10-bit YCbCr parallel transmission. A better solution is to transmit the YCbCr samples in time sequence in this fashion: Cb (the first sample following SAV) Y, Cr, Y', Cb ,Y, Cr, Y'... etc.

By interleaving the samples in this way, the overall sample rate for parallel operation becomes four times the sample rate for each YCbCrY' chunk, or 27 MHz.

Now we can calculate the number of samples that occur during each raster line:

$$\frac{\textbf{Sample Frequency}}{\textbf{H Frequency}} = \frac{\textbf{27 MHz}}{\textbf{15.734 kHz}} = \textbf{1716} \text{ (addresses 0000 to 1715)}$$

Data for each line are arranged as shown in Figure 7. This shows the SAV codes as samples 1712 through 1715. The first three are a preamble (3FF, 000, 000). This trio precedes both SAV and EAV and serves as a "heads-up" warning that the next code (shown as XYZ) is the actual sync word. The values of XYZ are coded to convey H, V and Field 1,2 information, as will be shown.

Following SAV, the first active sample, Cb, is followed by the remaing active samples in the line. A total of 1440 words make up the active (unblanked) part of each raster line. This is followed by a blanking period of 276 words that starts with EAV. The balance of the blanking period is available for other data, including embedded audio and other ancillary codes.

Levels: A to D

A 10-bit binary word ranges from 0 to 2^{10}—or 1024 discreet levels. However, not all levels are in use for video. The bottom and top of the range, 00 0000

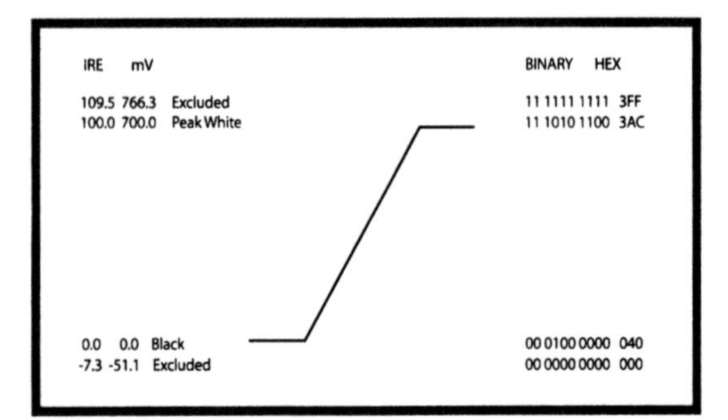

Figure 8. Conversion of analog levels to digital values for Y signals.

0000 and 11 1111 1111, are set aside exclusively for the preamble to the sync words. Figure 8 shows how levels are assigned in the 10-bit system for Y. The black level, 0 volts or 0 IRE is assigned the binary number 00 0100 000.

This is often difficult to remember, so a shorthand method of expressing binary numbers called "hex" is used. Hex stands for hexadecimal, a numbering system using the base 16. Thus, 00 0100 0000 in binary converts to 040 in hex.

It's easy to convert binary to hex and the reader might want to consult a basic text on numbering systems to find out. But the key hex numbers are easy to remember, and they will be called out as we run across them. (Look at the Calculator in Windows on your computer, switch it to Scientific and you have a dandy converter; from decimal to binary to hex and back again.)

Figure 8 shows the normal Y gamut—from black, at zero V and IRE, to peak white at 0.7 V or 100 IRE—to range from 00 0100 0000, 040 in hex, to 11 1010 1100 or 3AC in hex. This 3AC is another key hex number. It's

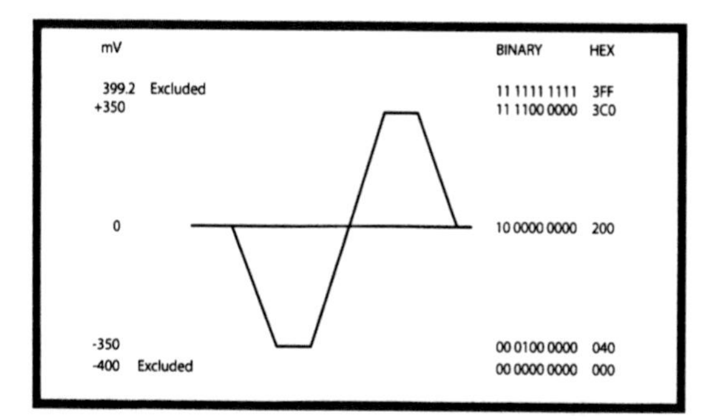

Figure 9. Conversion of analog levels to digital values for color (Cb/Cr) signals.

equivalent to 100 IRE. There is room in Figure 8 to allow for signals that range above and below 100 and 0 IRE. However the bottom and top of the hex range from 000 to 003 and 3FC to 3FF are excluded from use for video. The binary column in Figure 8 represents the number of wires (one for each of the ten places in the 10-bit words) that is required for parallel transmission. Transmission in serial form will be discussed shortly.

Levels for the chroma signals, Cb and Cr, are set up as shown in Figure 9. The chroma signals in analog swing above and below zero. (Although analog component waveform monitors set them on a 50 IRE pedestal so that they swing within the 0 to 100 IRE range on the graticule.) In digital, the 50 percent pedestal is part of the system, so that there is no need to deal with negative binary numbers.The pedestal in hex is 200; another key number. In any part of the signal where Cb and Cr go to zero, in white the white or black color bars, for example, the chroma signals collapse to the pedestal and the hex values become 200.

This is admittedly a dry subject that becomes

real when you use the waveform monitor to actually look at data. Figure 10 shows the 3rd page of the Digital menu of the LV 5100D waveform monitor. This display shows data in hex form for any selected raster line and digital address. A variable control is used to dial in either line number or digital address, depending upon which function is framed at the lower right of the screen. The line selected is 26. This is simply to get past the end of V blanking and into the active video area. The address has been set to show 1708 at the top to allow the observation of SAV, starting at address 1712. Note the precursor to sync with the data words 3FF, 000 and 000. The following word at address 1715 is the actual sync word, 31C in this instance. Information contained in this code tells what field of the two-field sequence we are in, whether we are in or out of the vertical blanking interval, and whether we are dealing with SAV or EAV.

The following shows the meaning of each of the bits in the sync word:

MSB									LSB
1	F	V	H	P3	P2	P1	P0	0	0

Here the most significant bit is always set to One. Reading from left to right, the next bit is labelled F to identify the field in the two-field sequence in interlaced systems. This bit is a "0" for Field 1 and a "1" for Field 2. The next bit, marked V, is set to 0 during active video and 1 during vertical blanking. The following bit, labled H, identifies SAV or EAV for each raster line. It is a 0 for SAV and a 1 for EAV.

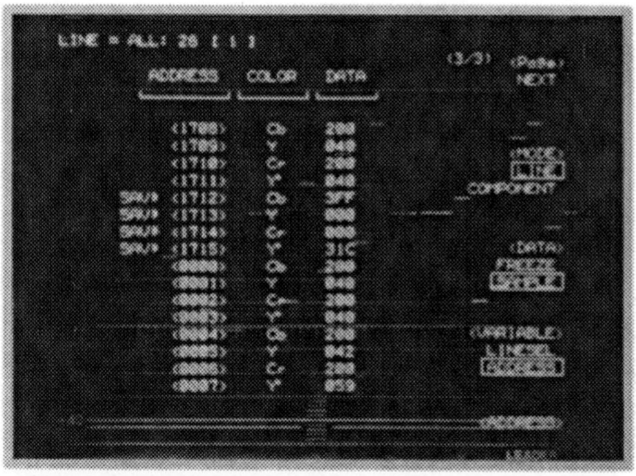

Figure 10. Data readout on the waveform monitor allow access to data values in hex for all pixels including the blanked areas. Pixels are designated by line number and data address.

The next four bits, labelled P3 to P0, form a Hamming code to correct an error in the most significant bits. This sync word works for 8-bit systems as well, but in 10-bit signals the two least significant bits are zero. The sync word is called TRS (Timing Reference Signal) and contains all the data, including SAV and EAV, shown above.

The data for the TRS shown in Figure 10 is 31C in hex. Let's see what that means in detail. The first thing to do is to convert 31C in hex to binary. This becomes 11 0001 1100. Using the table above, we see that the data captured is for Field 2, during the active part of the vertical scan and the timing signal, is SAV.

Following 1715, we see at address 0000 the first active sample, Cb. Its hex value is 200, the value of the chroma pedestal as shown in Figure 9. This means that the chroma value is zero. The signal used to take this picture was 100 percent color bars; the first bar is white so there is no chroma information. Thus, Cb and Cr will remain at 200 throughout the duration of the white bar and only begin to change when addresses are called up into the yellow bar (at about address 0201).

The Y signal, however, starts out at black, address 0001 at 040 hex, but it grows to 059 hex by address 0007. If we were to spool upwards in addresses we would find that Y' reaches 3AC (100 IRE) at address 0019. What you have looked at in data is the rise time of the left edge of the white bar.

It's doubtful that anyone will want to measure color bars in hex, but the point is that you can address any pixel in the picture, or any location where audio or ancillary data resides, and read the data. It's obvious that if we were monitoring live video instead of the relatively static color bars the hex reading might be expected to be a total blur.

In fact, data is captured at regular intervals of about one second, as evidenced by a tiny arrow that flashes opposite the word Data to indicate a data update. The operator has the option to "freeze" data at any time. The data display can also be set up to automatically be triggered by error. In effect the data display is blank, (all Xs in hex) until an error is detected, and at that time the data is captured and stored.

Serial Digital Interface (SDI)

The multiwire parallel-mode cable needed to interconnect system components is cumbersome and difficult to run for appreciable distances. Hence, a move to translate parallel data into time-

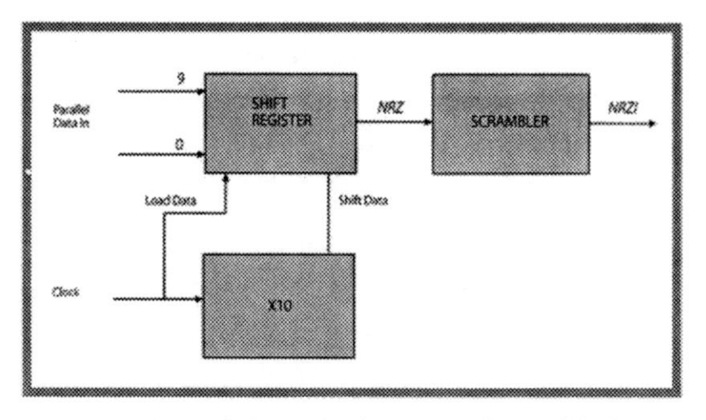

Figure 11. The serializer transforms parallel 10-bit data at 27 Mbps to serial data at 270 Mbps.

sequenced serial data was made early in digital development. Serial data is transmitted on a single coaxial cable using the familiar BNC connectors. The system used to serialize parallel data is shown simplified in Figure 11.

Parallel data in 10 lines is dumped into a shift register at each clock interval (27 Mbps). This sets the 10 cells of the register with the parallel data received at the time of the 27 Mbps "Load Data" signal. The clock is also fed into a X10 frequency multiplier (270 Mbps) whose output ripples the shift register to display the cells in time sequence (in serial form). Serial output from the shift register is in the NRZ (Non-Return to Zero) form, which means that the signal does not return to zero after every bit. A sequence of three ones means that the signal will remain high for those three bits.

Following the register, the signal is scrambled. Scrambling shuffles the data much like shuffling a deck of cards to break up former card sequences. The shuffling prevents long unchanged data sequences where there is little change in the picture, and avoids long strings of ones and zeros.

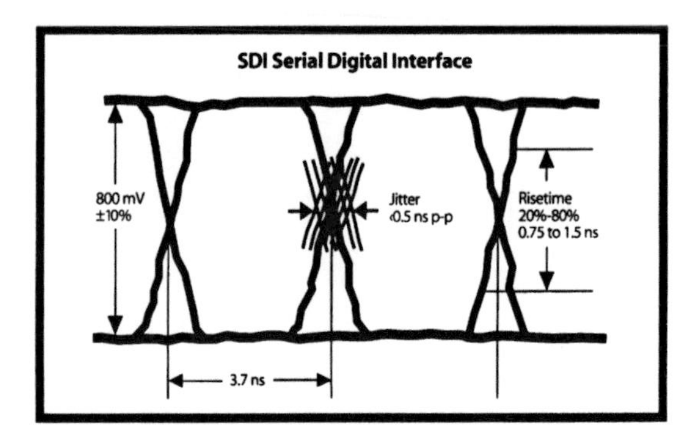

Figure 12. Waveform and specifications for the Serial Data Interface (SDI).

Unlike card shuffling, however, scrambling is not random. It is accomplished by a shift register of prescibed length with preset feedback loops. This makes it possible to unscramble the signal at the receiver by feeding the signal through a matching register. The scrambler also includes a data inverter that outputs signals in the NRZI (Non-Return to Zero Inverted) form. The unique attribute of NRZI is that binary Ones appear as signal transitions, zeros as an absence of transitions.

The serial data stream, while simplified to a single cable, is very difficult to handle due to the extreme bandwith required. The signal resembles square waves at the astounding bit rate of 270 Mbps. The duration of each bit is 1/270 Mbps = 3.7 nanoseconds. A square wave formed from a string of alternate 1s and 0s would appear as a square wave, however, whose full period is twice 3.7 nanoseconds, for a fundamental square-wave frequency 270/2=135 MHz.

But if you've ever dealt with square waves you

know that a square wave is made up of a fundamental frequency sine wave, plus sine waves at odd harmonic frequencies. The addition of harmonics steepens the rise and fall times and flattens the runs. This means that to preserve square waves the odd harmonics—the 3rd, 5th, etc.—must be preserved.

The third harmonic of 135 MHz is 405 MHz, the fifth is 675 MHz. Thus, a very wide band (and expensive) oscilloscope is required to observe the serial data stream. The drawing in Figure 12 shows how the SDI waveform would look, along with key specifications and tolerances. Keep in mind that a string of data taken over just a few data periods might look somewhat different, but the scope shows many such strings superimposed.

Observing the SDI Waveform, the "EYE" pattern

You can buy scopes of sufficient bandwidth (in excess of 400 MHz) to observe the SDI waveform. A very short time base, like 1 ns/div, is also needed. Fortunately video test equipment manufacturers have added the ability to monitor the SDI signal to digital waveform monitors.

A technique known as "sampling" is used to provide bandwidth equivalent to that which is needed. This makes use of the repetitive nature of the data stream. In effect, samples taken on one sweep hit a few points on the waveform and these are stored. On subsequent sweeps new samples are captured. The accumulation of points gathered in this way allows the waveform to be "rebuilt." Figure 13 shows the SDI waveform on a digital waveform monitor equipped to show the eye pattern, and using

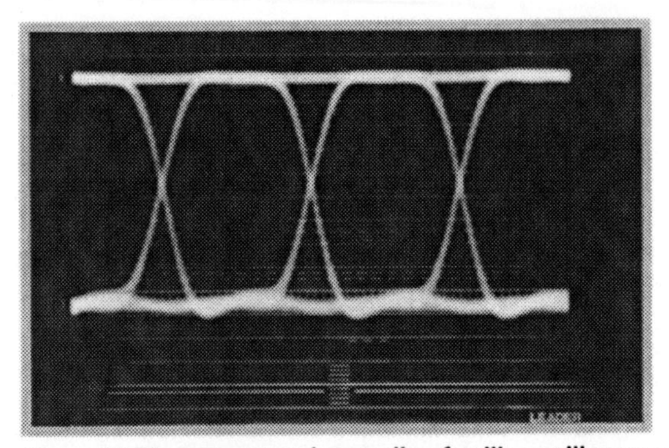

Figure 13. The eye pattern is actually a familiar oscilloscope display of the serial data stream, but the time base is very short, 1 nanosecond per division in this photo, and very wide bandwidth is needed.

a time base of one ns.

The term "eye pattern" has come into use for the normal oscilloscope display of the serial data stream shown in Figures 12 and 13. The reason is that the bit period, shown as 3.7 ns in Figure 12, and called the "Unit Interval" or UI, resembles an eye. The flats look like the upper and lower lids and the rise and fall transitions the corners.

The eye opening is critical to decoding. That is, after the signal has been converted back to parallel, whether the center of the unit interval represents a high or a low, a one or a zero.

The effects of coaxial cable losses, which increase with frequency, tend to close the eye. Signal attenuation brings the lids closer together. Loss of the high harmonics slows the steepness of the transitions, and other effects—such as phase shift between fundamental and harmonics, noise, reflections from cable discontinuities or bad

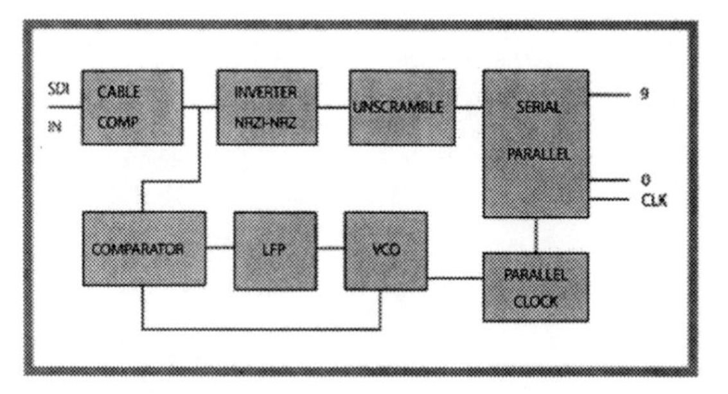

Figure 14. Serial receiver accepts the serial data stream, unscrambles it and produces data in parallel form.

terminations and jitter (not cable related)—act to close the eye.

The effect of closing the eye brings about an increase in the probability of decoding error. When a point is reached at which data can no longer be reclaimed at the receiver, the signal becomes meaningless and the so called "digital cliff effect" is at hand.

At this point it is a good idea to take a look at how the SDI receiver is set up. (See Figure 14.)

The first stage the SDI signal encounters performs cable compensation. This is an automatic circuit that looks at signal amplitude to establish how much cable is in use from an ideal source. This is based on the known attenuation characteristics of the cables commonly in use. This figure also provides the basis for correcting frequency response to restore rise and fall times and the shape of the eye pattern.

Many receivers, in digital DAs and elsewhere, perform the vital function of cable compensation. Some give a front-panel indication when signal degradation has reached the point where compensation will not be

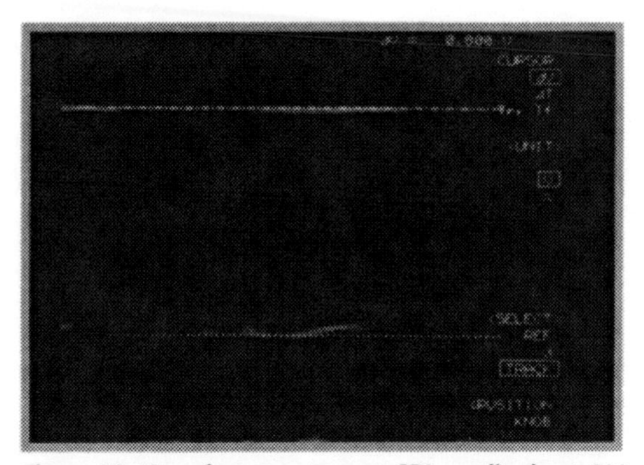

Figure 15. Use of cursors to spot SDI amplitude at 800 millivolts p-p. Time base is 500 picoseconds per division, and waveform brightness has been lowered so that the cursors stand out in the photo.

adequate. Following cable compensation, the signal is inverted to form NRZ, unscrambled and fed to load a shift register that is read out in parallel to reverse the process shown in Figure 11.

A second branch from the cable compensation drives the phase-lock-loop that recovers the 270 Mbps clock from the data stream itself. Here the data signal is compared with a sample from a crystal, voltage controlled oscillator. This comparison yields a DC correction voltage to bring the VCO into phase lock with the data. This correction voltage feeds through a low-pass filter that determines the speed at which the PLL can respond to changes or the range of jitter frequencies that the system can follow. The 270 MHz signal is divided down to 27 MHz to form the parallel clock drive for the register.

The waveform monitor equipped for eye display also provides the means to quantify signal

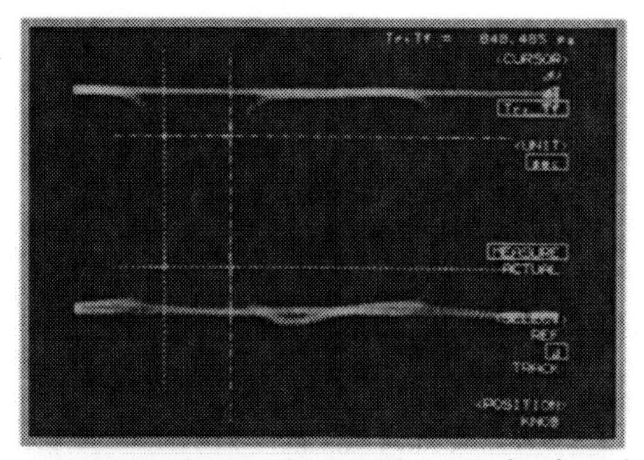

Figure 16. Waveform monitor setup for measuring rise and fall times employs horizontal lines to mark 20% and 80%, and calculates the effect of the instrument itself on the final reading.

characteristics in terms of voltage level, rise and fall times, and jitter. The latter is expressed in terms of the peak-to-peak spread of the transitions shown in Figure 12 (less than 0.5 ns p-p). However, it has become common practice to express jitter as a fraction of the unit interval (UI). Figure 15 shows the use of cursors to measure signal level. The timebase has been reduced to 500 ps per division, and brightness reduced to show the cursors more clearly.

Rise and fall time measurement (see Figure 16) calls up two sets of cursors. The horizontal set marks the 20 percent and 80 percent levels, between which rise and fall times are measured. The vertical (time) cursors are positioned to the points on the rise or fall where they cross the 20 and 80 percent marks. Note that two figures are given: Measure and Actual.

The first in ps (picaseconds) is that indicated when you position the time cursors properly. The

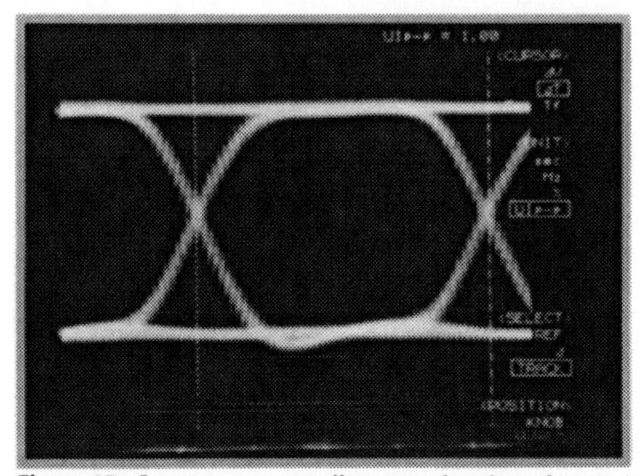
Figure 17. Setup to measure jitter as a fraction of UI (Unit Interval). Cursors are set to span the unit interval.

second (Actual) will always be shorter in time. Here the instrument figures in its own contribution to the slowing of rise/fall times due to the bandwidth limitation of the instrument itself.

Jitter

Jitter is measured by spanning the p-p rise/fall crossings that appear in the waveform with the vertical time cursors. The readout may be in picaseconds or in UI. Figure 17 shows the setup. The signal here is straight from the generator, so jitter is actually insignificant. The cursors have been set to span the unit interval, wherein the indicated UI is one.

Another aspect of jitter is the frequencies at which jitter occurs. A precise quantitative analysis of jitter frequencies can be performed with a spectrum analyzer, and to cover all frequencies (including a static offset), jitter should be measured against a stable clock reference.

However, a very useful guide to jitter frequencies can be had by switching the low-pass filter cutoff frequencies in the PLL employed in the waveform monitor. Jitter measured against the PLL clock is called "relative jitter."

The instrument used in this series offers low-pass filter cutoff frequencies of 10, 100 and 1000 Hz. If set to 10 Hz, for example, the PLL will follow all jitter components at frequencies below 10 Hz and they will not show on the waveform. Any jitter that does appear is therefore above that figure. The same is true for the 10 Hz and 1 kHz selections. Thus, by switching filters it is possible to narrow down the frequency range at which observed jitter occurs.

Relative jitter falls into two general bandwidth categories: Timing jitter measured from 10 Hz to a tenth of the clock rate, and Alignment jitter, from 1 kHz to a tenth of the clock rate.

Error Detection

As long as the numbers survive, and can be reclaimed at the receiver, the signal will be transmitted perfectly. That's what makes a digital system so rugged. The design of a digital facility is based on keeping SDI signals in the state where number reclamation is assured. This requires careful attention to SDI signal levels, the choice and routing of coax, close attention to terminations, the insertion of cable-compensating DAs when necessary, and selection of switchers and other processors.

The prime measurement of acceptance is whether data errors are occuring, and how often.

Thus, the key to evaluating system performance is a way to detect errors when they occur. Several systems are in use to detect and correct error in digital audio and ancillary data. These include parity checks and check sums.

The SAV/SAV codes, for example employ a Hamming code to correct single bit errors in those code words (4 of the 8 bits of the EAV/SAV codes are used for error correction). But the system used to detect error in the bulk of video data employs something called a CRC (Cyclic Redundancy Check) code.

Error Detection and Handling (EDH)

The basis for EDH is the insertion of a check code at the end of a video field that is calculated from all the data in the field. This code is calculated from received data in the receiver and compared with the code that has been tucked into the signal at the source. A lack of agreement indicates an error of a single bit in an entire field.

In practice, two CRC codes are implanted at the source. One is restricted to the active picture only (excluding data placed in the blanking intervals), called the APCRC. The second encompasses all the data in the Field, including audio and ancillary data—although excluding data on lines 9 to 11—and is called the FFCRC.

Calculation of the CRCs involves division of the data by a complex polynomial (X16 + X12 + X5 + 1). But this calculation is implemented by feeding the data through a shift register with prescribed feedback loops. The data left in the register at the end of the active or full field is the APCRC and the FFCRC. These code word are placed in the following vertical interval on lines 9 (Field 1) and —- (Field 2) at addresses 1690 through 1700.

You can spot the EDH codes in the type of data display shown in Figure10 by dialing in line 9 and address 1690. The preamble to EDH is two words of 3FF at addresses 1690 and 1691. The reason for the separate AP and FF CRCs is that some data changes may be expected in normal operations due to changes in ancillary data, such as user ID words, time code, etc.

So the operator may want ignore these errors, but the actual picture data should remain inviolate.

The Display of EDH error is handled in many different ways. Figure 18 shows the first of three status pages called up when the DIGITAL key is touched on the waveform monitor used for this series. The bottom entry, labled ERROR: displays the word FOUND if an error has been detected and follows that word with the time of day in hours, minutes and seconds at which the error occurred. This notice stays in effect until reset by touching the function key opposite <ERROR> RESET. Following reset, and until the next error is caught the display shows ERROR:—————-.

The remainder of the first status board is worth noting. The top, SIGNAL: PRESENT tells the operator that a valid 525/60 or 625/50 signal has been detected and is currently being processed. The next entry down, CABLE: <100 m, is of particular interest, as this readout is an indication of signal level for the input SDI data stream.

But instead of giving signal level in volts, the reading is converted to an equivalent length of coax of the type commonly used (such as Belden 8281) from an ideal, 800 mVp-p source. The reading is based on an amplitude measurement and the known characterisics of the coax. This gives the operator a short-hand look at signal conditions in a way that affects error count.

It is known that signal degradation due to high-frequency losses results in the sharp rise in error count called the "digital cliff." Experience has put this cable length at approximately 300 meters. Hence the operator can have some confidence in error-free operation if the reading is less than 300 meters—and the shorter the better. The reading of <100m shown in the figure alleviates concern.

The next entry, SIGNAL FORMAT: 525/60 tells the operator that the signal being processed meets U.S.A. standards at 525/59.94. The instrument will also handle 625/50 signals automatically, and so indicate that format here. The next three entries show the presence of ANC (ancillary) data, embedded digital audio, and the EDH codes.

The word CATCH at each of these entries shows that the signal currently contains ancillary data, embedded audio and the EDH CRCs. An EDH LED notice on the front panel also lights to tell the operator at a glance that EDH has been detected in the signal being processed. The extent of EDH implementation varies to some extent and is available from most test generators.

Error Flags

The handling part of EDH explains what to do about errors once they have been found. The use of error flags injected by receivers within a chain of processors makes it possible to troubleshoot the chain and localize the source of error. The flags are:

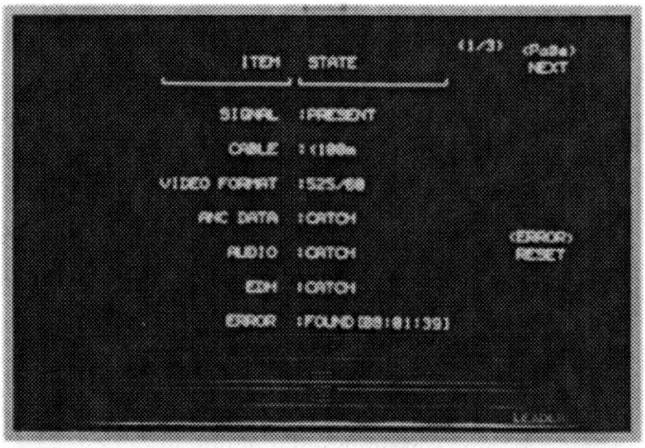

Figure 18. Status board of the waveform monitor shows the time at which an EDH error was detected. Also shown is the level of the SDI signal in terms of cable length from an ideal source.

EDH: Error Detected Here. This flag is injected as data in the reveiver when an error has been detected. It tells downstream processors that an error has been detected.

EDA: Error Detected Already. This flag warns the operator that the error detected has been spotted upstream in the system. EDA flags should be passed through to to downstream equipment, and locally detected EDH should be changed to EDA for transmission downstream.

IDH: Internal Device Error. Warns downstream processors that an internal error was spotted in the local unit.

IDA: Internal Device Error Detected Already. Similar to EDA in warning downstream processors that an internal error has been reported upstream.

UES: Unknown Error Status. Warns operators downstream that the signal being propagated has not

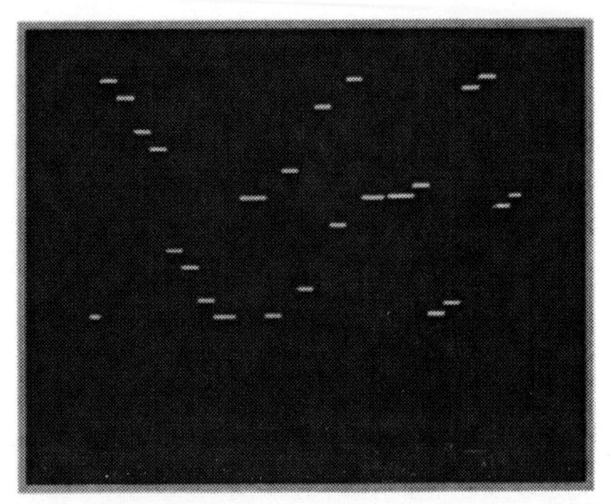

Figure 19. Parade display for 100% color bars for a 1080i HDTV signal. Note the precipitate drop in the Y signal at the green-magenta interface resulting from the formula for Y.

been checked for errors. This flag should be relayed to downstream units.

The error flags are set up for full-field, active picture and ancillary data. Implementation of the use of error flags is sparse at the time of this writing. However the system is in place to draw on in future applications. The waveform monitor in use for this chapter reports on the presence of error flags in the data stream.

HDTV Test and Measurement

Much of what has been covered earlier applies to high definition television (HDTV) signals as well. Data is carried in 10-bit words and the digital levels for Y, Cb and Cr are the same as those shown in Figures 8 and 9. This section will stress the differences.

Chromaticity

If you have grown up with NTSC and 525/60 components, you might be taken aback when you first see the YCbCr parade waveform for 720p or 1080i HDTV signals. They look much different.

Look at Figure 19, and compare this waveform for 100 percent color bars with the set shown in Figure 1. Note the precipitate drop in the Y signal at the transition of the green-magenta bars in Figure 19. This signifies that Y is composed of more green and less red and blue. The reason is that the formula for Y has changed to reflect changes in phosphors and other factors that have taken place over the years.

The Y formula given in SMPTE RP-177, and repeated in SMPTE 274M 1995 is :

(1) $Y = 0.2126\ R + 0.7152\ G + 0.0722\ B$

Compare this with the Y formula for NTSC:

(2) $Y = 0.299\ R + 0.587\ G + 0.114\ B$

Note that the later standard has been carried out to four decimal places rather than three, and that there is a lot more green and less blue and red.

Once you get used to these differences, there is little to affect level checks. Peak white remains at 100 percent or 0.7 volts. The p-p span of Cb and Cr is once again scaled to fit between zero and 0.7 Vf or 100 percent bars. The Cb/Cr span for 75 percent color bars is again 75 percent or 0.525 Vp-p. Calibration of the vectorscope targets must be changed to reflect the change in standards.

It should be noted that an interim formula for Y had been in effect prior to that given in SMPTE 274M. This formula, found in SMPTE 240M, is Y = 0.212 R + 0.701 G + 0.087 B. This formulation is very close to that given in (1), and should have a minimal effect on routine operations. The differences will not alter level settings as the peak Y and p-p chroma signals are not affected. However, small changes will be noted in waveform and vector displays if older material is monitored on an instrument set up to comply with the later standard.

Sample Rates

HDTV signals pack a lot more pixels into the viewing area so we can expect a dramatic rise in bits per second. The following develops the bit rates for 720p (720 lines displayed non-interlaced, called progressive scanning) and 1080i (1080 lines displayed with interlaced scanning).

For 1080i: The format provides for 1920 pixels horizontally by 1080 interlaced lines displayed. There are 1920 active pixels per line, plus 280 blanked for a total of 2200 pixels per line. There are also 1080 lines displayed plus 45 blanked for a total of 1125 lines per frame.

Multiplying the frame rate of 29.97 fps by 1125 gives the horizontal frequency (Hf) of 33.716 kHz. Taking the reciprocal of Hf yields the period of the H scan (Ht) at 29.659 ms (microseconds).

Unlike parallel operation in SDTV where Cb,Y, Cr, Y' are multiplexed on a single cable, in HDTV, Y/Y' and Cb/CR are multiplexed on separate cables. For either set we can calculate the sample rate by dividing the horizontal line period Ht by the total number of pixels per line.

$$\text{Thus: } \frac{Ht}{\text{total y pixels}} = \frac{29.659us}{2200} = 13.481ns$$

$$1/13.481ns = 74.17 \text{ Mbps.}$$

The same calculation applies to Cb/Cr. For the serial data output Cb Y Cr Y' are multiplexed before being serialized and as a result the final parallel clock is twice the clock rate for the YY' and CbCr sets, or 148.34 Mbps. This figure is multiplied by 10 to change parallel to serial and yield the serial clock rate of 1.483 Gbs. This data rate is referred to loosely as 1.5 Gbs in the literature.

At this time it appears that the 29.97 Hz frame rate developed for NTSC might revert to the 30 Hz frame rate that was in use prior to NTSC. Repeating the above calculations for a 30 Hz frame rate yields a horizontal frequency of 33.750 kHz and the SDI sample data rate of 1.485 GBs.

For 720p: There are 1280 horizontal pixels by 720 lines displayed (progressive scan). Also, 1280 active pixels per line, plus 370 blanked, for a total of 1650 total pixels per line. There are also 720 lines displayed, plus 30 blanked, for a total of 750 total raster lines

$$\text{Thus: } Hf = 59.94 \text{ Hz} \times 750 = 44.995 \text{ kHz}, Ht = 1/Hf = 22.244us$$

$$\frac{22.244us}{1650} = 13.481ns \text{ (clock period)}$$

Again, this is the parallel sample rate for Y/Y' and CbCr which doubles to 148.34 Mbs prior to serialization. Serializing multiplies the rate by 10 to yield the SDI data rate of 1.483 Gbps. Note that the data rate for 1080i and 720p is the same at 1.483 Mbs. Redoing the above for a frame rate of 60 Hz again yields the data rate of 1.485 Gbps. Also note that the sample rates are identical for 720p and 1080i systems.

Practical Aspects

The enormous increase in data rates for HDTV production standards causes a revision in many standard operating procedures. For example, high-frequency cable losses are much more severe at 1.5 Gbps than at 270 Mbps. (Harmonics must be preserved to several GHz.) This has prompted the move to improved, low-loss cables and the consideration of fiber-optic cable for signal distribution within the plant.

Loop-through input connections are disappearing because the problem of preventing return loss and reflections from attempted loop through connections are very large. A single input BNC connector is more common, with a precision, low SWR internal 75 Ω termination. And while 300 meters of cable has been the accepted rule of thumb for the proximity of the digital cliff, the figure is closer to 100 meters for 1.5 Gbps data rates.

Error Detection in HDTV

A system similar to EDH in SDTV systems has been developed for 720p and 1080i signals as well. It employes CRCs that are calculated in the same way by dividing the data by a specified polynomial.(Again a shift register with prescribed feed back loops carries out this calculation.)

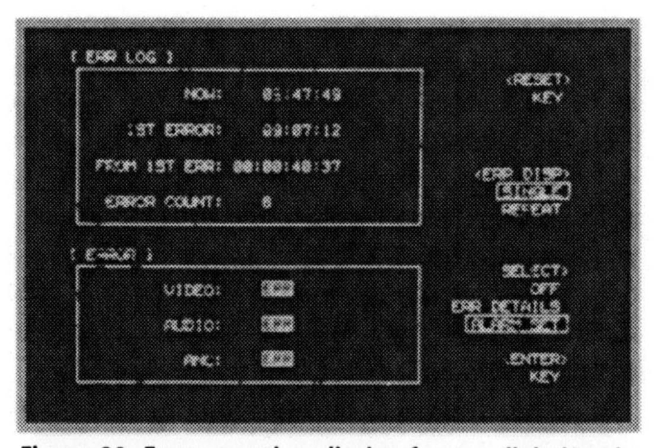

Figure 20. Error-reporting display from a digital/analog waveform monitor capable of handling 720p and 1080i.

However, the calculation does not include the data for an entire field, but is done on a line-by line basis. Thus, the CRC codes are placed following EAV and a two-word code that identifies the line number. Since Y and Cb/Cr are carried in two separate cables for parallel operation, two sets of TRS and two sets of CRCs—one for Y and the other for C—are inserted prior to the serializer. This makes it possible to detect error in Y and C separately. The calculation starts at the first active word in the line and finshes at the end of the line-number codes.

Figure 20 shows the error-status board called up on an digital/analog waveform monitor capable of handling both 720p and 1080i signals. The ERR LOG frame at the top gives a run-down on error activities up to the present time. The NOW: reading shows the present time of day in hours, minutes and seconds. Below that is the time at which the first error was detected. The instrument continues to record errors, and the accumulated number appears to the right of ERROR COUNT:.

In addition, the time duration from the point of the first detected error is given. From elapsed time and total error count it is possible to determine the BER (Bit Error Rate).

The lower frame in Figure 20 permits the operator to find out where the errors occurred: in video, audio or ancillary data. Details as to the nature of the error are also available by framing the VIDEO, AUDIO or ANC headings when ERR DETAILS is selected. The latter, for example, shows video error in Y and C.

Also accessed in the lower frame is the ability to set alarms to indicate error in the selected category (VIDEO, AUDIO, or ANC). The alarm is registered on the front panel of the instrument (an LED) , and may be wired to a remote location from a rear-panel connector.

Digital System and Component Tests

When a new digital facility is set up, even at a temporary site designed to cover a one-time event, the system should be tested for the one failure mode that is most likely to degrade performance—data errors. The system could be monitored over a considerable length of time to establish acceptable bit error rates of 1 per day or per week. But time is a luxury, and methods have been developed to speed up the process and develop confidence in the system. The idea is to stress the system, to put it to work in situations in which data errors are more likely to occur.

The simplest "stress test" is simply to add more coaxial cable. Earlier discussions noted the fact that data errors increase sharply when cable runs reach 300 meters (100 meters for 1.5 Gbps signals).

Therefore, once a system has been set up and no errors have been detected, add 50 meters of cable. If no errors are detected, the operator can have some degree of confidence that the system will be at least 50 meters back from the digital cliff when the test length is removed. A rise in error count with the test length in the system calls for system changes such as the addition of cable-compensating DAs at suspected locations.

Several test-equipment manufacturers offer dummy cables of fixed equivalent lengths to be used for this purpose. The dummy cables are made up of fixed components designed to immitate the characteristics of known cable types. They are small and portable, and eliminate the need for a bulky reel of cable.

Pathological Check Field

Let's look at some worst-case data recovery situations. A long string of zeros in the serial data stream stresses the phase lock loop in the receiver, because the absence of signal transitions removes the reference in the phase comparator, and the crystal oscillator tends to revert to its natural free-running frequency. The short term correction when ones resume tends to cause jitter.

Long strings of ones, on the other hand, tend to introduce low-frequency components that upset the action of automatic cable compensation. Either of these actions affects the decoding process and tends to raise the error count. But the scrambling that takes place in the serializer acts to shuffle the signal and break up long strings of repetitive data.

However, within the framework of scambling, certain data combinations can arise that do, in fact,

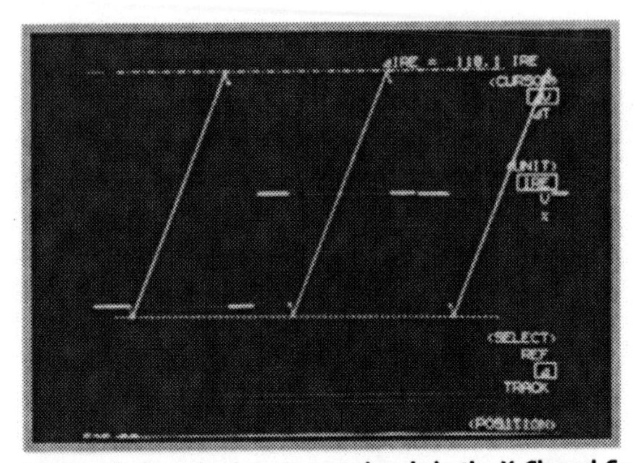

Figure 21. Oversized ramp test signals in the Y, Cb and Cr channels check D/A decoders and subsequent analog processors.

lead to long strings of either ones or zeros. The pathological check field is a test signal made up of those unique code combinations. It is a split-field test pattern in which the top half is designed to stress the cable compensator in the receiver, and the bottom half stresses the PLL. (The longest string of zeros is 19.)

The Pathological Check Field is a unique stress test, and its use adds to confidence in error-free operation. Most digital test generators include this test pattern.

Other Test Signals

Digital signal generators provide many test patterns that are familar as standard references such as color bars (100 percent and 75 percent). Others are designed to check digital decoders and the analog circuits they might drive. These include multiburst and line-sweep to check frequency response, pulse-

Figure 22. Shallow ramps reveal decoding errors in the least significant binary numbers.

bar to check for transient distortion, the Bowtie to check for timing errors between the three-signal components, and the stairstep or ramp to check linearity. These are test signals that have been in use for some time in analog operations.

The ramp, however, is of particular importance in digital operations, and is sometimes included in split-field combination with color bars to form a dual-purpose test signal. In providing a uniform ascension of digital numbers, the ramp checks the ability of the decoder at a wide range of levels.

Some generators provide three levels of ramp signals in each of the Y, Cb and Cr channels. One level is an oversized ramp that extends from below black (040 in hex) to above 100 percent (3AC in hex) to check decoding accuracy in the normal video gamut. Figure 21 shows ramp signals of this type.

A larger ramp is the "Digital Limit" ramp. This signal covers the entire range of signal

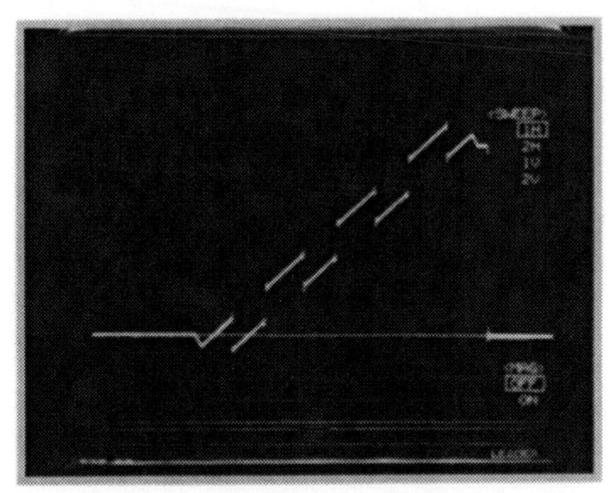

Figure 23. An example of a "stuck bit" in the Y channel.

excursion, except for the excluded data values at and close to 000 and 3FF. The third type of ramp is the shallow ramp shown in Figure 22. This is actually a series of 10 shallow ramps at 10 different levels. The shallow ramps spot decoding errors in the least significant bits.

Errors in coding and decoding might be difficult to spot. Wrong numbers, for example, might make color bars come out at incorrect values and give very confusing results. But the ramps help to spot coding errors and can narrow down the error to particular channels.

Figure 23 shows an example. This is the result of "a stuck bit" in the parallel input to a serializer. A stuck bit is a constant 1 or a 0; depending on the circuit fault. The apparent frequency and amplitude of the square wave that appears to be riding on the ramp will vary with the "place" from 0 to 9 of the stuck bit to give a clue as to which bit is stuck. When in doubt about confusing conditions, go to the ramps.

Picture Display

Most digital waveform monitors offer a picture display as a handy way for quick identification of program material if a picture monitor is not readily available. The picture display is naturally monochrome and is made from the decoded Y or G signal. (The picture is black and green in waveform monitors equipped with green-phosphor CRTs and black-and-white in white-phosphor CRTs. The latter has become standard issue to help prevent the color vision of editors from being temporarily altered by glancing at green images.)

But the picture display provides a useful check of signal status when operated in the EAV/SAV PASS mode. This brings to light data that is carried in the blanking intervals.

Figure 24 shows an example. The signal is color bars with EAV/SAV set to PASS. SAV and EAV appear as very thin (and dim) vertical lines to the left and right of the active picture area. But the bright vertical column to the right of the display shows the presence of four channels of embedded audio. So a glance at the picture display shows if embedded audio is present.

The presence of the EDH codes also appears as a faint dash at the top-left of the picture. It extends to the left of the SAV line just below the 120 mark on the graticule. It should be noted that the ability to see embedded audio, and the EDH codes in the picture display does not extend to HDTV

Figure 24. The picture display with SAV/EAV set to PASS reveals signals hidden in blanking, such as embedded audio and the EDH codes.

operations. The reason is that in 720p and 1080i siganls, embedded audio is placed in Cb and Cr addresses (and the picture is made from Y). Error-catching CRCs are also placed at the end of each line.

Presets

No discussion of waveform monitors would be complete without mention of the use of memory presets. The waveform monitors used for this chapter have a relatively clean front panel that tends to hide a very wide range.of operating options.

For example, older instruments had front panel selection sweep controls for time bases 1H, 2H, 1V, 2V and MAG ON/OFF. To alter sweep speed on the current waveform monitor, the SWEEP key is touched. This brings up the sweep menu with the choices listed. But the use of menu-driven control, while giving the operator an enormous range of operating choices, tends to slow things down by the number of key strokes needed for a particular setup. The solution to this problem is the ability to store front-panel and menu settings in the preset mode.

Using the preset mode, the operator sets the instrument for a particular observation. It may be waveform, vector, timing (for Bowtie) or data, with specialized settings such as line select, and cursors. Once the observation has been set up as desired, the operator goes into the PRESET mode and assigns a preset number (from 1 to 10). This action can be repeated for up to 10 observations that are deemed to be routine. Thereafter each observation may be recalled, complete with all settings including line-select number, cursors as originally set and position (centering) settings. Presets may be recalled with a single keystroke, or may be recalled by remote control using rear panel connections.

Gerry McGinty *is a former Engineer for RCA (and was present at the birth of NTSC), assistant vice president of engineering for Sony and currently a consultant for the test & measurement industry. His current clients include JVC, Panasonic, Sony and Leader Instruments Corp.*

Lighting

If there is a point where science gives way to art in video production, it surely must be in the control and quality of light. Creative manipulation of light can elicit stunning images from a modest consumer camcorder, while poor lighting will cripple the most expensive, state-of-the art broadcast camera.

Light is the radiant energy that transforms the dull, nondescript two-dimensional television image into a three-dimensional illusion which can stimulate the imagination of an audience. Through light, television's "world" is created. Whether that world is a dreary, stormy, terrifying night or a sunny, warm, cheerful day, lighting is the key to what we see in the television image.

As the definition suggests, truly creative lighting is an art form learned through years of study, experimentation and imagination. There are no formulas for good lighting. Each situation is different and requires of the lighting designer a combination of basic knowledge, good tools, common sense and the willingness to experiment.

The development of sensitive CCD cameras has changed the rules in video lighting. The word "quantity" has been replaced by "quality" in the lexicon of the video lighting designer. The days are long gone when video cameras needed mega-watt blasts of light just to make an acceptable image. Miniature fixtures capable of precisely controlling light are the trend in location video lighting. Modeling of light, use of shadow control, diffusion and color all help to create the mood of a scene, and are now just as important to the quality of the video image as they are to film.

It is a mistake to conclude that the low light capabilities of CCD cameras so heavily promoted by camera manufacturers are a reason not to take great care with lighting. The fact that a CCD camera can make a flat, dull, two-dimensional image with almost no light is fine for the occasional emergency newsgathering shot, but it means nothing in the creation of compelling images.

A Few Basics

Generally, video production encounters three kinds of light: Outdoor daylight (the sun), indoor tungsten (lamp fixtures), or some combination of the two.

Daylight changes qualities according to time of day, weather, direction of the sun, etc. Images of subjects made at mid-day with the bright sun directly overhead are often harsh and have dark shadows. However, if a cloud moves over the sun, the light may become diffused and change to a soft, pleasant, shadowless illumination. Reflectors and artificial fill lights may be used to supplement the deficiencies of sunlight for illumination.

Tungsten refers to the filament (lamp coil) found in many indoor lighting fixtures for video. Such lamps differ in color temperature from daylight. This color temperature is measured in degrees Kelvin (K). While daylight color temperature is about 6,000K, tungsten lamps range from 3,200 to 3,400K.

When daylight and tungsten fixtures are mixed, the tungsten color temperature is usually converted to daylight color temperature by use of a filter (more on this later).

Light can be hard or soft. Hard light, usually from direct sunlight or a directional spot-type lighting fixture, is used for modeling surfaces. It creates strong highlights, emphasizing form and texture, while yielding dark shadows. Soft light, on the other hand, is greatly diffused, producing an almost shadowless, gentle, flattering light. Most lighting designers use a combination of hard and soft light for video productions.

Most of the traditional rules of television and film lighting have been altered or modified through the years. But an understanding of the basics of traditional lighting techniques and tools offers a good starting point for anyone lighting a video set. A basic traditional lighting setup for a person or object involves the use of four lights. Each has a purpose.

Keylight is just that, the "key" source of illumination. On an outdoor shoot, the sun may serve as the keylight. Indoors, that light source may suggest an environmental source, such as a window, lamp, candle, etc. Placement of the "hard" keylight is critical because it determines the form, texture and principal shadow content of the scene.

Fill light is a "soft" illumination that lightens the shadows caused by the keylight and controls the contrast ratio of the scene. No new shadows should be added to the scene by fill. The fill light is usually placed on the opposite side of the camera lens from the keylight.

Backlight is a "hard" rim of light behind the subject. It comes from a lamp mounted above and behind the subject. Its purpose is to create tonal separation of the subject from the background. The illusion of depth created by backlight helps create a three-dimensional image for television.

Background light is illumination for the background of the set. As with backlight, background light helps separate the subject from the background. However, background light is aimed the other way—in the direction of the set, not the subject.

In addition to these four major types of lights, there are many variations of accent lighting which single out an object or subject (or features of a subject) for special attention. For example, a tiny light mounted on the camera can add a twinkle to the subject's eyes. A kicker light mounted at approximately eye level and three-quarters to the background can add character and "glow" to the un-keyed side of the sunject's face. Other accent lights are often used for hair, clothes, effects and objects.

Light Fixtures

The lighting designer's "toolbox" should include a range of fixtures and accessories which allow for the easy manipulation of light. Fixtures most common in video production use tungsten or tungsten-halogen lamps. HMI fixtures, a more expensive lighting system that produces illumination of near-daylight color temperature, use gas discharge from large studio units with maximum light output to tiny miniaturized versions for highly portable applications.

The *spotlight* (or "spot") is often used as a "hard" keylight and/or backlight. The intensity of the light beam on most spots for video is adjustable. Some spots are open-faced while other designs have a front lens (fresnel). Open-faced designs are lighter in weight and have greater light output per watt of electricity than fresnel designs. Fresnel fixtures, on the other hand, have better shadow quality and offer softer edges of light, which makes for a more seamless blend of several lighting instruments.

Until recently, most video field productions used the lighter, open-faced spots while fresnel spots were mainly relegated to the studio environment. This is no longer the case. Digital CCD cameras are more sensitive and can operate with lower light levels, and lighting manufacturers have developed a new generation of smaller, lighter fresnel fixtures. Field video crews today are just as likely to have a kit of 300-, 650- and 1,000-watt fresnel lights as they are to have open-faced units.

Broad lights are non-focusing fixtures which produce a semi-hard light. Such devices are designed to spread an even beam of light over a large coverage area. These fixtures are commonly used for fill or background light.

Softlights are large instruments which produce a pleasant, flattering illumination with a minimum of shadows. With a softlight, lamp radiation bounces off an interior reflecting surface in the fixture before hitting the subject. Such light is easy on the eyes and very flattering to subjects. Softlights also make excellent fill fixtures and can even be used as a single light source.

Taking Control of the Light

Choosing the fixture is just the first decision. Controlling the light from that fixture is essential to success in video lighting. A wide range of accessories are available to help the lighting designer gain control. Here are some of the most popular ones:

• *Barndoors* are two or more black panels on hinges that fit onto a rotatable frame which mounts on the front of the light fixture. The individual doors are positioned in order to cut off the light beam from selected areas of the set.

• *Flags* are panels which are also used to block light. Varying in size and usually mounted on a light stand, a flag helps to control light spill and can be used to create shadow.

• A *scrim* is a wire mesh screen used to reduce the intensity of light. The scrim, which mounts in front of the fixture, offers no diffusion of the light.

• A *diffuser* spreads light, making hard light softer. It also reduces the level of light output. Diffusers, which are placed close to the front of the fixture, can be made of glass or gel. Other materials can be used if installed at a safe distance from the lamp. Diffusers are especially useful in softening highlights and shadows.

• *Reflectors* are panels that can concentrate or re-direct rays of light. Reflectors are very useful for providing fill light on outdoor location shoots.

• An *umbrella* is a reflective parasol which, when mounted to a spot or broad light fixture, can diffuse and soften the illumination.

• *Dichronic filters* are used to correct the color temperature of tungsten light to daylight. Such filters are made of glass with a vapor-deposited coating which blocks the undesirable portions of the light spectrum.

• *Gels* (gelatins) are a wide variety of thin, film-like, heat-resistant materials which can be placed over light fixtures, windows or other light sources to change the color, amount or quality of the illumination. For example, a gel can be used instead of a dichronic filter to convert tungsten lighting to daylight. Gels can be supported by gel frames mounted in front of the fixture, secured to barndoors by wooden clothespins or simply taped over windows or fluorescent lights.

•A *butterfly* is a very large frame which holds a fabric or net to diffuse light. It is often used to reduce the effects of harsh sunlight.

•A *cookaloris* (or "cucoloris," "cuke," "kook," or "cookie") is a perforated panel which, when placed in front of a light source, throws shadows, dappled light or patterns on a bare wall. They can be made of hard (tin) or soft (celophane or foil) material and are especially useful to video crews shooting against bare walls in hotel or conference rooms.

• A *snoot* is a "tube" that, when mounted on the front of a light fixture, narrows the light to a precise area on the set. Snoots come in a variety of lengths to suit various needs. Generally, a longer snoot will create a well-defined circle of light, while a shorter snoot will illuminate a larger area.

Electrical Power

For the video crew working on location without the benefit of a portable generator, the availability of electrical power is a major consideration in lighting. It can be embarrassing when a shoot comes to a halt while a production assistant searches for the right fuse at the local hardware store.

To determine the number of amps needed for your lighting set-up, divide the number of watts of light by the voltage of your lighting equipment. In the U.S., a simple formula is to divide the number of watts by 100. Thus, a 1,000-watt lighting fixture requires 10 amps of electricity.

Don't judge the amount of light available to you by the wattage of your fixtures; some light fixtures and lamp models are more efficient than others. Hard lights put out more light than soft lights. Gel and diffusion material affect light output. HMI lighting equipment emits far more light for a given amount of electrical energy than tungsten lighting. It pays to thoroughly investigate the specifications of your lighting hardware and lamps before the shoot.

Basic Lighting For Video

by Ross Lowell

Ross Lowell, a multiple Academy Award nominee, is a veteran documentary director, producer, cameraman, writer, teacher and inventor. In 1959, he founded Lowel-Light Manufacturing, makers of portable lighting equipment for video and film production. Mr. Lowell received an Academy Award technical certificate for lighting design in 1980.

In his book Matters of Light and Depth *(published by Lowel-Light), Lowell offers a warning: "It is all too easy to confuse effects with effective lighting, startling images with unforgettable ones, quantity of footcandles with quality of light. Today's sensitive equipment means that merely recording an image is not the real challenge. Creating separation of planes, implying depth, revealing the character and subtleties of the subject and establishing a meaningful mood are at the heart of our miraculous craft."*

The following is an excerpt from Mr. Lowell's writings on that craft.

The One-Light Approach

Beautiful and dramatic images are possible when you use only a single light source which has been placed carefully in relation to your subject and camera.

Unfortunately, the worst place to position a light is on top of your video camera. Such single-source lighting close to the lens-subject axis results in texture-less, character-less illumination with washed-out foregrounds, distractingly shadowed or totally black backgrounds and little sense of depth. Those without a choice, such as fast-moving news crews, should try to diffuse and, if possible, reduce the intensity of the camera-mounted light so that any existing sources are not overwhelmed and shadows are softened.

When working with one light that is not camera-mounted, it is advisable to use a relatively large, soft source, preferably one with barndoors or an egg crate. If an umbrella rig is used, it is a good idea to have flags or large cards to control lens flare and to provide subtle shading of parts of the subject or background. The flags can also be positioned to reduce overall subject brightness, allowing more light to fall on the distant, presumably darker background in order to reduce contrast, increase separation or prevent the background from disappearing. Conversely, a flag can be set to reduce an overly bright wall, perhaps making it darker toward the edges or top of the frame.

The reason a soft source is often preferable to a hard one is that a large, diffused source helps to convey the subject's character as a result of subtle gradation between broad highlights and soft shadows. Also, spill from the softlight can provide fill illumination that will reduce contrast ratio. If

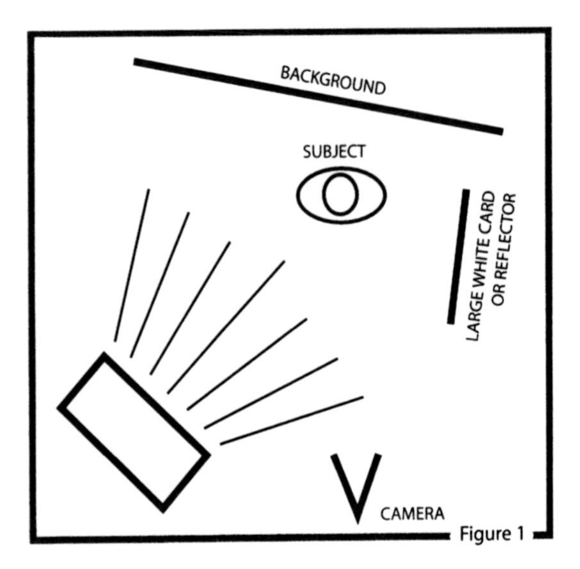

Figure 1

contrast is still too great, some subtle fill (front) or kicker (side-back position) can be added by using a large white card or a soft-silver reflector placed on a stand and angled to reflect spill light from the same single source.

There is no one perfect position for the single light appropriate to all subjects and moods, yet the exact position of the source is important. Movement of the light or subject by only a few degrees can change the overall look significantly.

To find the best angle for the light as quickly as possible, it may help to mount it on a small boom with casters so it can be swung, elevated and rolled around easily. If time allows, try different lighting angles and evaluate the reasons for success, failure or mediocrity of each. Later, experience will determine where to place the light in order to emphasize the significant planes with little wasted motion.

It should be remembered that many subjects, settings and styles are inappropriate for this single-light treatment.

Two-Light Techniques

There are many situations when one light cannot adequately model complex, multiple-plane forms or illuminate and separate foreground, middle-ground and background or control contrast. A second light source can help solve some of these problems.

Traditionally the second light is used to soften the harsh shadows and dark areas left by the first source. If there is a lot of spill from the first light, or if dark shadows and high contrast are desired, this may not be necessary. If, however, you do need fill light, the second source should be soft enough so that it does not introduce any new shadows; diffusion materials are especially useful if a large, soft source is not available. The amount of fill should be appropriate to the subject and mood, but avoid overkill-fill.

If the dark edges of the subject disappear into a black background, there are two ways to create some separation. The second light can be put to work to brighten the background behind the subject.

The light should be positioned above and/or to the side to emphasize shapes and textures and to avoid casting shadows on the background.

Another way to separate the subject from the background is with backlight. Position the second light above and somewhat behind the subject, aimed toward the camera. Keeping flare out of the lens is generally accomplished by adding an extension flap

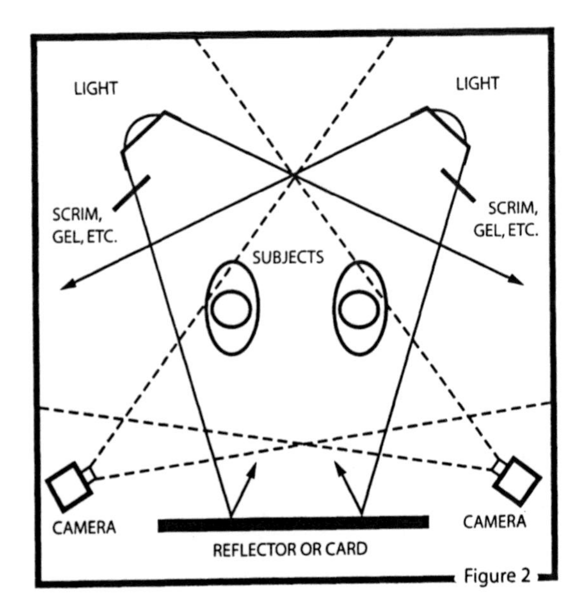

Figure 2

to the top barndoor on the backlight or using an opaque flag near the light or camera. Backlight, when used with reflective surfaces, is partially glare light, so a little bit goes a long way. It is most successful when it seems to be motivated by a credible source within the shot, such as a window.

Another limitation of the one-light approach becomes apparent when photographing two people who are facing each other, especially if reverse angle, over-the-shoulder shots are planned. Generally, each subject is lit by a separate source from the opposite direction. The unit that illuminates the front of one subject can perform double-duty and backlight the hair and clothes of the other. Barndoors, half-scrims, nets or gels can be positioned to reduce the backlight relative to the front light. Some fill illumination, perhaps from a reflector or large white cards, will probably be necessary.

Complex subjects such as appliances, furniture and machinery with many planes that must be revealed often require a second light. Try not to have both sources at equal heights, equal angles or equal intensities. Symmetry in lighting is seldom a virtue. Each plane or surface of the subject should have a different brightness, with the top or side planes, perhaps, appearing to be lighter than the front.

Sometimes Several Lights Are Necessary

As suggested above, a second light should be used: 1) if contrast is too great; 2) if the subject doesn't separate from the background; or 3) if a single-source can't successfully model multi-plane forms. Naturally, if several of these or other problems exist simultaneously, a second light will not be enough and three, four or more lights may be needed.

At times, multiple keylights are required because two lights do not have enough output, the areas being shot are too large, dramatic effects are desired or the subject moves around the room and looks in different directions. In such cases, restricting each light's beam-spread to separate areas of the scene prevents unattractive multiple shadows. On the other hand, you may decide to convert most of your resources into an apparent single source key by diffusing them or bouncing them using umbrellas, a white wall or reflective panels.

In video work, camera movement and, most importantly, subject movement often dictates the use of multiple lights. Take, for example, the common situation of an actor walking down a narrow hallway toward the camera (camera either stationary or moving with the subject). There are several ways to handle it.

In a news-type situation, the light is almost certainly on top of or behind the camera. It's quick and easy but results in the character-less lighting we find on nightly newscasts.

There are, however, ways to emphasize movement, depth and drama. Attach small broad lights to the ceiling at intervals of five or more feet. The trick is to hide them and cut lens flare when ceilings are low. With dropped ceilings it is possible to tuck them into the space available when acoustic tile panels are removed. But beware of flammable materials, wiring and automatic sprinkler heads. If practical, lights can be positioned on stands behind doorways so they will "spill out" into the hallway to create areas of light and dark, through which the subjects walk.

Obviously, when there is opportunity for rehearsal on your newly lit set, exploit it to judge the look and make adjustments if needed. When there isn't lots of time to light, some sort of workable illumination is still possible. While I don't believe in "formula lighting," there is one formula-like setup which can offer more-than-adequate light while also allowing for considerable freedom of both subject and camera movement.

The setup requires three fairly small, wide-angle broad lights. They should be positioned high enough to stay out of the shot while low enough to illuminate the subject's eyes. The units should be fairly equally spaced, one each in adjacent corners, for example, and one on the opposite wall. To

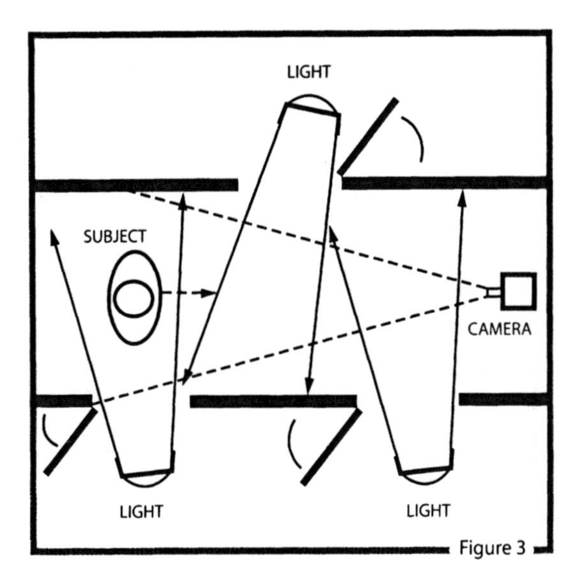

Figure 3

motivate these sources, position the lights near windows or other existing sources. Or, choose mounting places that offer pipes or beams for clamping, or use a door-top or wall-mounting device to eliminate stands.

This versatile setup allows for unrestricted, 360-degree shooting if the cables are hidden. Wherever the camera is, subjects will have some front light, some side and some back light. If the exposure you need allows, add frost gel diffusion to the lights or bounce them if walls and ceilings are not green.

There was a time when few self-respecting cameramen would consider a subject properly lit without a key, fill, backlight, background lights, kicker, eyelight and clothes light. This type of elaborate lighting has disappeared because video, film and lenses are "faster," actors and non-actors

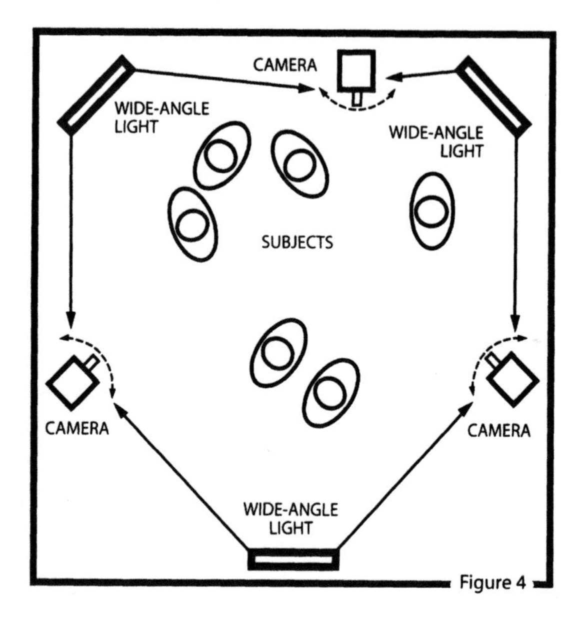

Figure 4

have been granted more freedom of movement and lighting styles, or, if you will, fashions, have become more natural.

Much of the craft of lighting interiors, as discussed above, also applies to exteriors. The principles are unchanged even though the tools may differ. The sun, the sky, the clouds become your light sources, as do white walls of buildings, battery operated lights and reflectors. Here, shade may be your best friend and you will soon discover the many flavors of exterior shade. Your palette of tools for night-time shooting may extend to street lights, flares, camp fires and automobile headlights, real or suggested.

Whatever the sources, whether outside or indoors, the most important resources you have are: a good plan, a good alternative and a good eye.

Lighting For Video vs. Film

The following text is reprinted from American Cinematographer *magazine.*

There is a great deal of talk about a "film look" as opposed to a "tape look" and it is important to understand exactly what the difference is and the reasons for it. To what extent is the difference really a difference in working methods rather than a difference inherent in the recording medium itself? When most people talk about a "tape look," they are generally referring to the kind of lighting associated with multiple camera shows done tape. To a large extent, the "look" of the show is more a function of the fact it is lit for multiple cameras than the fact that it is shot and recorded electronically.

The use of multiple cameras, that may be simultaneously shooting reverse angles as well as long shots and closeups, imposes restrictions on the lighting style that have a radical effect on the "look" of the show, regardless of whether it is on film or tape. The problems of lighting for multiple cameras are not really what we are concerned with here, although they may be the first thing to come to a videographer's mind when they contemplate shooting for tape rather than for film.

There is obviously no law that says electronic cinematography has to employ multiple cameras. It has traditionally relied on multiple cameras because of its origins in "live" broadcasting and its association with stage shows performed before an audience. There is a trend emerging, however, towards electronic cinematography using single-camera techniques of the sort traditionally associated with film. As the working styles of film and tape productions converge, there is an increasing demand in tape productions for cinematographers experienced in single-camera lighting and shooting techniques; it behooves every cinematographer to understand whether or how lighting for an electronic camera differs from lighting for a film camera.

In a broad, general sense, it is now realistic to say that there is no difference in lighting for tape and lighting for film, given state-of-the-art electronic cameras and recorders. Leonard South, an ASC member, insists that he would make no changes at all in lighting the set for a multiple-camera show if he were told that a decision had been made to switch from film to tape.

Or, as lighting director/designer Greg Brunton puts it, "There is no real major difference in lighting. A camera is a camera, and light is light. It is only the style in which you are shooting that requires you to light the way you do."

This has not always been true, and in certain situations there are still differences between film and tape which can affect the lighting. For the most part, however, the differences in the lighting of a videotape production and a film production are a result of working methods and personnel. If a cinematographer wants to achieve "film style" lighting in a videotape production, it is helpful to know how and why things are normally done in a tape production.

Contrast Ratio

The most important inherent difference between film and video is the brightness range or contrast ratio which each can successfully reproduce. Film is generally considered to have a contrast ratio of at least 100:1 (a range of between 6 and 7 stops) while video is limited to a contrast ratio of about 30:1 (or about five stops). This difference is compounded by the difference in the viewing conditions for each medium. A film image projected onto a screen in a darkened room can obviously reproduce a much greater brightness range than an electronic image viewed on a television tube in a fully-lit room. The television screen itself is never fully black, and the viewer's eye will never adjust to differences in the brightness of a television screen in the way it would to differences in the brightness of a large theater screen.

A normal home receiver can be considered to have a contrast ratio of about 20:1 (although this will change with the new generation of digital television sets). If a film is being shot for television broadcast, then of course it is subjected to the same viewing conditions, and its effective contrast ratio is reduced as well. But inherent in the electronic system is a limitation of the contrast ratio relative to what film can handle.

Exposure Control

Because highlights in a video image tend to be more problematic than shadow areas, the practice in electronic cinematography is to set the exposure for the highlights and let the shadows fall where they will. As with film the exposure is controlled by means of the f-stop. In low light situations it is possible to increase the video gain in a way comparable to force-developing film. There is usually a switch which will permit an increase in the video gain level in six dB increments. Each 6dB increment is the equivalent to pushing film one stop, and boosting the video gain in this manner results in an increase in the noise level of the video image, which is the video equivalent of increased grain in force-developed film.

Normally with video it is considered advisable to set the white level so that face tones will be about 80 percent of peak brightness. In most studio conditions this is usually feasible, although there may be instances where it is difficult. If a performer, for example, is wearing a shiny white satin dress, it is possible that setting the video gain to bring the white of the dress down to the proper level may result in dark face tones. In such a case, some kind of compromise is necessary. Either the dress must be allowed to exceed the ideal peak brightness or the face will have to appear dark. If the dress does exceed peak white, there will be a loss of detail in the dress. Fortunately the electronic cameraman does not have to wait for his dailies to come back from the lab to see how bad the problem will be. He can see it right away on a monitor as he is rehearsing the shot.

In addition to setting the white level, the video operator has control over two other elements of the video image. He can "raise and lower the pedestal" or "stretch the blacks." These are two distinct alterations of the video signal, and their effects are a bit difficult to describe in words. Raising the pedestal is perhaps most comparable to flashing the film. It increases the average overall brightness of the image without raising the peak of the signal (without raising the white level).

This is similar to turning up the brightness control on a television set. Stretching the blacks is an alteration of the video signal that brings out detail in the shadow areas without raising the pedestal or the black level. Raising the pedestal will make blacks in the scene turn gray. Stretching the blacks will keep some blacks in the scene at the level of the pedestal, but will increase the separation for tones in the lower end of the brightness range. It is also possible for the videographer to alter the gamma of the video signal to produce yet another alteration in the overall look of the image.

Light Levels

Some electronic cameras can operate well in light levels as low as 10 to 15 footcandles (fc) and yield acceptable images. Generally this is accomplished by boosting the gain, and generally 125 to 150 fc is considered a normal light level for studio electronic cinematography. Some television technicians still light a set to 200 or 250 fc just as a matter of habit from the days when video cameras required that much light to function properly. Most cameras today are designed to operate at much lower light levels.

Lighting director George Riesenberger shot a test at one footcandle, literally using one candle one foot from the camera and got an image. The lowest light level he has actually worked at, however, is 10 fc, and that was for a camera demonstration at a National Association of Broadcasters convention. Generally the only time a cameraman would work at light levels this low is in taping a stage show or some other event where he had no control over the lighting.

When fellow lighting director Bill Klages was called upon to light Leonard Nimoy's one-man show on artist Vincent Van Gogh, he was faced with the problem of incorporating images projected onto a screen behind Nimoy. Since it was not feasible to brighten the images on the background screen, it was necessary to light Nimoy at 15 footcandles. He was able to do this, and the show was successfully recorded on tape.

Highlight Detail

One consideration when comparing the latitude of film and video is that a television image originally shot on film and then transferred to tape can sometimes show more detail in highlights than the same scene recorded directly on tape. Although any telecine system used to broadcast film or transfer it to tape has a 30:1 contrast ratio, just like a live camera, there can sometimes be compression of highlights in a film image due to the "knee" at the top end of the H & D curve.

It is possible for highlight detail which would be outside the range of an electronic camera to be captured on film and compressed so that some or all of the detail in the processed film image would fall within a 30:1 contrast range. This would mean that the detail could be preserved when the film image is converted into an electronic image. Most electronic cameras now have circuits which attempt to duplicate the highlight compression caused by the "knee" in a film curve, but none of them can achieve the 100:1 contrast ratio of film.

The difference between a 30:1 and a 100:1 contrast ratio may sound more drastic than it is in practice. It is probably only in extreme situations that the cinematographer is going to feel restricted by what he can do in lighting for tape. He may need to put slightly more fill light into shadow areas of a low-key scene than he would with film, or he may have to be more careful about hot spots in the frame, but basically he can still achieve the same kinds of lighting effects with tape that he does with film.

Color Balance

Lighting for video must involve the same considerations of color temperature as lighting for film. Electronic camera control units are generally equipped with a switch which can be set for daylight or tungsten light. Rather than filtering the light as it enters the lens or changing to a different film emulsion, the operator of an electronic camera can adjust the color balance of his image by adjusting the amplification of the three color signals. He can also use a filter in the same way a film cameraman does.

The fact that an electronic camera generally involves a beam splitter and processes the color components of the image separately provides the cameraman with a very powerful tool for controlling color in electronic cinematography. One of the members of a video crew is the video operator, whose responsibility it is to insure appropriate brightness levels and consistent color balance in the signal being generated by each camera. If the cinematographer communicates effectively with his video operator, it is as if he has a timer from the lab on the set giving him instantaneous reports on the lights at which the scenes are printing. In many instances the video operator can correct problems on the set which a timer would be hard pressed to correct in making an answer print.

For example, video productions which are essentially stage shows or concerts often have to use a follow spot with a different color temperature from the rest of the lighting. Sometimes it is not possible to filter the spotlight without cutting the light output too much. In many instances the color balance of the camera can be custom-tailored to the situation, achieving results which would be very difficult to reproduce by timing a negative.

Similarly, video productions often involve the use of dimmers to control all the lights. Color temperature of the lights may vary when they are dimmed. It is possible to compensate for these variations by adjusting the levels of each of the color signals in the camera for each new setup.

The ability to custom-tailor the color balance of an electronic camera can be used creatively as well. Color effects which might normally be achieved by filtering the lights or the lens can be accomplished electronically by the video man. One advantage this technique offers is the ability to slightly alter the color effect from one setup to the next with great ease.

Greg Brunton, for example, introduced a sepia effect into a sequence in a video production by having the video operator electronically "paint" the scenes. He was able to use a more saturated sepia effect for wide shots and a less saturated effect for closer shots simply by having the video operator tweak a few knobs at every setup.

In addition to the color balance and the brightness level, the video operator can also vary the contrast or the gamma of the image, in the same way a home viewer can adjust the contrast on his receiver. While the video operator will normally set the gamma for certain specifications which are considered standard, there is no reason why the ability to control this aspect of the image cannot be used creatively by the cinematographer as well.

As Anton Wilson (author of "Anton Wilson's Cinema Workshop") is fond of pointing out, electronic cinematography is really like having a custom-made emulsion for every scene. The speed, contrast, and color balance can be modified to help achieve whatever effect the cinematographer desires. In a sense, "lighting" for video involves electronic manipulation of the image after is it captured by the cameras as well as the use of lights, filters, scrims, cutters, etc. on the set.

The Video Operator

It should be clear that while lighting for video can be governed by the same principals as lighting for film, there are nonetheless certain tools and working relationships which are unique to video. The working relationship between a cinematographer and the video operator is a prime example. The principle tool that the video operator uses is a waveform monitor, and any cinematographer who is going to work with an electronic camera should at least be conversant with a waveform monitor.

A waveform monitor is essentially an oscilloscope displaying the waveform of the signal corresponding to each scan line of the image (see related chapter elsewhere in this book). The screen of the monitor retains the wave form of each scan line long enough for it to be combined with the wave forms for every scan line in an individual frame. What it displays is in effect a cumulative light reading for every spot in the scene.

The video operator refers to the waveform monitor in order to set levels for peak white and for apparent black. Although many video operators understand more about the characteristics of electrical waves than they do about the art of lighting, they can be powerful allies in achieving specific lighting effects.

The Color Monitor

The second unique tool the cinematographer has in working with an electronic camera is the color monitor. A color monitor can function as instant dailies or as an instant wedge test on every scene. The cinematographer can see what they are getting with an immediacy impossible with film. Even with a Polaroid "instantmatic" camera, the photographer has to wait 60 seconds to see the results.

In video, the images are processed at the speed of light. It is essential, however, to ensure that the monitor being used to evaluate the lighting has been properly aligned so that it reflects accurately what is actually being recorded on the tape. An inadequate or improperly aligned monitor can do more harm than good.

It is also important to make sure that anyone attempting to evaluate the lighting is looking at a monitor that is comparable to the one being used by the videographer. In many instances, the monitor being viewed by a director or producer may be in another part of the studio, and the image may be entirely different if the monitor is not properly aligned beforehand. Conversations about lighting between two parties who are looking at inadequate monitors rapidly become totally counterproductive.

If all the monitors are properly aligned,

however, it becomes easier to have intelligent discussions about lighting effects than it is with film. Every cinematographer knows the difficulty of discussing a lighting style on the set with inexperienced producers or directors who cannot visualize the difference between the way a set looks and the way the scene will look on film. Generally the cinematographer must simply assure his colleagues that the image will look right, and wait for dailies to find out how the director or producer feels about the lighting. With electronic cinematography there is no need to explain a lighting effect in words.

There is, of course, a drawback to this possibility that many cinematographers may view with apprehension. The ability to see every lighting effect immediately can open the door to lighting by committee, resulting in a decrease in both the efficiency of the production and the integrity of the lighting style. If the cinematographer has the respect and trust of his director and producer, however, he should not be any more hesitant to discuss lighting with the help of a monitor than he would be to discuss it at a screening of dailies. What a good color monitor offers a cinematographer and his director is a means of improved communication and more fruitful collaboration.

Lighting for the Video Camera
by William M. Klages

Much has been said about the problems and techniques of lighting for the film camera as well as lighting for the video camera. In all circumstances, the two areas have been treated as separate, distinct worlds, never to be considered or even mentioned in the same context. In the general sense, there is absolutely no reason for this. In the specific sense, we need to be aware of the major technical differences between the two systems.

The Problem

Speaking as a "video" person, it has been difficult to get filmmakers to admit that the video image is "photographic" or "cinematic." The serious film image-maker usually has great difficulty in applying the term "photographic" to describe the efforts of the video image-maker. But the video camera is a reproduction device. An image recorded on videotape can be transmitted on a television signal equally as well as one recorded from a film camera. What then is the problem? Why this lack of acceptance?

It is difficult to believe that it is due to a reluctance to accept this "new" technology, now more than 50 years old. I believe this attitude is the result of an honest feeling that the photographic results from the video camera are inferior from a creative standpoint to those obtained with a film camera.

Here we'll limit the scope of our discussion to the subject of lighting for television transmission, whether the recording device is the film or video camera. I will not touch upon the subject of using the video camera as the recording device for theatrical motion pictures. At present, there is no practical method utilizing this technique that can approach the quality of an image recorded directly on 35mm film and projected on a screen.

Emperor's New Clothes

Let's discuss some of the "differences" between lighting and production techniques for television programming using either the film camera or the electronic camera. Some of the examples may seem superficial; my point is that most production situations are not unique to either video or film.

Great mystery must surround our tools. We find that the result takes a back seat to the technique involved. Filmmakers and videomakers alike can be accused of promulgating these great mysteries. The most basic mystery is the prevailing jargon. God help the lighting artist who makes a terrible slip by referring to a "Siamese adapter" when "two-fer" (or "martingale") is the required password. "Density" is hardly in common usage in a television studio and "signal level," although closely related, is never heard on a film set. Hence the popularity of the glossary. As we all have seen, terms which must be interpreted for each local situation become self-defeating.

Many years ago, I was assigned to light one of a series of automobile commercials which had previously been shot on film. The client was forced to do the commercial on videotape because of an immediate air date. He was not pleased and chose to find fault with anything and everything concerned with the videotape operation. One of the elements that received his direct attention was a "missing" reflector directly overhead and slightly downstage of the automobile. No amount of discussion (I was much less experienced then) could convince him that this reflector would accomplish nothing. As a result I had my crew suspend and light the reflector.

Needless to say, it had no effect on the image.

We then went on to solve other problems. The element of mystery had been added — one step forward for Madison Avenue, and one step backward for the visual sciences.

In a television studio, I asked the purpose of a piece of spun glass covering the front of a 4K softlight. The lighting man who had used the diffusion over the softlight was not in attendance to defend himself nor to observe the simple test that I performed. I demonstrated that he could have saved a great deal of spun glass by merely turning off half of the lamps in each softlight to achieve the identical quality of illumination.

The mysteries also give birth to other more alarming enigmas. The collapsible four-way door, a necessity in a multiple-camera situation for convenience, speed and practicality, is never included in film production lighting equipment complements. Why? Allow me to tell a favorite story. It might have taken place in a sound stage (which it didn't) as well as television studio (which it did). I was lighting a weekly variety show. During the first show of the season, the 20 backup singers appeared in raincoats whose reflectance was nearly equal to the pure white of magnesium oxide. Although during the first show the raincoated group was in the background and controllable, I knew that we would eventually have an impossible situation wherein the group would move into the foreground with the star. We would then have to give the raincoats billing as a result of their visual predominance. I spoke to our costume designer about the unacceptability of the raincoats. She was sympathetic and seemed to understand the problem.

The following week saw our singers prepared

for inclement weather and grouped around our star, who for some reason did not have a raincoat, but his favorite cashmere sweater. The television picture was a disaster. When I complained to my costume designer associate, I heard what has become a show business tradition: "I cannot understand your problem. We used them before." Life goes on.

All of these examples should have a familiar ring. The environment of a film production is basically similar to that of video production. Certainly the same elusive, subjective thinking is present in each discipline. Only certain pieces of hardware are different.

Video Removes Mystery

The video camera enters the scene with the promise of removing all mysteries. Or does it? We see the results of our efforts immediately in instant "dailies." However, Murphy's Law is basic to electronics. A whole new crop of dilemmas present themselves. We are told of strict rules that must be applied lest catastrophe result. The glossary becomes so loaded that its seams are bursting. The lighting becomes so technical that there seems little hope for the "photographic." And, of course, we must adhere to the tradition of multiple-camera shooting.

Multiple-camera shooting is the single factor that has most restricted the videomaker in his quest for superior photographic results. Luck, at times, will create exceptions to this generalization, but hardly proves the statement incorrect. No matter what lighting style you may choose—"high key," "natural," "film look," "single source," "low contrast" or "source"—you are visualizing a single viewpoint. You expect to maintain the same visual style throughout.

For each shot, the basic lighting setup is altered so that the style is consistent. When lighting for multiple cameras, you cannot make these individual alterations. I must add, at this point, that this situation has become even more aggravated by the use of a complete vertical structure, a recording channel for each camera. The compromises are even more severe.

But is the photographic quality of a multiple-camera film shoot any better than its video counterpart? The problem of multiple viewpoints,. the mechanics of equipment and personnel displacement are common to both situations. As a result, the photographic quality of both is compromised. We should be sympathetic to image-makers with high standards who must cope with the heartaches of the multi-camera operation.

Television production using the electronic camera has been primarily multi-camera. However, single-camera television production, with proper care, can result in high-quality, "photographic" images. Since this shooting method is exercised so infrequently, it is no surprise that filmmakers have such a poor opinion of video's cinematic qualities. However, quality results require an understanding of the shortcomings of the video camera. Awareness of these considerations should form the basis of your approach to lighting for the electronic camera.

Important Differences

Probably the most disconcerting difference confronting an experienced film lighting person operating in the video environment is the attempt to evaluate his efforts on a television screen. Usually he can see a number of screens, all with the same image, reproduced in what appears to be every combination of hue, brightness, color intensity and contrast imaginable. At this point he will probably hear a common showbiz statement: "If you want to see what it really looks like, watch the video engineer's monitor." Our poor hero, completely frustrated by this time, will not realize that the video man's monitor has been set for high color saturation and low brightness to assist the engineer in making his operating adjustments.

The truth, unfortunately, is this: the performance of the cathode ray tube (CRT), upon which the entire system's image reproduction specification is based, is not consistent. Adjustment of a television monitor or receiver is, at best, subjective. There is a great difference or opinion among technical personnel responsible for the adjustment of this equipment.

It does take some experience and time to be able to evaluate the image on a monitor not in perfect adjustment or, even worse, on a receiver with a non-standard transfer characteristic. Today this is a very common situation as small, portable receivers are adapted for monitoring. Even after adjustment by the same individual, there is no guarantee that the screens will agree. A good trick is to use a black & white monitor to evaluate image brightness relationships. These relationships are quite apparent even on a monochrome monitor that is not in proper adjustment.

The next step, evaluation of the color, is even more elusive. You must rely on some very evasive indicators. The exposure is generally set for the camera to give an accurate reproduction of human skin tone. Knowing the quality of the illumination upon your subject, if you feel that the monitor is showing a true representation of this subject, assume that the monitor is properly adjusted.

Judging fine graduations of color saturation and hue is not easy considering the lack of conformity in the television system monitoring. Initially, I would suggest not being too critical until you have enough experience to see the relationships that actually do exist, from a color standpoint, between the subject and the result on the television receiver. It will take many hours before one feels at ease with this aspect of the system.

The next difference is easier to deal with. The television image, due to the standards by which the system transmits, has relatively low resolution. No matter what the definition of the image focused on a negative or on the image surface of a video camera's pickup tube, it is limited to the maximum resolution allowed by the system parameters. Even with a state-of-the-art prime lens on the taking camera (film or electronic), the final image will not be any sharper than the system is capable of delivering to the screen.

To improve the apparent resolution, we must keep the main areas of interest to as small a number as possible. Items of secondary interest should be eliminated or placed in unimportant positions in your composition. Rely heavily on contrast to replace the lack of resolution.

The last difference is most important to obtaining the photographic image from the video camera. It is also the difference that those proficient in lighting for the film camera will have the most difficulty in accommodating. The problem is the video system's inability to reproduce a great range of brightness. This in itself might not be too debilitating were it not for the additional problems introduced as a result of exceeding this narrow range.

At the top of the brightness scale, the system does not reproduce any definition for subjects whose brightness exceeds the system's limit. Also, these high brightness areas cause seriously adverse electronic effects that the pickup tube introduces into the picture under these conditions. Since the overall brightness range capability of the system is about 20 or 30 to 1 due to our original enemy, the television picture tube, we are quite heavily restricted in the ways that we can include the complete range of subject brightness.

We can slide the scale downwards to increase the detail in the highlights, but at the cost of losing information in the lower end of the scale. With only a 30 to 1 range, the result can be an awful picture. We can also alter the transfer characteristics (gamma). We do improve the low light reproduction, but find the range of adjustment is not sufficient to maintain highlight detail. (The system's signal-to-noise ratio may be lowered to an unacceptable value.)

Other "fixes" using different transfer characteristics within the brightness range have had little success. However, there have been some hardware innovations that decrease the adverse electronic effects caused by extreme highlights.

To illustrate the practical limitations imposed as a result, let's say we are shooting outdoors on a sunny day. We find that there is not sufficient latitude available to expose the shadow areas when dealing with a backlighted subject. The resulting image from the video camera can hardly be described as "photographic." Determining the required amount of fill light is most difficult. The proper amount usually results in a very unrealistic image with little visual appeal.

Anyone lighting for video must realize that the video camera is not forgiving. Careful attention must be paid to controlling the brightness values of all areas. Use the primary area of interest as the reference. The limits are exceedingly narrow. It is necessary to maintain a very precise exposure level on people to provide a fleshtone reference. The videomaker will discover that he is always working to the limits of the system's brightness range.

In other words, beware of the white raincoat—it takes many forms.

***William M. Klages** a multiple Emmy-winning lighting director. He is CEO of Klages Group, Hollywood, CA.*

New Battery Technologies

There has been a great deal of talk regarding new battery types in the market recently. "Smaller, lighter, more powerful, and less expensive,"—who hasn't heard these wishes from a battery user? In fact, in all battery-powered markets, batteries are the number one area in which customers would like to see improvements. In the computer and cellular telephone markets, requests for improvements in battery life (runtime) and weight/size come before processing speed and cellular coverage.

Of course, the broadcast and professional video industry is no exception. Since the very first portable cameras, cameramen have looked for lighter and more powerful batteries.

Unfortunately, the quest for the "perfect" battery has led to many unsuitable battery types being marketed over the years. Some manufacturers have offered (and still offer) batteries of incorrect voltage, unsuitable size and insufficient packaging to meet the requirements of a video professional. Because these batteries were touted as "smaller, lighter, cheaper" and because the uninformed view is often that "a battery is a battery", these products were purchased thinking that they would be suitable for a professional.

Many of these, such as NP-types, were reconfigured by equipment manufacturers from consumer products to allow the company to offer a turn-key camera package. Professionals soon found out that problems with these batteries were insurmountable. Terms like "memory" (which does not exist in practical application) were coined to explain the inadequate operation of poorly designed and/or misapplied batteries.

Once these batteries were in operation, users looked for ways to salvage their NP investments. For example, we are all familiar with the variety of rejuvenators, reconditioners, de-memorizers, revitalizers and other such gadgets marketed in an attempt to salvage the large inventories of NP batteries in the marketplace. After investing thousands of dollars and hundreds of hours of maintenance time on their NP batteries, users found out too late that poor design and misapplication problems never really go away. Thus, an NP user typically carries up to four times the amount of batteries that should actually be needed and replaces them twice as often.

For a dozen years since the NP battery was introduced on the first Betacam cameras, users were looking for a way to "fix" them. Over the years this exercise has prompted many products—which unfortunately is like trying to fix a mis-registered camera by buying a new lens.

The quest for the "Holy Grail" of video batteries has taken its most recent turn in the introduction of exotic cell types introduced into the cellular and computer markets. These new cell types addressed many of the size and weight issues for mobile communications and computing products. And rightfully so, since the market drivers for these products are several orders of magnitude greater than all camcorders—consumer and broadcast, put together.

The cell manufacturer who could design a cell that could be used in a battery for notebooks and cell phones was designing a product for the largest growth markets the battery industry has ever seen. Typically 6 volt systems which had typical power requirements of less than 10 watts (and often less than 5 watts) made the job much easier. And if their service life was short, so much the better.

The publicity these new technologies—e.g., nickel metal hydride (NiMH) and lithium ion (Li-Ion)—have received for mobile communications and computing have made them seem like the answer to all battery problems. Indeed, there's been so much talk in the trade press about them that the impression is that all new batteries are NiMH or Li-Ion.

This is not so, even in the mobile communications markets.

Let's look at a few irrefutable facts:

(1) Nickel Cadmium (NiCd) technology has been commercial for over 40 years with real viability for about 25 years. Everyone remember their first "dustbuster?" In 1994, about 1.5 million cells were shipped; in 1996, over 1.6 million cells. Today NiCd accounts for almost 70 percent of the world's total of rechargeable cells produced.

(2) NiMH cell technology was commercialized less than 10 years ago with real viability of less than five years. In 1994, 200 million cells shipped; in 1996, 450 million cells shipped. Today, NiMH technology represents more than 20 percent of the total cells produced for the world's consumption.

(3) Lithium ion technology has been commercialized for less than five years, with real viability of less than three years. In 1994, about 15 million cells were shipped; in 1996, 140 million cells . Today, lithium ion represents a mere 10 percent of the world's total of rechargeable cylindrical cells.

(4) NiMH has taken over the computer industry, perhaps the closest application to video in the mobile communications market. In the U.S., for

example, NiMH accounts for an estimated 70 percent of all notebook batteries. Lithium ion accounts for less than 30 percent.

(5) About 80 percent of all cell telephone batteries are NiCd. Less than 2 percent are lithium ion. The rest are NiMH.

(6) A typical notebook computer draws less than 1 amp (with hard drive and back lit color LCD screen) usually at 12 volts or about 10 watts.

(7) A typical cell phone draws less than ½ amp at typically 5 volts or well less than 3 watts.

(8) There is a big difference in cells versus batteries. The largest capacity NiMH cell applicable in video today has a capacity of well over 8 watt hours. The largest lithium ion cell has a usable capacity of over 10 watt hours, while the largest NiCd cell provides about 6 watt hours.

However, when these cells are put into a 14.4 volt series configuration and discharged at 50 watts (a camcorder and light), look at how the runtime numbers are different:

NiMH: 2 hour, Li-Ion: ¾ hours, NiCd: 1.5 hours

By looking at the numbers, one could assume that lithium ion has more capacity than the other two technologies and that NiCd has the least, but this is not the case. Lithium ion has a voltage advantage of 3.6 to 1.2 per cell for nickel-based cells. Very simply this means that lithium ion needs only four cells to power a 12 volt device where nickel based technologies require 10 to 12. But its capacity is virtually the same as a NiCd.

The Ni-MH and lithium ion cells available are a small size which, although greater in capacity than a NiCd cell of the same size, are limited in their ability to discharge at the same rates as the NiCd, and therefore are de-rated in actual use.

The cell sizes that can be effectively and safely constructed in NiMH and lithium ion are limited. Therefore, the batteries that can be made from them are limited because they must use the smaller cell sizes. To obtain the capacity of the same voltage NiCd battery, for example, two or three lithium ion cells must be paralleled or "stacked".

By paralleling cells, theoretically, "larger" cells can be created from smaller cells, matching the capacity of the nickel-based technologies, then put into a series configuration to obtain the voltage necessary. But the volume (smaller size) advantage is all but lost.

Paralleling or stacking cells theoretically creates larger cells, because manufacturing consistency—both in cell and battery assembly—is critical to this practice. However, in a young technology such as lithium ion, given its track record since its introduction, the totally new manufacturing techniques involved, and taking into account the controls required to safely charge and discharge this technology, no one in the battery industry assumes that today this practice is viable to all product applications.

Now let's look at some of the criteria for professional video batteries:

(1) A typical Betacam SP or DVCPRO camcorder draws about 2 amps at 12 volts, or about 24 watts in Record. (As an aside, "save" modes don't usually save all that much; even if someone uses it—which they usually don't). Many versions of new digital format cameras (disk, Digital-S, Betacam SX and others) as well as the new high definition equipment, draw almost double that of the state of the art Betacam SP camcorder.

(2) The typical on-camera light used today draws 25-50 watts. The typical focusable or dimming type light will always draw 50 watts.

(3) New formats have recording times on a single medium of 60 to 120 minutes or more (versus the 20-30 minute standard recording time of Betacam SP)—an increase of three to six times. Therefore, the power necessary to record a single tape has increased by up to six times.

(4) Nearly ⅔ of the weight of a camcorder (with lens) is forward of the center of gravity point. Compensating for this unbalanced weight has been

determined as the cause of fatigue and back strain for cameramen. Although cameras are getting smaller and lighter, camera lenses must remain out front, unbalancing the camera. A 3-5 pound (2kg) battery actually balances today's camcorders perfectly while a lighter battery can actually add to the fatigue factor. Balance not weight is an overriding ergonomic design consideration on a camcorder.

Thus, the answer to the question, "Why aren't all these new battery types used for my camcorder?," should now be clear: A camcorder used by a video professional has different power and ergonomic requirements than a cell phone used by a soccer mom.

Let's look at what is happening in today's work environment with each technology and how it is applicable to professional video.

Lithium Ion

This technology is being employed primarily in two-cell configurations, in the cellular industry and in the computer industries, where the primary considerations are weight and size. Its major disadvantages are made obvious by the absolute requirement for on-board "protection" electronics to prevent overcharge (that results in catastrophic failure) or over-discharge (which renders the battery useless). Moreover the devices they are used with, such as computers and telephones, have additional battery monitoring programs that can improve performance and reliability.

Lithium ion cells also retain their charge for a somewhat longer time than other technologies. However, the practical application of this feature is offset by the fact that the recoverable capacity of the cell never returns to 100 percent after storage. Therefore, lithium ion batteries stored for any time irreversibly lose capacity.

Another drawback to lithium ion technology as a video battery is its ability to address high rate discharge. In practice this means that no lithium ion battery on the market is capable of powering both a camera at 25 watts and an on camera light at 50 watts. Either the protection circuitry (required to protect the cells from over-current) will operate or the voltage regulation of the camera will limit the draw of the light—rendering it virtually useless. Since the camcorder and light configuration is the most popular and economical operating arrangement in professional video, the practicality of existing lithium ion batteries is limited.

Much of the technical discussion in the battery industry regarding lithium ion has to do with some well founded safety concerns. The technology of lithium ion differs dramatically from any other rechargeable chemistry due to the nature of its electrolyte (the liquid medium that allows the transfer of electrons from the positive to the negative plates) and the volatility of lithium metal (which can be formed under certain abuse situations).

Current lithium ion cells use an organic electrolyte that is highly flammable. This means that the cell itself can support a fire, unlike other chemistries which use an aqueous (water-based) potassium hydroxide electrolyte. The battery industry is actively pursuing this concern and development efforts are underway to address this issue.

Recently, cell manufacturers working on lithium ion have been experimenting with different electrolytes, especially in the area of inorganic (non-flammable) and fire retardant electrolyte formulations.

These changes, as well as volumetric improvements in energy density, may pave the way for a appropriate design for professional video.

Nickel Metal Hydride

Advancements in NiMH have moved this technology to a similar energy density by volume to lithium ion cells of the same size. This means that in a given size (cell or battery) the watt hours per volume are the virtually the same. The weight of a lithium ion cell is less, but this is offset significantly by the complication of controls required for safe operation and the incompatibility with nickel based charger designs.

Early NiMH cells were intended to be "drop-in replacements" for NiCad applications. The cells have the same voltage as their NiCad cousins, with the ability to store more energy due to the porous metal hydride electrode. C-rate charging with temperature cutoff(TCO), -ΔV and/or timed cutoffs were represented to be appropriate methods to terminate charge. [-ΔV, or "minus delta vee," is a term used to describe the negative voltage inflection of a battery at end of charge.] This would obviously be ideal as unsophisticated conventional NiCad chargers take advantage of the ability of cells to withstand high rate charging and overcharge with minimal consequence.

In practical application today's NiMH cells have a low tolerance for high rate charge (excessive heat buildup lowers charge acceptance) and overcharge (degrades performance and cycle life). In fact, the cutoff methods employed for NiCad products by conventional chargers will not protect NiMH cells from damage (for example the requirement for cutoff is twice as stringent as with

NiCad). The inflection -ΔV in NiMH is less than ½ of that exhibited by a NiCd cell, thereby necessitating more electronic resolution in monitoring voltage.

The only precision cutoff methodology for NiMH is a dT/Dt (change in temperature over a specified period of time). This methodology has been implemented in the computer industry since the early 1990s due to the availability of "smart" batteries and sophisticated processing of temperature information supplied by the battery.

Early NiMH cells were restricted by limited low temperature performance as well as high temperature cycle-life limitations. However recent improvements in NiMH chemistry have virtually eliminated these concerns.

Nickel Cadmium

The world of rechargeable batteries will continue to be based on NiCad technology for years to come, especially in high power applications such as power tools and professional video. Continued development of higher energy NiCad formulations and improved manufacturing techniques have kept this technology in the mainstream of portable power. With the advent of worldwide recycling and reclamation programs, the environmental concerns of the 1980s regarding the disposal of nickel cadmium cells have been addressed by the battery industry. Today NiCd cells are handled in recycling programs around the world similar to recycling glass or cardboard.

In the many applications of greater than 40 watt power requirements (such as a camcorder and on-camera light), NiCad remains the only acceptable rechargeable technology for optimizing reliability, runtime and service life. Charge times for NiCd batteries of about one hour are up to three times faster than either NiMH or lithium ion, making NiCd indispensable to a fast paced professional.

What Works Best

In the end, how does one determine which battery is "best?"

It is important to recognize that choosing a battery system today is as important a decision as deciding on a recording format. In most cases the choice of batteries outlasts the choice of cameras. The "best" battery is one that can be consistently and dependably used in every way the operator wishes to use his equipment. The battery to power a 40-watt digital format camera with an on-camera light is not necessarily the same battery to power a 25-watt camcorder without a light.

Ultimately, each application and operation is different and should demand different battery types. No one battery in video, or in any industry, today can be called "universal." A battery system, with features adopted by every major equipment manufacturer (consisting of batteries of multiple sizes, chemistry and cost), that can all be addressed on a single upgradeable charger is the only "universal" solution.

The text for this chapter previously appeared in a supplement to The Video Battery Handbook, *by Anton/Bauer (located in Shelton, CT), and is reprinted here with their kind permission.*

Digital Audio for Video

by Lon Neumann

The decade of the Eighties saw the introduction of digital audio technology to the world of entertainment production. Technology, later to be applied as professional digital audio, was earlier employed on satellites for deep space probes. It was first used for entertainment purposes in the music industry. Later it found its way into the production, post-production, and broadcast industries of film and video.

Prior to the arrival of digital technology, advancements to the state of the art were evolutionary in nature. Systems were made better by a process of continual refinement. Engineers continued to learn ways of improving circuit designs over the decades since the 1930s. However, the arrival of digital technology was not an evolution of what had come before. Rather, it was completely revolutionary.

There is very little about the details of analog audio technology that is useful in the digital world. This fact creates a big problem. There are many well educated and experienced engineers around who suddenly find themselves ill-equipped to deal with the day-to-day realities of designing, fixing, and using digital systems.

This means having to learn the basics all over again, yet there seems to be no way around it. We now find ourselves living in a digital world. Production and post-production processes are now

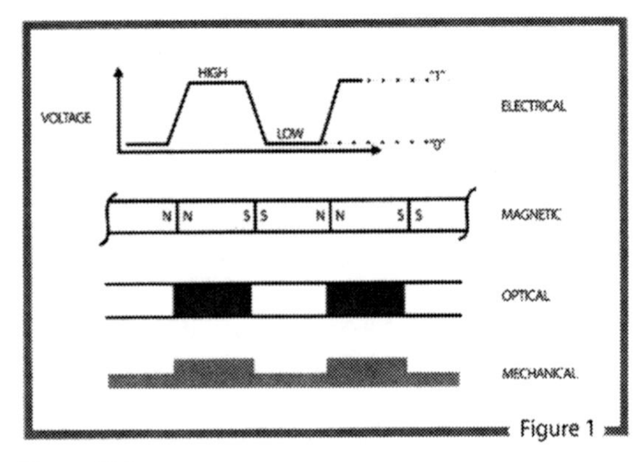

Figure 1

Binary States

being converted to digital processes. This is sure to be an ongoing phenomenon with time. There is no going back.

It is worthwhile reviewing just why it is that we bother converting to digital technology. After all, wasn't everything working just fine before digital came along? Well, yes and no.

Analog technology was working, but there were problems. Many of the attributes of digital technology are best appreciated as benefits when they are compared to similar aspects of analog technology. Some of the benefits of digital technology are entirely new, for which there is no comparable aspect in analog technology.

Let's start with a look at tape recording. Some of the problems inherent in analog tape recording that are solved by digital technology include: wow and flutter; remanant high frequency response/self-erasure; low frequency head bumps; modulation noise; bias rocks; tape saturation; print-through; azimuth shift; head alignment and its matching machine to machine; tape-to-head spacing loss; stereo image shift; poor signal-to-noise ratio; and generation losses. All of these problems are completely eliminated with digital technology.

To understand better why this is true, it is important to understand some of the fundamental principles at work with digital. Much of what makes digital beneficial comes from the fact that all of the information of interest is represented by a binary code. Without getting too technical regarding the rules of using binary codes, first just consider how it is that binary itself helps.

It all stems from the fact that the audio signal is represented by a code system of just two values. That is the real beauty of it. Just two *states* say it all. This makes life much easier. As shown in Figure 1, there are all sorts of systems of two opposing states that can be used, such as off/on, north/south, high/low, up/down, etc. In each of these systems, we have a case where one state representing a binary *zero* is completely opposite, or at least very different, from the state used to represent a binary *one*.

In tape recording, this can be tape saturation with a *north* polarity being used to represent a binary "zero", and tape saturation with *south* polarity representing a binary "one." When playing back the tape, as long as you can discriminate a one from a zero, you will be able to extract all of our original information.

Since the ones and zeroes have been recorded as full saturation of opposite polarities, it is going to be very easy to tell them apart. They are not even close to each other in value. They are completely opposite, to the extremes possible, from each other. Even in the presence of very high tape noise, distortion, interference, etc., we are still going to be able to tell the difference between full north saturation and full south saturation.

In fact, the ratio between the off-tape data signal and the background noise can be as bad as only 20db (very bad indeed), and still all of the original data can be extracted that will yield an analog signal with a signal-to-noise ratio of 120 db or more.

What a miracle! Instead of having to continually fight against the noise that is inherent in tape recording, it just does not matter much anymore. As long as we use two states that are easy to tell apart, we can easily record, process, and transmit all our binary data.

By contrast, analog signals are very delicate and fragile voltage waveforms. Making analog systems work is all about preserving the delicate little nuances of these waveforms. There are forces at work in the universe that are constantly conspiring to compromise these subtle little nuances. With digital technology, once the signal is in the data domain, we have a system that is so robust that we scarcely have to worry about it any longer.

In analog, the laws of magnetic tape recording dictate that as soon a signal is recorded, the high frequency information recorded on tape begins to diminish through a process known as *self-erasure*. This occurs even with the tape just sitting on the shelf. It also occurs as a result of coming near partially magnetized surfaces. That is why technicians must always take pains to thoroughly degauss the analog tape path of tape recorders. None the less, surfaces the tape comes in contact with tend to accumulate magnetic charges.

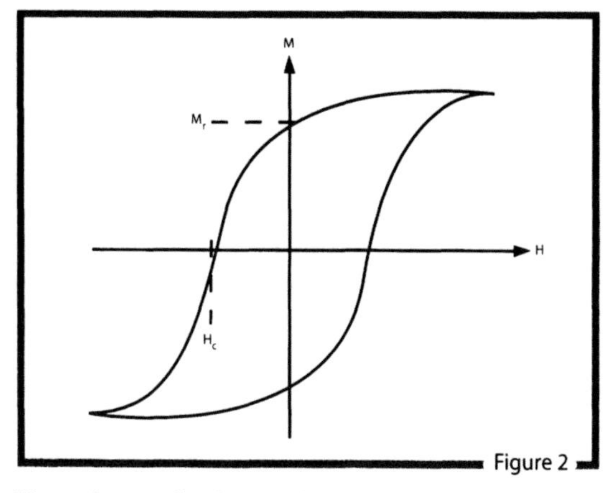

Magnetic recording hysteresis curve

Some of the problems with analog tape recording come about from having to use bias. Magnetic tape as a recording medium is not inherently linear. During World War II, engineers were struggling with the fact that magnetic tape has an inherent hysteresis characteristic.

The familiar hysteresis curve shown in Figure 2 shows that it takes a disproportionately high amount of positive energy to magnetize tape with a north polarity at low levels. Likewise, when recording the other side of the waveform, it takes an excessive amount of negative polarity energy to magnetize the tape with a south polarity. Tape does not like to be magnetized with low-level signals close to 0 volts. Every time the waveform wants to swing from positive to negative there will be *crossover distortion* when passing through zero.

Ultimately, German engineers discovered that by combining an ultrasonic high frequency *bias* signal to the audio input, the tape could effectively

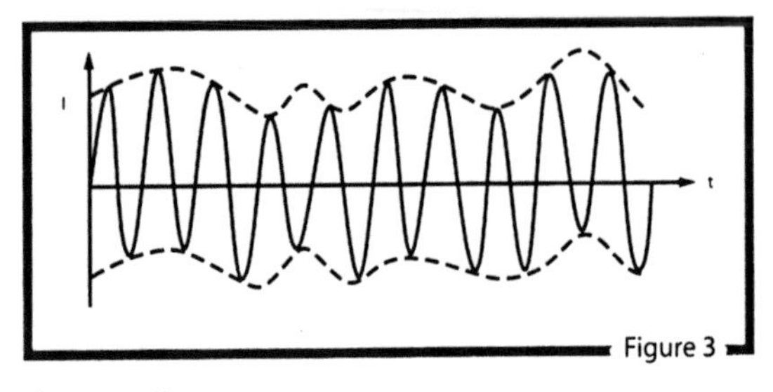

Bias recording

be kept operating in its more linear region that is somewhat outside the zone close to the 0-volts baseline. All modern analog audio tape recorders actually record audio that is riding on a high frequency bias signal, as illustrated in Figure 3.

On playback, the very high frequency bias signal is filtered out, yielding the underlying original audio signal. As far as the human ear is concerned, the audio frequencies are recorded on tape in its linear region. In Figure 3, the dashed lines represent the audio waveform. Bias is shown as the sinusoidal waveform drawn with solid lines.

It works, but there are problems with it. Every tape formulation has an optimum bias recording level that is a trade-off between high frequency response and noise and distortion. This optimum point is rather narrow. It must be carefully adjusted fairly often on every channel of every recorder.

Also, bias recording introduces its own set of spurious artifacts, such as intermodulation distortion, etc. *Bias rocks* are a curious phenomenon that is well known to analog audio engineers. When low frequencies are recorded at low level on tape, the careful listener can hear a sort of garbled, low level, rocky-sounding noise.

There are a whole host of noise sources at work in analog recording: bias noise, DC noise, modulation noise, surface noise, etc. All of these are in addition to the noise that inherently exists in all the electronic circuits in the chain that the signal must pass through. It is no wonder that noise reduction systems have come to be required for analog audio recording to be acceptable.

Then there are a number of limitations imposed by the recording/playback heads and head-to-tape interface problems. The heads have frequency response problems inherent in the physics of the necessary head gap, eddy current losses in the head laminations, inductive problems inherent in the coils of the heads, and so on. Head-to-tape interface issues include such things as spacing losses, so-called low frequency *head bumps* inherent in the contour required on head faces, etc.

Then there are the issues of tape speed and tape path geometry. In analog audio tape recording, all record and playback speed irregularities are converted directly to proportionate irregularities in the resultant signals. Anomalies such as wow and flutter are well known. With digital audio, the data that is played back off tape is fed to FIFO (First In, First Out) memory banks configured so as to buffer the data stream. The concept is somewhat akin to placing a holding tank in a water flow.

Basically, just like the holding tank, the buffer memory is designed to be half full at normal play speed. Data is removed from the buffer under control of a precision timing circuit, just as the water flow out of the tank is regulated by the output valve. The output flow rate is made very smooth and precise by the action of this clock circuit.

At normal play speed, the data will be clocked out at the same rate that it is coming in to the buffer. If the tape speeds up slightly, it will start to fill the buffer faster. But the data will still be clocked out of the buffer memory at precisely the correct speed. The buffer will become more than half full, but the output data will be precisely on speed.

Conversely, if the tape should slow down, the buffer will not be loaded as fast, but will still be clocked out precisely on speed. The buffer will then be less than half full. As long as the FIFO buffer memory is large enough to absorb all speed variations, all the speed irregularities will be completely removed by this buffering action. The output data rate will be correct to the limits of the precision of the output clock. Such clocks can be made to be ultra-precise with quartz crystal clocks. All speed variations are effectively and completely removed.

In addition to purely longitudinal tape speed variations, analog audio tape recorders also suffer from other geometrical errors of tape path and the tape-to-head interface. *Azimuth shift* is a common geometrical error in the tape path. A static azimuth error will excessively attenuate high frequencies and skew a stereo image.

Often azimuth error is dynamically changing as the tape plays with a weaving pattern past the head. Under this circumstance, high frequency response and stereo imaging will be dynamically skewed proportionately.

Tape-to-head contact pressure can also vary both with long term variation and short term dynamics. This can be the result of things like *holdback tension* variations--due to the size of the tape pack on the reels--and other irregularities. In most cases, high frequency fluctuations will occur.

These are just some of the limitations and failure mechanisms inherent in analog audio recording that are completely removed by digital audio recording. A truly exhaustive list of such problems would be too large to list here.

Digital audio recording systems usually have frequency responses that are as flat as rulers throughout their passbands. From the lowest frequencies of interest to the very highest frequencies, not only is the response completely flat, but it is continuously so. There are no short-term fluctuations or other variations with time. Frequency response is constant with time, and play speed is also rock solid.

Likewise, stereo imaging is completely stable. There is no print-through and no generation losses. Copies can be made of copies with no increase in noise or distortion. These copies are said to be *clones* of the original since, as long as the system is operating within its limits, the original data is actually recreated on the clones. The clones, therefore, are recreations of the originals, not just copies.

The ability to clone data gives rise to one of the very important benefits inherent in digital technology. Since there is no loss or other penalty in either cascading successive stages or successively copying from one medium to another, audio engineers are now able to design systems that are convenient and efficient. Such things as non-linear and non-destructive editing were never feasible before the arrival of digital.

It also provides that things like routing switchers are entirely transparent to the audio. This has never been the case with analog audio. Analog audio routing switchers have always added noise, distortion, high frequency rolloff and cross talk.

At a time when the audience has become accustomed to ultra high-quality digital audio multi-track playback through very high-quality amplifier/speaker systems, the consequence is that there is a greatly heightened requirement for even higher performance audio environments for production and post-production facilities. Consumers now demand that their audio be transmitted to them with an extremely wide dynamic range, with a very broad frequency response extending from nearly sub-sonic to ultra-sonic, and that all the phase information at all frequencies be rock solid so as to maintain the phantom imaging of the complex surround-sound field. The best way to achieve this is to employ a digital infrastructure.

There are two fundamental precepts to adhere to for successful digital audio projects in post-production. The basic ideas are to 1) digitize once, and 2) to do it at the earliest possible stage. In other words, it should be ensured that on any given project an audio signal should, first of all, only be digitized once.

This means that a signal should not go through successive stages of analog-to-digital and digital-to-analog converters. It should be digitized once, and then kept digital all the way through the entire post-production process. Going through successive A/D & D/A stages is akin to generation losses with analog audiotape.

The conversions from analog-to-digital and digital-to-analog are the two areas of digital technology where the signal is guaranteed to be degraded. Great care is taken to minimize the inherent degradation of conversion, but the best results are achieved if it is done only once during the whole production/post-production process. Once the signal is converted to data, it's best to keep it as data straight through to the final delivery. Every time a signal is converted from digital back to analog just so some sort of analog processing can go on, and then converted back to digital, the audio is degraded beyond what would be the case if some digital process had been used instead.

The second precept to observe is that the earlier the digitizing is done the better. Digitizing at the earliest possible stage ensures that a minimum of noise, distortion, phase shift, flutter, and other spurious artifacts are added to the audio. These degradations always accrue cumulatively from analog audio stages. Ideally, the best possible stage to digitize would be right at the output of the microphone. Microphones with digital outputs have begun to appear on the market. There will no doubt be increased utilization of digitizing microphones as time goes on.

In some ways, digital audio is more similar to traditional analog video than it is to traditional audio. As in video, scanning the program material with precision timing is at the core of the technology. In video, input program material is captured as about 30 still picture frames every second. Each of these individual frames is very carefully scanned one line at a time.

Every frame is made up of 525 horizontal lines. As each line is scanned, luminance and chroma values are very carefully measured continuously as the scanner continues left to right across the line. At the end of each line, the scanner retraces to the beginning of the next. This continues over and over until the bottom of the frame is reached. At the bottom of the frame, the scanner retraces vertically to the top of the picture, and the whole process begins again.

All of this continues at the rate of about 30 frames per second. This process begins with a camera and ultimately concludes at a monitor. For the system to work, the scanning in the monitor must be precisely synchronized with the scanning action of the camera. When the camera begins scanning the first line, the monitor must also begin scanning the first line. The two scanning systems must remain precisely locked together, or synchronized, as they trace across each line, retrace at the end of each line, and vertically retrace at the bottom of each frame. Precision timing of synchronization is of the essence of the system.

There is nothing new about any of this. It has been successfully practiced worldwide for 50 years. What is new is that these principles are applied to audio in a very similar fashion. Traditionally, timing and synchronization had been an issue for audio only in as much as audio needed to stay synchronized with picture to the extent of maintaining the illusion of lip-sync. Up to a frame or two of loose sync this way or that was no big deal. There was no special requirement for high precision timing as a fundamental of the medium. With digital audio, all that has changed. In digital audio, precision timing is fundamental to the technology.

As in video, digital audio is a scanned system. Digital audio "scans" the input program material 48,000 times per second. Every 20 microseconds, the input sampler takes a snapshot of the audio signal voltage.

This snapshot voltage value is converted to a binary representation of ones and zeroes, with precision from 16-bit to 24-bit. With this, the audio has just entered the digital data domain. From here on out, the laws that apply to data hold sway. From processing, to storage, to dubbing, to transmission, it's all data until it is converted back to analog audio for listening.

And, all along the way, just as in video, timing is at the core. In the first place, precise timing must be applied to the original sampling. Instability of the timing of sampling is known as *jitter*. Jitter in sampling results in audible distortion that will be irrevocably attached to the program material.

Then there is the timing required in interconnecting systems. Each of the data *words* must be passed from one stage to the next at just the instant this next stage is prepared to receive it--much like traditional analog video. The receiving stage needs to be running at precisely the same data rate as well. In fact, succeeding stages need to be precisely locked in synchronization for successful operation. Their operating rates must be locked together by some means.

When all is said and done, this is one of the areas that presents the greatest possibility for failure in the field. Synchronization must be maintained. If it is not, the result will be garbage. It happens. The possible failure modalities are too numerous to mention here. It is important for audio engineers to take pains to ensure that proper sync is maintained from start to finish.

Sampling

In digital audio systems designed for professional applications, Pulse Code Modulation (PCM) is the standard for encoding analog audio signals as binary data. The fundamental operation of PCM is that the audio waveform is measured 48,000 times per second and assigned a binary number representing the instantaneous voltage at the instant of measurement. The process consists of two separate operations, *sampling* and *quantizing*.

The Nyquist Theorem states that as long as the sampling process is done at least twice as often as the rate of the highest frequency of interest, nothing will be lost by the sampling process.

To begin the PCM process, the input signal is measured periodically. This is known as sampling. The input waveform is essentially cut up into tiny slices for quick voltage measurement. The period of measurement is very short. It must occur 48,000 times each second.

In a classic linear PCM converter, the input sampling function is usually fed first to a device known as a *sample-and-hold* circuit. Even though the sampling process is relatively fast, the subsequent quantizing process is not infinitely fast. It takes time to quantize; therefore, it is not enough to merely "slice" a signal. The sampled value must also be held for a discrete period of time for the quantizer to have time to do its function.

During sampling, it is imperative to have minimal jitter in the clock that regulates when each sample is taken. The regularity of the sampling process is critical. Not only must it happen at a very high rate, but also it must happen with great

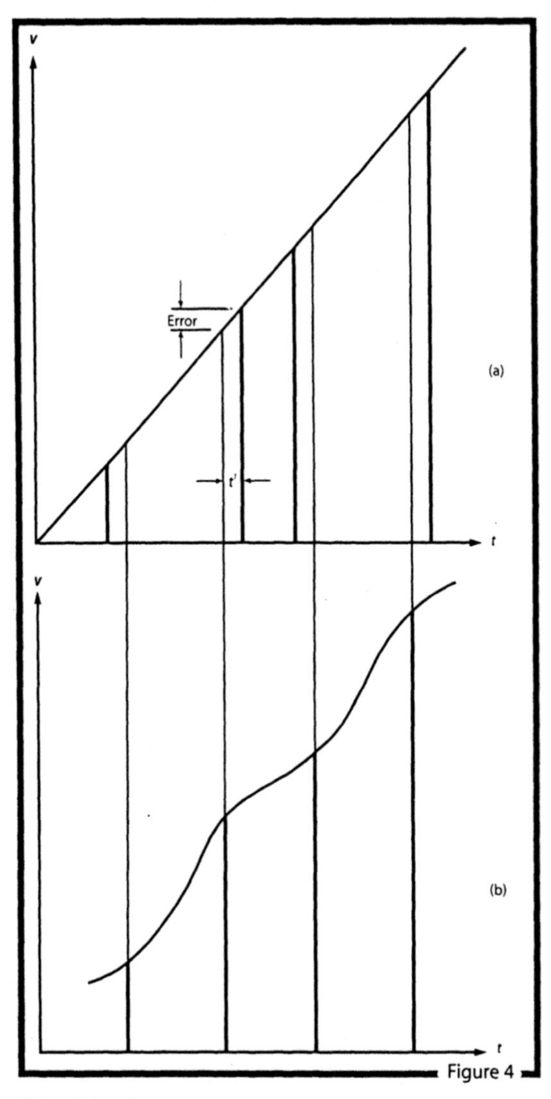

Figure 4

Jitter distortion

precision. Specifically, it must happen at exactly every 0.00002 seconds, or every 20 microseconds.

The degree of precision required here is on the order of +/- .000,000,001 seconds, 1 nanosecond, or better. This is a high degree of precision, but it is necessary in a well-designed professional system. Any jitter in the sampling process yields a distortion that is permanently attached to the signal as it is passed to each following stage, as shown in Figure 3. In this figure, t^1 represents the timing error, jitter. The lower waveform shows the distortion induced by jitter in the sampling clock. This distortion becomes a permanent artifact of the data representing the original audio.

In this regard, it is totally unlike the characteristic of *transmission jitter*. Transmission jitter is removed by reclocking data out of a FIFO buffer memory. Sampling-induced jitter distortion is permanent. There is no removing it later. That is why it is of the utmost importance to have a stable ultra-low jitter sampling system.

At interconnected installations any more elaborate than a simple isolated island suite, it becomes important to not just generate a low-jitter sampling clock, but also to distribute this common sampling sync reference throughout the facility in a way that retains the integrity of its jitter performance. There needs to be just one digital audio sync reference common to entire production facilities.

This single digital audio sync reference needs to be distributed throughout the facility and received at the sync inputs of all sampling systems--the analog-to-digital converters. In other words, the sync distribution system needs to maintain the

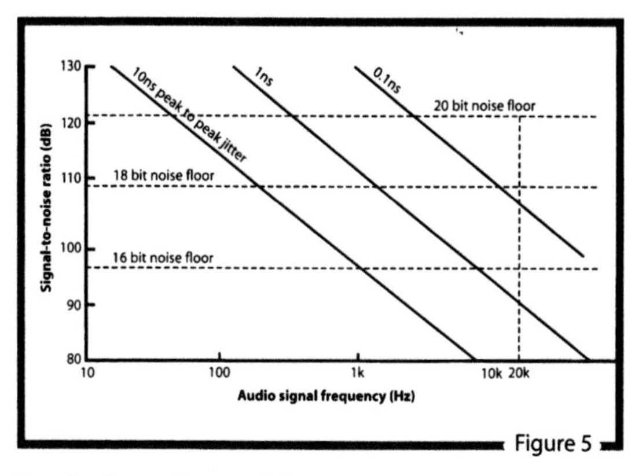

Figure 5

Required sampling precision

ultra-low jitter performance of the sync reference too. The jitter performance that is required of sampling clocks increases with digital word length. Although +/- 1 nanosecond of sampling-clock jitter may be adequate for 16-bit systems, as shown in Figure 4, 24-bit systems have even more stringent requirements.

If sampled signals include frequency components that exceed a rate greater than half the sampling frequency, an unfortunate phenomenon known as *aliasing* occurs. In normal audio terms, this means that if frequencies higher than 24 kHz are sampled, there will be aliasing. Great care must be taken to ensure that aliasing does not occur.

Aliasing is a particularly obnoxious form of distortion. It is especially objectionable in that there is no harmonic relationship with the fundamental signal. It is extremely dissonant and very obvious. Harmonic distortion, given its relationship with the fundamental, can exist at surprisingly high levels before it is audible.

This is not so with aliasing. Very small levels of aliasing are glaringly obvious. With classic PCM converters, this meant the application of analog "brick wall" anti-aliasing filters (low-pass filters with a very steep cutoff characteristic at the upper edge of the pass band) prior to the sampler. With the advent of oversampling converters, the filtering paradigm is shifted into a new domain.

Given the disastrous result of sampled frequencies higher than the Nyquist cutoff frequency, before oversampling converters became viable, anti-aliasing filters needed to have brick wall characteristics.

These theoretical limits could never actually be achieved in the real world. The simple truth is that the sharper the slope of the filter, the greater the phase-shift anomalies in the pass band. That is, some of the frequencies of the program content would be delayed in time relative to other frequencies. *Phase-shift*, or group delay, a type of distortion, can be more audible in some circumstances than others, but it is always a departure from the original signal. Those early anti-aliasing filters did introduce audible spurious artifacts in the program material. Even then, this was much less of problem than any aliasing would have been.

Later on, over-sampling converters became the most popular approach to eliminate the problems associated with analog brick wall filters. *Over-sampling* simply means sampling at a rate that is higher, usually much higher, than what is required by the Nyquist Theorem, and then, via some clever digital signal processing, deriving the desired data at the sampling rate of interest.

Quantizing

At the completion of the sampling process, there is a string of 48,000 measured voltage steps per second. *Quantizing* is the process of converting each of these measured voltages to data.

First, each sample is assigned a number representing its instantaneous voltage level. This base-ten number is then converted to its binary equivalent of ones and zeros. The number of data bits used for this encoding determines the resolution and dynamic range available. Sixteen-bit systems have 65,536 voltage steps that can be encoded.

When converting the data back to analog waveforms, the resultant voltage step that is created represents the value midway between the adjacent steps, as illustrated in Figure 6. This may not represent the exact level that was originally converted. This discrepancy between the resultant analog output voltage and the original analog input voltage is known as *quantizing distortion.*

Quantizing distortion in the presence of mid- to low-level signals is barely perceptible as low level background noise. However, lower level signals combine with quantization distortion for an effect that is perceived as *granularity* in the signal itself. This granularity in low-level signals is much more objectionable than simple background noise.

The solution is *dither*. Dither is a means of decorrelating the quantizing error from the signal of interest. The result is a system noise floor (the low-level noise inherent in the system) that sounds and behaves like a conventional analog audio system. Figure 7 illustrates the resultant averaged transfer function from adding dither to the raw analog output voltage waveform.

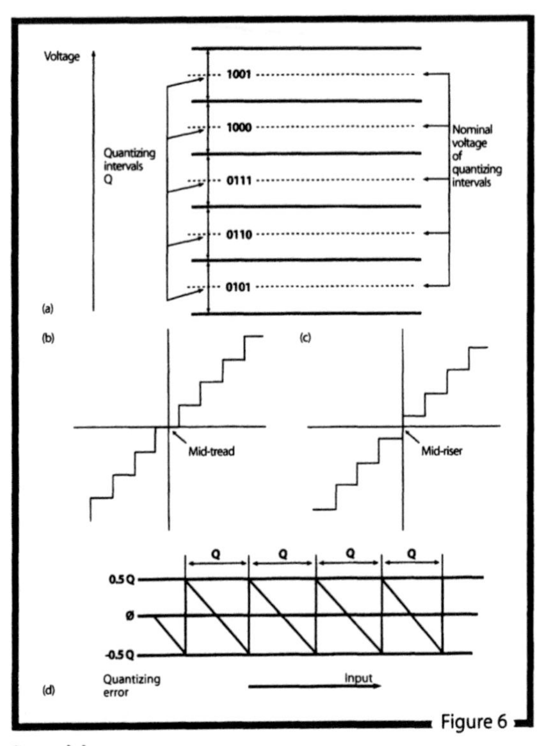

Figure 6

Quantizing error

Some signals of interest, for example reverb tails or ambient room tones, tend to operate at the lower operating levels. In these cases, when the signal is digitized with dither, they seem to merely decay down into and even below the noise floor. This is the same sensation as has always been the case with analog audiotape noise, for example. Without dither, these low-level signals become very grainy and objectionable.

Dither is actually a random noise signal that is added to the low level quantizing. The spectrum of the dither can be totally random white noise. On the other hand, spectral shaping may be applied to the noise for psycho-acoustic benefits. The optimum spectral shaping of this additive noise signal is a topic of discussion.

Whatever the shape of the applied dither should be, it is important to understand that all of the benefits it imparts are contained in the lowest-order bits, or perhaps even in just the least significant bit (LSB). Any process that would remove the LSB would remove the dithered information, and thereby eliminate all its former benefits.

There are two common practices that do just that, *truncation* and *digital signal processing* (DSP). When a signal that is converted with 20-bit precision is to be fed to a 16-bit system, something must happen with the remaining four bits.

The lowest order bits represent the smallest signal variations. Thus, it makes sense that the lowest order bits could be removed to yield a 16-bit signal. If the low order bits are simply sliced off from 20-bit data to yield 16-bit, this is known as *truncating.* Truncating is one way of interfacing 20-bit A/D converters to 16-bit recorders. The problem is that not only has the low-level information been removed, but also the dither has been removed in the process. Low level output granularity is once again the result.

A better approach is to reintroduce dither at the level of the new LSB, the 16th bit in this example. This is known as redithering. Unfortunately, truncation is not the only process that would conspire to relieve us of the benefits of our dithering. Virtually every DSP stage also strips out the dither information internally. DSP

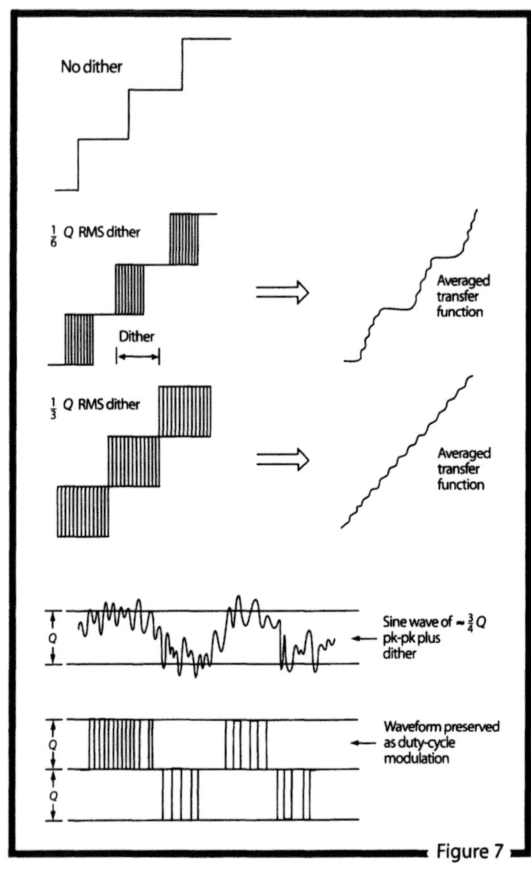

Figure 7

Dither

includes such things as level adjustments, mixing, EQ, etc. Often DSP will appear in unexpected places such as the output of tape recorders. Some tape recorders provide the ability to digitally adjust their output levels.

As we have said, it should be obvious that if the level is being adjusted digitally, the dither has been lost. What is not so obvious is that DSP may be occurring when you least expect it, such as when the controls are set so that the signal should be output at the same level as the input. In other words, even when it seems that signal level has not been altered, sometimes its level is in reality something like 99.9 percent of the original.

This level shift, in and of itself, would not be so objectionable. But it will strip the dithered information out of the data, even though you might not even know that any DSP at all has been applied. True data recorders never have such a problem. No such DSP would ever be automatically applied to the output of a data recorder. These cases all require redithering to regain the original smooth noise floor. Fortunately, many digital audio workstations and other post-production systems do provide the ability to digitally redither with a high degree of control.

Level

In professional audio systems in North America, Standard Operating Level (SOL) has traditionally been 0VU, 0.775 Vrms. This same operating level persists with professional digital audio systems as well. However, the characteristic operations above and below SOL are different between digital and analog audio tape recording systems. Both have noise floors that are the limiting factors at their low ends. But the high level operation is different.

In analog audio, SOL was chosen as being the optimum compromise between being adequately far from the noise floor on the one hand and just below the gradually increasing onset of distortion with increasing level on the other hand. The ultimate high-level limit, or saturation point, was often some agreed upon but arbitrary level of distortion, sometimes as high as 10 percent. Generally, SOL was hoped to be at a point in the curve safely below saturation.

This range between SOL and saturation is known as *headroom*. In the range of headroom, distortion definitely is higher than in the linear range, yet it is still less than at the saturation point. The distortion is too high in this range for standard operation, but if the signal was attenuated enough to completely stay out this region, its signal-to-noise ratio would be proportionately diminished to its detriment. On the other hand, if you set aside the headroom region for just quick transient signals, the increased distortion of the transients is less likely to be noticed. The human ear is less sensitive to transient distortion.

Digital audio signals have a completely different characteristic at high levels. Instead of increasing distortion with increasing levels exceeding SOL, distortion actually decreases in levels above SOL. This is because the primary distortion component of digital audio systems is low-level quantization error.

Up to the clipping point, the farther away from the low-level quantization error the signal is, the lower will be its figure for distortion--specified as THD+N (Total Harmonic Distortion plus Noise). However, at the ultimate limit, there is no forgiving gentle onset of high-level distortion as in analog audio systems. Instead, there is an abrupt ceiling of hard clipping. Any signal excursions that are attempting to be quantized at a level that is higher than all bits set in the quantizer are simply chopped off at the limit.

There are no more remaining values available than all bits turned on. *Clipping* is the most severe form of harmonic distortion. In actual fact, it may well be that clipping of the very fastest transients may be hard to detect. However, most self-respecting audio engineers would usually not admit to knowingly clipping fast transients. It is important to allow enough room above SOL to accommodate fast transients that often accompany lower-level RMS fundamental signals.

Just how much room really must be left above SOL for transients is a debate that has raged for years. The standard practice throughout North America is to allow 20db above SOL before clipping. Since SOL is 0VU, or +4dBm, clipping occurs 20db above at +24dBm--a good match for most professional audio systems. But there is no clearly defined pivot point, or knee in the curve, as is the case with analog. So the operating level is more a matter of general agreement between audio engineers rather than parameters inherent in the medium as in analog.

In North America there is general agreement about what constitutes SOL, but Europe, for example, generally has a different practice. In some parts of Europe, they have elected to set their SOL with 18db of headroom. There are also different opinions about what is represented by Full Scale Digital (FSD). When all the bits of the data word have been set, or turned "on," we have Full Scale Digital, the largest analog signal amplitude that can be encoded. The analog output of D/A converters can be adjusted up and down. FSD could be adjusted

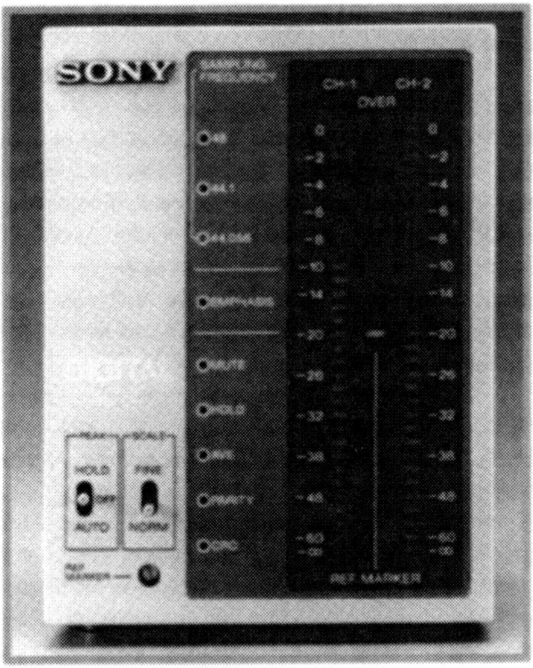

Figure 8. A standard digital audio meter.

to represent +22dBm, or it could be adjusted to +28dBm. In North America, by general agreement, FSD is taken to represent +24dBm.

In professional digital audio systems, different conventions for metering signals have been developed. Traditional metering systems such as VU meters are generally employed to monitor analog signal levels as they are fed to the A/D converter. After the signal is converted to data, metering is generally done with digital meters.

Digital meters are generally calibrated with a scale that indicates headroom remaining before clipping. In contrast to VU meters, a reading of 0db is put at the top of the scale. It indicates that there is 0db remaining before the clipping point. Down scale from there, levels are indicated with negative numbers (e.g., -15). This means that there would be 15db of headroom remaining above that level. These displays can generally stretch the input pulses so that we can be sure of displaying the true level of even the fastest transients. The meter becomes a powerful device for knowing the real levels of even the fastest peaks. Analog meters have generally never been quick enough to show the fast transients. One generally had to use good judgment about just how much headroom to allocate above the displayed RMS value of a VU meter.

In North America, SOL is set for -20db on standard digital meters, as shown in Figure 8. This means that at 0VU there is 20db of headroom remaining. An analog console or preamp with an output of 0VU should register -20 on the standard digital meter.

It is useful to have a display to indicate clipping. This could be set to display at the analog level of +24dBm. It's more direct, however, to derive the "clipping light" by directly monitoring the digital audio data, as indicated by the "OVER" light at the top of the display in Figure 8. The problem is that having all bits "on" is not a problem, per se, but it is the level at which the system is about to clip. Just having all the bits set is not enough to know that clipping has occurred. However, if many successive samples are set with all bits on, it is reasonable to deduce that clipping must have occurred.

The waveform that would be decoded results in its top being clipped off at the maximum allowable level. Some digital metering systems are designed so as to give the engineer the ability to make the judgment that some selected number of consecutive full-scale samples represents that clipping has occurred. Engineers would generally agree that a single, full-scale sample should be allowed, but that eight consecutive full-scale samples is clearly too many. Just how many full-scale samples ought to be allowed to pass before setting the "over" display can be a matter of personal judgment.

Emphasis

In the early days of professional digital audio, not all A/D and D/A converters were up to professional standards. In fact, many were not. It was difficult to make commercially viable converters that were adequate for the needs of professional audio engineers. A system known as *pre-emphasis* (or just "emphasis") was devised to allow acceptable operation with some of these lesser converters.

The issue was *dynamic range* because converters were noisy. Bear in mind that, in the early days, even 14-bit systems were pressed into service. Engineers recalled that analog audiotape had always been a noisy medium that had been made more acceptable by a system of emphasis/de-emphasis--the familiar Record/Playback EQ.

The noise spectrum of tape was perceived as more objectionable at the high frequency end of the spectrum. That fact, combined with the realization that the real high frequency content of most real-world signals is at a much lower level than mid-band signals, gave rise to the standard practice of pre-emphasizing the high frequency content of signals about to be recorded. In playback, a complementary or inverse EQ curve was applied that put the high frequency content back at the original relative levels.

The benefits of this approach derived from at least two attributes: 1) High frequencies were recorded at a level much higher above the noise than would otherwise have been the case; and 2) High frequency tape noise was suppressed by the Playback EQ. The overall high frequency signal-to-noise ratio was thus much improved. Mid-band signal-to-noise was less affected.

This same system of complementary high frequency EQ was applied to the A/D and D/A conversion processes. Pre-emphasis of high frequency content before digitizing, when used in conjunction with the complementary de-emphasis equalization after the digital-to-analog conversion process, allowed successful professional applications of some of the early marginally-acceptable converters.

The interesting aspect here is that, contrary to what had always been the case with audiotape, emphasis was never universally applied. Rather, it has always been selectively applied. Some people liked it sometimes for some applications, but not everybody liked it all the time. Therefore, a method was developed for signaling to the playback circuits, whether or not emphasis had been used during the A-to-D process.

The playback circuits use this information to determine whether to switch the de-emphasis EQ circuits in. Since emphasis was first devised, there has always been a way to indicate whether or not to use de-emphasis EQ on playback.

In SDIF data there is a simple flag that is set in the serial data stream. If the playback circuit sees this bit turned on, it will know that pre-emphasis EQ was used during recording, and will switch on the playback de-emphasis EQ so as to have normal frequency response of the resultant program signal.

In AES data it is a little bit different. Emphasis signaling information is contained in the respective byte of the *Channel Status Block*. These days it is rare to see emphasis applied for post-production work. Converter technology has progressed to the point that it is unusual to have an application where emphasis would be necessary.

Many professional systems are now designed for post-production which make the assumption that emphasis will not be used in the professional environment. The issue is that, when editing a program together, if the editor intercuts between emphasized and non-emphasized material, unwanted muting may occur when playing back the edited program. De-emphasis circuits do not switch in and out of circuit especially fast. Usually some time is needed for the circuits to settle down after switching. Many systems will mute for a short period to give the EQ circuits a moment to settle down.

Common practice for many post-production facilities is to dispense with emphasis altogether. If there is no switching in and out of de-emphasis circuits, there will be none of the possible muting of edited material. But the signaling system still exists.

Other problems can arise in using emphasized data in professional systems. The practice of stipulating that no emphasis will be used has become so widespread that some systems designers assume it as a given. Now we have the case that some post-production systems simply will not accept data with the emphasis flag set.

Although this may now seem to be a little extreme, there was a time when emphasis switching came to be seen as causing more problems than it solved. One solution is to process the emphasized data through a Digital Audio Workstation and digitally de-emphasize the data before cutting the clip into the program.

Short of that, sometimes a de-emphasized analog output must be resampled by a non-emphasized digitizer. This would be an unfortunate compromise. Once digitized, it is always better to keep the signal in the digital domain if at all possible. A more common approach is to just stay away from emphasis altogether. No emphasis, no de-emphasis switching problems.

Having said this, it may be worth remembering that there may still be cases where emphasis can do some good. There have been cases where a recording engineer is faced with imposed uncertainty in setting record levels. The case might be that some historic or otherwise important one-time event needs to be recorded. If there is no way of reliably predicting the needed gain settings and record levels, the most prudent thing to do is back way off on the record levels, leaving much more headroom than normal (say some 40db, for example).

If there was any chance that the signal so recorded would be pushed up in the final mix, in other words, listened to at high level, then one would be better off if that signal had been recorded with emphasis. There will be less high frequency noise associated with it. In fact, any time that a signal must be recorded at a low level and subsequently brought up in level, one is generally in the position of needing to decide if emphasis should be used or not.

One final point about emphasis. Emphasis should never be used to record high level high-frequency signals. The high frequency content of most natural acoustic sounds is fairly low, relative to mid-band frequencies. That is not always the case, however. Synthesizers can generate high frequencies at arbitrarily high levels, and even some acoustically generated signals can have tremendous high frequency content. If such signals are recorded at high level with emphasis in circuit, high frequency distortion will likely occur. If the emphasis equalizer pushes some program content beyond +24dBm, it will be clipped.

Standard Interface

In 1985, the Audio Engineering Society (AES) and the European Broadcasting Union (EBU) developed a format for standardized interchange of digital audio data, known as AES3-1985. Prior to that time, there was no standard that was common to all systems. Therefore, there was no assurance of being able to make a digital interface between systems.

Subsequently, the standard was amended in 1992. The new title is AES3-1992, and is also known as ANSI standard S4.40-1992. Later on, the standard was adapted for interface on coaxial cable. SMPTE first published its standard, SMPTE 276M-1995, "Transmission of AES/EBU Digital Audio Signals Over Coaxial Cable". AES followed suit with its AES3-ID.

Given the worldwide adoption of the AES/EBU standard, audio engineers have the comfort of knowing that, as long as systems meet the standard, digital audio data can be reliably interfaced between all compliant systems. Needless to say, this is an important consideration for facilities considering doing digital audio work in production/post-production. It is important to understand what is contained in the standard so as to assure compliance.

AES/EBU

The AES Digital Standards Committee was given the task of developing a format for digital audio interface that would ensure interconnection between equipment without concern of manufacture at either end. Some of their design goals were to utilize existing installed audio cabling, and to develop a format that is both self-clocking and self-synchronizing that would permit a complete stereo interface on one cable. Subsequent experience has proven that it is not a good idea to interface AES data on standard audio cable, but most of the rest of the goals have been met.

Electrical Interface

(*Please refer to Figure 9.*) From this diagram we can see many of the important parameters to be observed in the electrical interconnect circuitry of AES3-1992 data. The cable is a shielded twisted pair. It is used as a balanced circuit to interconnect a balanced transmitter with a balanced receiver. The driver output impedance is 110 ohms, the receiver impedance is 110 ohms, and the characteristic impedance of the cable should be 110 ohms at the frequency of interest, 3.072MHz at 48kHz sampling.

The driver needs to produce output waveforms of between 2V and 7V, peak-to-peak (p-p), into such impedances. With contemporary 110-

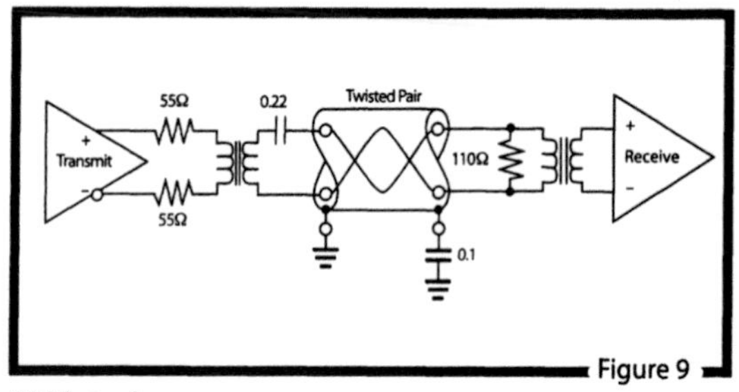

AES interface

ohm cable designed for AES/EBU interface, it is not uncommon to see successful interface at distances of up to 1,000 feet. It is possible to extend that distance by using receivers with transmission line equalizers designed to square up rounded pulses. Figure 10 shows an EQ curve that would be useful for that purpose.

The standard is written for point-to-point interface. This means that each transmitter will connect to just one receiver. Although not written into the standard, there are cases where it makes good sense to connect a transmitter to more than one receiver. Sync distribution is a common example.

In such a case, it would not be unusual to see a central AES sync generator needing to be widely distributed to the sync inputs of systems throughout a plant. Typically, engineers will develop a tree of distribution amplifiers for distributing this sync signal. By employing loop-though inputs on the distribution amplifiers (as has been common in the video industry for decades) the number of required distribution amplifiers can be greatly reduced. But looping through multiple inputs of the DAs represents taking the AES3 output of the sync generator to more than one destination. Though this

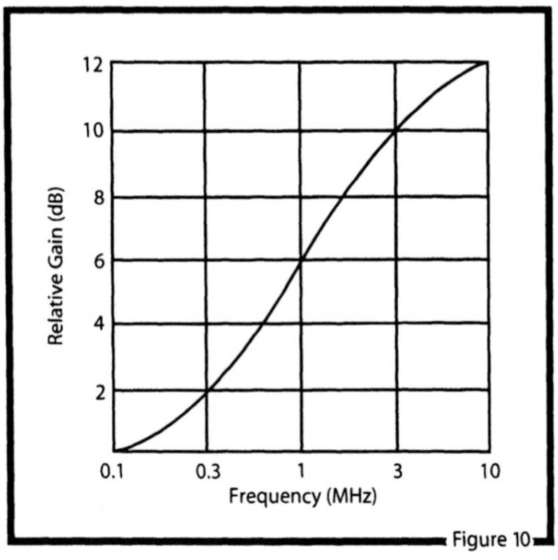

Figure 10

AES EQ

need was not anticipated by the drafters of the standard, it can work. However, it does mean that the impedance of the looped-through inputs need to be convertible to high impedance so as to not upset the nominal impedance of the interface seen by the output feeding it.

Figure 11 shows the interface circuit details for connecting coaxial cable per AES3-ID or SMPTE 279M. All data formatting and channel coding remain the same as for AES3-1992. Only the electrical interface is changed. This approach was designed to take advantage of the huge installed base of coaxial cable previously employed for analog video interface. All source, cable, and destination termination values and signal levels are the same as for analog video, i.e., 75-ohm impedances and 1-volt peak-to-peak, respectively.

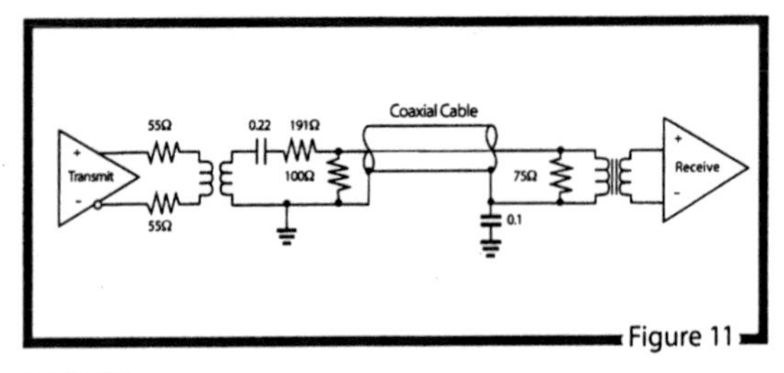

Figure 11

AES3-ID

Since the data rate of AES3-ID data is roughly equivalent to baseband video, this approach sometimes is the obvious choice. However, it is recommended to keep AES3-ID data away from other legacy infrastructure devices such as video distribution amplifiers. The fast rise times of data edges is often more than older distribution amplifiers may handle gracefully. Better to use distribution amplifiers designed specifically for AES3-ID data.

Eye Pattern

(*See Eye Pattern illustration, Figure 12*) If an oscilloscope is fed from a transmission line carrying AES data, a pattern similar to the illustration can be displayed. This pattern is known as an *eye pattern.* The name is derived from the fact that the pattern actually looks somewhat like eyes. Eye patterns are one of the most useful tools available to an engineer for judging the quality of data generation, transmission, storage, etc. This one simple pattern includes the important operating parameters of amplitude, noise, and jitter.

As shown in the illustration, the vertical dimension relates to amplitude. The clear space

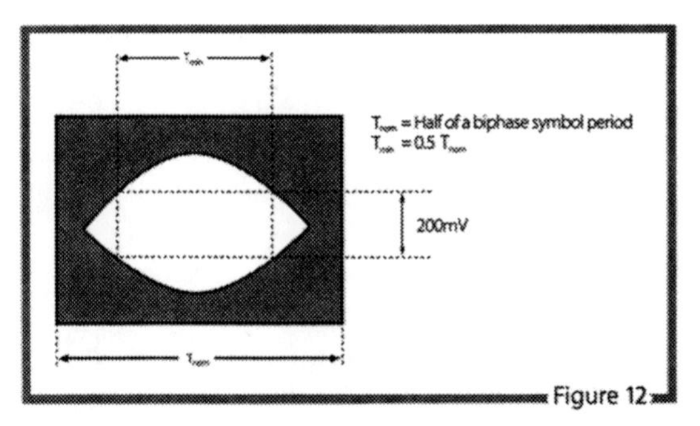

Figure 12

inside the eye needs to represent a minimum of 200mV on the vertical axis at points that are a minimum of 1/2 of a biphase symbol period apart. The thickness of the horizontal lines indicates how much noise is present. The width of the zero-crossing region of the eye is an indication of the timing jitter of the data.

Sometimes it is necessary to quantify these parameters. But part of the beauty of using eye patterns is that much can be learned by just having a quick look. The object is to keep the eyes open. Open eyes indicate good data. When the eyes start closing down along either axis, horizontal or vertical, it is time to become concerned. If equipment is built to meet AES specification, it must be able to decode the data represented by the minimally acceptable eye pattern of 200mV at a width of 1/2 of a biphase symbol period.

Channel Code

In Figure 13 we see a timing diagram that explains the *channel code* for transmitting AES data. Raw data is not transmitted directly. It needs to be put into a form more suitable for transmission. Think of it as a container for the data. There are many different channel codes in existence. The channel code used for transmitting AES data goes by different names, such as "Manchester Code" or "bi-phase mark." Perhaps the most descriptive name is simply FM (Frequency Modulation).

As depicted by the diagram, this channel code applies a kind of frequency modulation to the data. There is one frequency to indicate data "ones," and another frequency to indicate data "zeroes." Part of the beauty of this approach is its simplicity. There are no complex formulas involved. Note that when the input data goes to the high state, indicating a data one, the resultant output will be a waveform with four transitions between high and low during the period of the input bit, yielding two high states and two low states. Conversely, a data zero at the input will yield an output waveform with two transitions during the period of the input bit, one high state and one low state.

Concealed in the simplicity of this are some very important properties. Even with long strings of the same input data bits, whether ones or zeroes, there will be no long direct current (DC) states, where the data would be represented by a relatively long period of either the low voltage or the high voltage. This is very important for data transmission. As shown in the drawing, long strings of ones or zeroes produce transmission frequencies of either one frequency or another, but no long DC states.

Also note that there is always a transition at the beginning of the bit cell period. Thus, it is possible to easily derive a downstream data clock. This provides self-clocking data. There is no need to run an extra cable to carry a clock signal for locking downstream data receivers. Also, this scheme is insensitive to

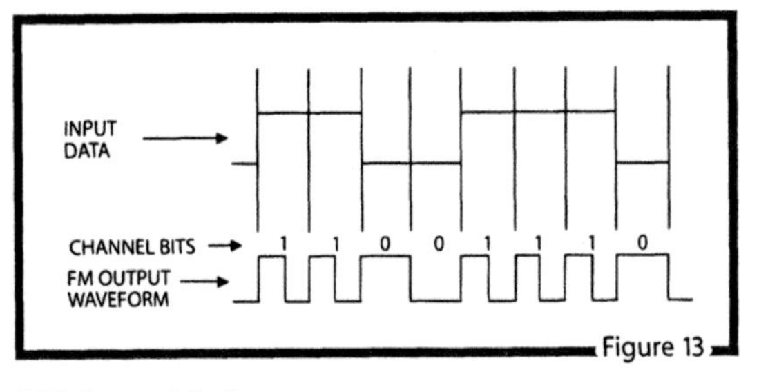

AES Channel Code

polarity of balanced circuits. It is unimportant whether a given bit is represented by a high or low state. Rather, the important thing is the frequency of transitions. It matters not whether a twisted pair cable is wired with the correct polarity at its connectors.

This scheme provides for good jitter rejection. Timing jitter of up to half a data bit can be rejected. Also note that since there are only two frequencies of interest for transmission, and that they are only one octave apart, the job of designing equalizers for the transmission line is not a complex matter.

Frame Format

In Figure 14, we see the basic frame structure of AES3 data. What we are seeing is actually one subframe. (A full frame consists of two subframes.) Two audio channels are transported by one AES3 data stream. The two channels are represented by the two subframes, A and B. The two subframes alternate, one after the other.

As such, the two channels should be considered to be time-division multiplexed. The frame rate is the same as sampling frequency. There

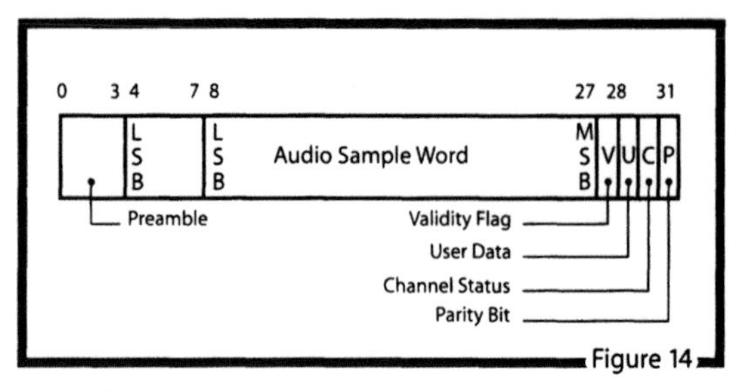

AES subframe

is one frame per each sampling period, left and right. The bit rate at 48kHz sampling is therefore 3.072 Mbps.

Subframe Format

Each *subframe* consists of a 32-bit space for the audio data plus considerable overhead. The primary audio data space is the 20-bit space between bits number 8 and 27. To carry 24-bit data, the 4-bit auxiliary data space between bits number 4 and 7 are used. These four bits are otherwise generally not used. Whether it is 16-bit data, 20-bit data, or 24-bit data, the most significant bit (MSB) is located at bit 27. If the data is shorter than 20 bits, the leading bits should be set to zero. The overhead, or housekeeping, data comprises the remainder of each subframe.

At the beginning of each subframe there are four bits known as the *preamble.* The preamble constitutes a code violation. The unique patterns of the preambles violate the timing rules of bit-cell timing in ways that cannot occur in any other pattern of data combinations. The purpose of these deliberate code violations is to facilitate simple recognition of them as sync patterns.

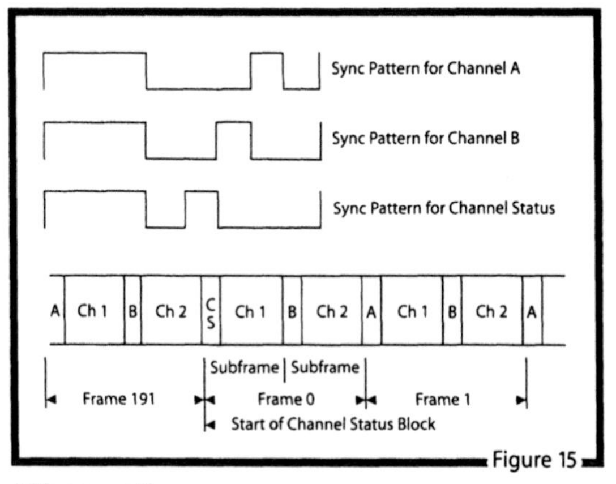

Figure 15

AES sync patterns

Nowhere else will there be such violations. Therefore, any such violations must be one of the sync patterns. There are three of these different sync patterns. As shown in Figure 15, there is one pattern to identify the beginning of "A" subframes, another to identify the beginning of "B" subframes, and a third to indicate block start. Subframes are collected into larger groups known as *blocks*. (Block structure will be discussed in more detail below.)

For now, suffice it to say that after every 192 subframes, the third sync pattern is used to indicate the start of a new block. Consistent with the other properties of the bi-phase channel coding, each of these sync patterns is also DC-free and indifferent to polarity.

At the end of the subframe are four status bits, V, U, C, and P (for *Validity Flag, User Data, Channel Status,* and *Parity Bit*, respectively). "V", the validity flag, is intended to be used to indicate that the associated data is suitable for conversion to an analog audio signal. A zero here indicates that it is a sample that is valid for audio. A one here indicates that this data should not be used for conversion to analog audio.

Experience has shown a tendency for the usage of this bit to be somewhat problematic. Generally, there are perhaps better ways to indicate non-audio application. If there is persistent difficulty in using a given AES3 data stream, it might be worthwhile determining just how this bit is being set, and just how downstream equipment reacts to such a state, or just what such equipment actually expects to see there.

"P," the parity bit, is set so that adding up the sum of all bits in the subframe will yield an even number. This is known as *even parity*. It is a simple form of error detection. In error checking later, if the sum of all bits in the subframe add up to an odd number, something is wrong and that data should be considered invalid.

With "U" and "C," the user data bit and channel status bits, we have a couple of slightly different cases that are similar to each other. In both cases, the bits are available to be extracted downstream, one bit at a time from every subframe, and assembled into separate serial data streams. One bit per subframe may not seem like very much, but it adds up fast. In fact, each of these serial data streams represent a serial data transmission rate of 6 Kbaud.

Channel Status Block

The channel status serial data that is derived by stringing together the "C" bits from each subframe is

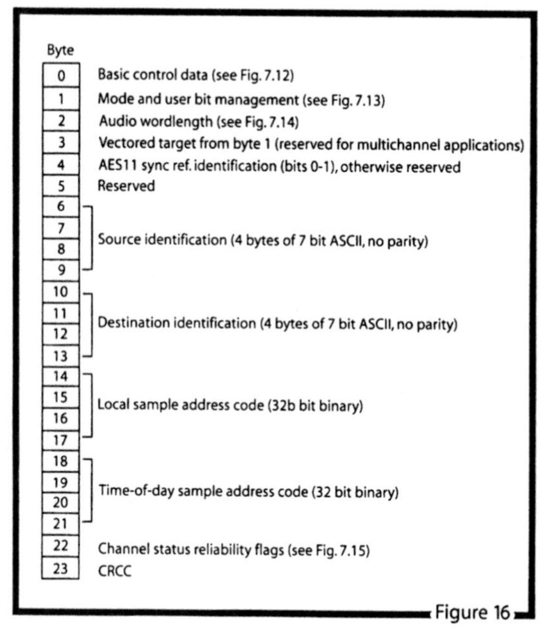

Figure 16

AES channel status block.

used to build up a 24-byte channel status block as shown in Figure 16. These 24, 8-bit bytes, the channel status block, include much important information about the system. At 48kHz sampling, the entire 24-byte block is rewritten every 4 milliseconds (192 subframes), therefore updating at a rate of 250Hz.

Figure 16 shows the 24 bytes of the Channel Status Block. Out of the 24 bytes of the channel status block, there are really only four that currently have much day-to-day relevance in the real world of digital audio production; Byte 0, Byte 1, Byte 2, and Byte 22.

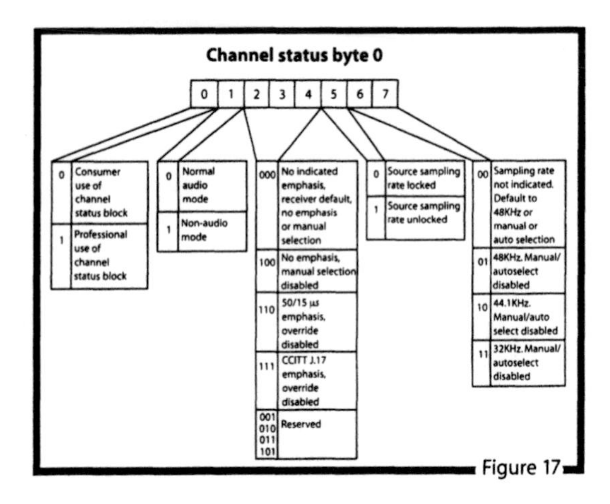

Figure 17

Figure 17 shows channel status byte 0. The first bit in this byte indicates whether the application is professional or a consumer version. The consumer version of AES3 data is known as SPDIF or IEC 958 and is found on RCA connectors on the back of some CD players and other consumer gear. Except for the channel status block information, SPDIF data is virtually identical to AES3 data. The electrical interface is a little different, being nominally 500mVp-p data on an RCA connector.

Bit 1 indicates non-audio modes. Passing AC-3 or Dolby E data though an AES3 channel is an example of a non-audio application. (It may have originated as audio, but by the time it has become AC-3 data, it has been heavily compressed, multiplexed, and otherwise processed to a state where it will no longer simply convert to audio directly.)

Bits 2, 3, and 4 create a three-bit binary code for indicating whether emphasis has been used, and

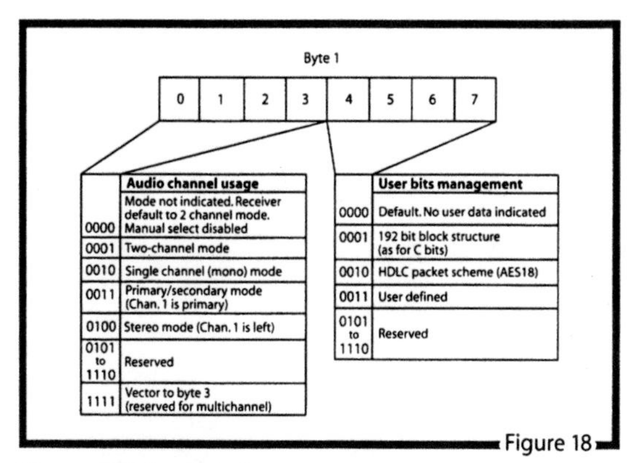

Figure 18

Channel Status Byte 1

therefore whether de-emphasis EQ circuits should be switched in during D-to-A conversion. In cases where emphasis is used, it will also indicate the type of de-emphasis to be used. It should be noted that more than one version of emphasis has been devised over time. Only these first four of the possible eight three-bit codes are currently in use.

Bit 5 shows whether the sampling rate was locked or unlocked. There may be applications that need to know such a thing. The last two bits, 6 and 7, form a two-bit binary code of four states for indication of sampling rate. The default state, 00, indicates 48kHz sampling, but allows for manual override.

Figure 18 shows the organization of Byte 1, the channel usage byte. The first four bits form a four-bit binary code to indicate various states of stereo, two-channel, and mono usage. The last four bits indicate how the user bit information is organized. There will be a discussion of user data utilization below.

Audio word length is dealt with in Byte 2, as show in Figure 19.

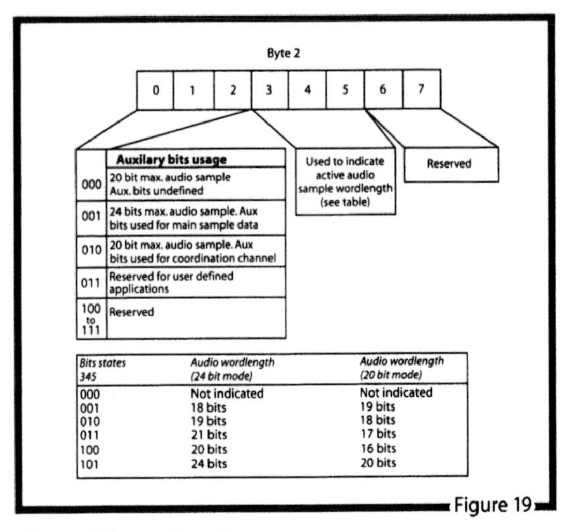

Bits states 345	*Audio wordlength (24 bit mode)*	*Audio wordlength (20 bit mode)*
000	Not indicated	Not indicated
001	18 bits	19 bits
010	19 bits	18 bits
011	21 bits	17 bits
100	20 bits	16 bits
101	24 bits	20 bits

Figure 19

Channel Status Byte 2

The first three bits indicate how the auxiliary bits of the AES3 subframe will be utilized. These auxiliary bits have some flexibility in how they might get used. For many applications, 20-bit resolution audio is quite adequate, being far better than CD-quality. In these cases, the four auxiliary bits may be used for voice-grade communication. This could be used for such things as talkback, etc.

However, if 24-bit resolution is desired, the four auxiliary bits of each subframe are combined with the 20 primary bits to yield 24-bit data. Bits 3, 4, and 5 of Byte 2, in conjunction with bits 0, 1, and 2, define just what the audio word length is.

Byte 22 contains channel status data reliability flags. (This can be seen in Figure 20.) Channel status data is mostly stationary. If a block or a portion of a block becomes corrupted, usually it is adequate to

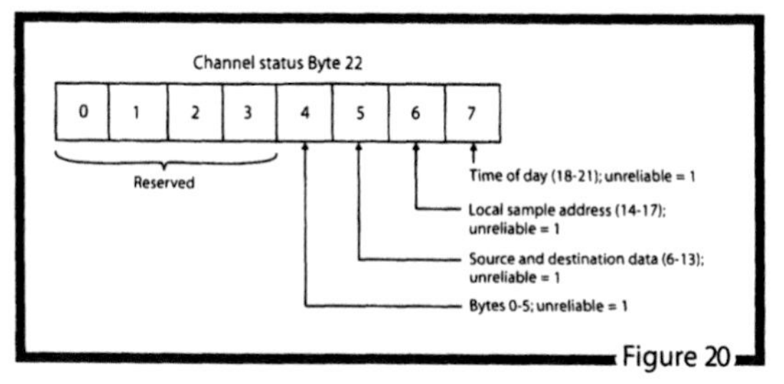

Channel Status Byte 22

simply ignore the corrupted block and wait for the succeeding one. With the use of the information in Byte 22, it is also possible to ignore just selected portions of the channel status block.

Byte 4 contains one bit that is used for identifying a sync source as an AES11 reference. Byte 5 is reserved for future use.

Bytes 6 through 9 are used as 7-bit ASCII 4-character alphanumeric data about the channel origin. They are to be set for odd parity.

Likewise, Bytes 10 through 13 are for 7-bit ASCII, four-character alphanumeric data about the intended destination. These two areas, Bytes 6-9 and Bytes 10-13, could conceivably be employed for automated routing.

Bytes 14 through 17 provide a relative 32-bit index counter of each audio sample and a means for identifying individual samples relative to an arbitrary starting point.

Bytes 18 through 21 are a 32-bit binary time-of-day clock. The AES had intended that true time-of-day timecode, starting at zero for midnight, could be encoded in this space at the time of recording. However, this practice has never seen widespread adoptance.

The last byte in the block, Byte 23, is a *Cyclic Redundancy Check Code* codeword that is used for error detection of the channel status block. As mentioned earlier, there is hardly any point in bothering to employ error correction here, since channel status data is essentially static data. But, it is available for use none the less.

User Data

The *User Data Bit* is the other subframe status bit that is extracted bit-by-bit, one per subframe, and assembled into another serial data stream. The usage of this data is unconstrained. Virtually any digital format could be assigned to this data. It has been recommended that the same block size as the channel status block ought to be used, but even that is not a hard-and-fast rule.

There have been some clever suggestions for using this space for labels. Some of the suggested uses include the following:

Time and date of program origin
Program and identification number
Take number
Program duration
Cue information
Act or scene number
Timecode-related information
Network information
Radio-data information
Generation number (for recording)
Copyright ownership code
Editing information
Signal source information
(e.g. originating microphone)

These suggestions are merely offered as examples of the kinds of things that might have some utility as labels in user data. Neither the presence nor the absence of user data will impair the primary interface function in any way. To date, there has been very little utilization of this capability of the AES3 interface.

Digital Tools

Production

After a long day of shooting film on location or the sound stage, the day's work is usually transferred, along with picture, for subsequent viewing of what is known as "dailies." This same transfer is usually used for the editorial process and other post-production work. Generally speaking, images for high-end video productions (TV movies, documentaries, sitcoms and commercial spots) are originated on film shot at 24 frames per second, while production audio is recorded with 48 kHz sampling.

Typically, dailies are viewed on video, perhaps 3/4-inch U-Matic or VHS video cassettes. Likewise, post-production is commonly completed on video. Unfortunately, video and film do not share identical frame rates. Film runs at 24 frames per second. Video runs at 29.97 frames per second. Through the magic of the 3:2 pulldown cadence in telecine transfer, the resultant difference of speed in film-to-video transfer is .1 percent. This means that for the audio being transferred to match the resultant video picture, its speed must be changed by .1 percent.

This is one of the problems to be addressed by the audio engineer at the beginning of a new project.

There are many variations on this theme. There are also many ways to get into to trouble. In general, the best way to avoid problems is by communication and testing. The responsible audio engineer needs to make it his business to be in close communication with the supervising editor long before commencing operations on the first day of shooting. Make sure there are no misunderstandings about anything to do with frame rates, sample rates, and timecode during the process of production through post-production.

It is also vitally important to include the audio transfer facility in the discussions. Make sure no incorrect assumptions are made about the capabilities of the transfer facility. Once it is certain that everyone concerned is reading from the same page, it is highly recommended that you test the entire process to be certain that it will yield the results expected by the editor and the director. Ideally, this testing process should also include shooting with the camera, so as to shake out any of the variables that may be introduced that are specific to camera usage, such as timecode referencing, slating, etc.

This process should also include utilizing the transfer facility. Test dailies should be viewed, and the editor should confirm that all elements are performing as per their expectations in the editing environment of choice. Later on, similar processes should occur for the ADR, Foley, music scoring, and final dub mixing stages.

The primary task at hand during the transfer process is to adjust the audio rate and timecode to match rate changes that will also be going on with the picture. As mentioned before, there will typically be a .1 percent change in the speed of the audio. In the days of analog, this was not such a big deal. A simple .1 percent speed change of analog audiotapes is barely perceptible when listening.

With digital it is different. When transferring from any digital audio source to any digital audio destination, the source and destination systems must be "locked" (synchronized). The degree of synchronization is similar to what has always been required by traditional analog video. It is not enough for the systems to be speed-locked adequately for maintaining lip sync. A much higher degree of sync is required for the system to work at all.

During transfer, the destination system must lock on to incoming data so that its data reception circuits are running at absolutely the same speed as the incoming data. Every bit in the data stream must be clocked in to input buffer memories at the precise instant it is expected.

In most cases, AES-format data is used for post-production work. As we have seen above, AES data is self-clocking, so no separate sync lines are needed. But still, synchronization must be achieved. Some further issues complicate this. The goal is a system that is or will be locked to the video material. In fact, this destination will need to be locked to both video and digital audio simultaneously.

This brings us back to the original problem of doing all this with a .1 percent speed change. There are two approaches to solving this problem: 1) Shoot .1 percent fast (48.048 kHz sampling) so that standard referencing during transfer will automatically achieve the correct pull-down of .1 percent by locking to the 48 kHz destination; or 2) Reference the transfer with sync running .1 percent slow at 47.952 kHz.

The decision of which method to use is in large part decided by the capabilities of the recording equipment, the transfer facility, and the personal preference of the editor. It is important for everyone involved with a production to be talking early on so that there are no surprises during the dailies transfer and subsequent editorial processes.

There are some interesting considerations that flow out of the real-world applications of some of the equipment that is used during the transfer process. Many of the problems that are encountered fall into three categories: 1) Recordings that were incorrectly referenced; 2) Playback by systems that do not lock to the reference of interest; 3) Playback by systems that do not lock to any reference.

There are two solutions that work in all these cases; a good solution and a not-so-good solution. Using the analog output from a digital audio playback device and redigitizing at the input to the target recording device is not recommended. This will yield an inevitable generation loss that is easily avoided by staying in the digital domain.

A much better solution is to use a sampling rate converter. Sample rate converters are well known for converting between 44.1 kHz digital audio (CD-rate) and 48 kHz "post-production-rate" digital audio. What is less appreciated is the ability provided by well designed sample rate converters to lock data transfers between two systems that are running at nominally identical rates, e.g., with both running at nominally 48 kHz.

However, being nominally identical is not adequate. Successful application requires that every bit be clocked in right on time. Any slight speed differences between source and destination

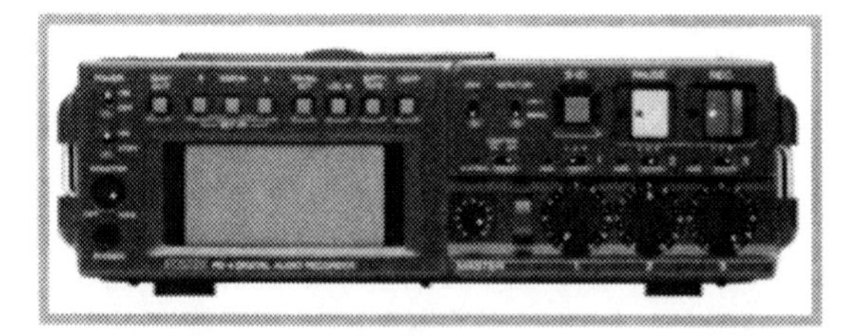

Figure 21. A portable DAT recorder

systems will yield a transfer with, at best, pops and clicks. More extreme cases will result in no data transferred at all. The solution is to use a good quality sample rate converter. It will remove data rate differences, however small, and yield data that is perfectly locked to the destination. It is a powerful tool that has saved many an errant source element.

These days, an audio engineer has many different options to choose from for recording digital audio on location. There are tape recorders of different digital audio formats, hard disk recorders, and even random access memory (RAM) recorders.

In tape recorders, the Digital Audio Tape (DAT) format is popular. Figure 21 illustrates a state-of-the-art example of such a device, the Fostex PD-4. It provides many of the features that location recordists require. One of the essentials that all production audio recorders must offer is flexible timecode recording. It is not uncommon to generate timecode internally in a production recorder. But, it must offer timecode at many different rates and in different formats. The ability to "jam sync" timecode from an external source has become very important.

It is important to understand the needs of post-production and transfer in planning the correct

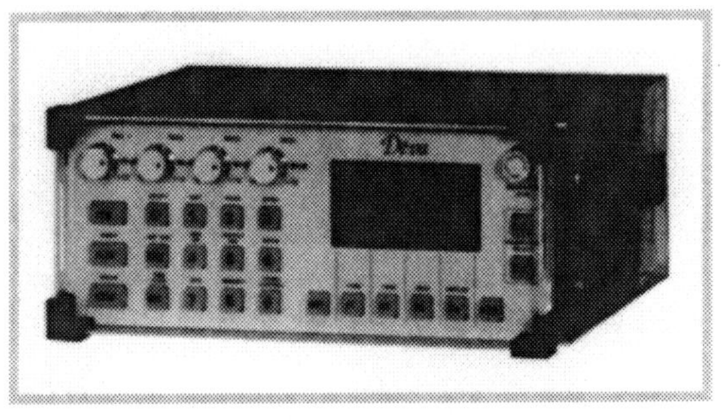

Figure 22. A portable hard disk recorder

timecode and its referencing, if any. Needless to say, all location production recorders must be rugged and reliable.

It is also very important to have the ability of confidence monitoring while recording. Confidence monitoring is the ability to listen to the decoded output of the data that has actually been recorded on tape while it is happening. This is contrast to merely monitoring incoming audio and simply presuming that everything is recording acceptably during the actual takes. If there are any problems, it is much better to know about them as they occur, rather than during the playback of what the director thought might be the keeper take. Other features like *phantom powering* for microphones and battery life are also important considerations.

Figure 22 illustrates a popular hard disk recorder for location production work, the Deva, from Zaxcom, Inc. Besides the usual features that would be expected of a location recorder, the Deva offers the benefits that are inherent to disk media, those that derive from random access. As with all disk media, there is no need to wait for tape to shuttle to

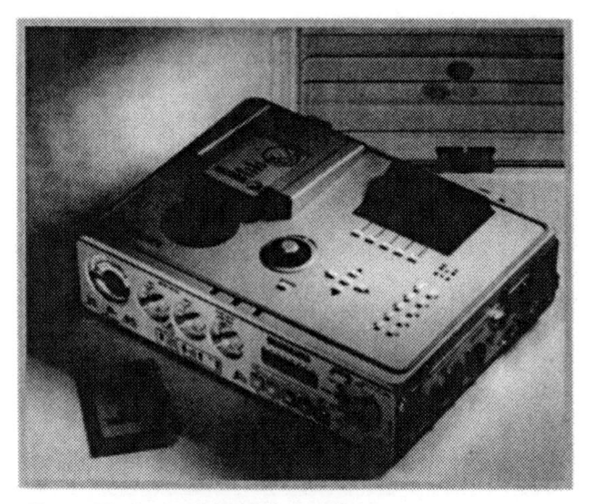

Figure 23. A portable RAM recorder

the circled takes during transfer or any other playback. The heads in the hard disk system merely step immediately to the position of interest. The Deva also offers four audio channels of 24-bit audio. DAT recorders are limited to two 16-bit channels.

Figure 23 shows another approach to location recording. The Nagra ARES-C is a RAM recorder. It records directly onto PCMCIA Flash RAM cards. This approach to recording seems to offer a lot of promise for the future.

As shown in Figure 24, Nagra now also produces another digital audio recorder for location production work, called the Nagra-D. The Nagra-D is a helically scanned reel-to-reel digital audio recorder. This system, shown in Figure ND, has also become popular for feature films and other discriminating production projects.

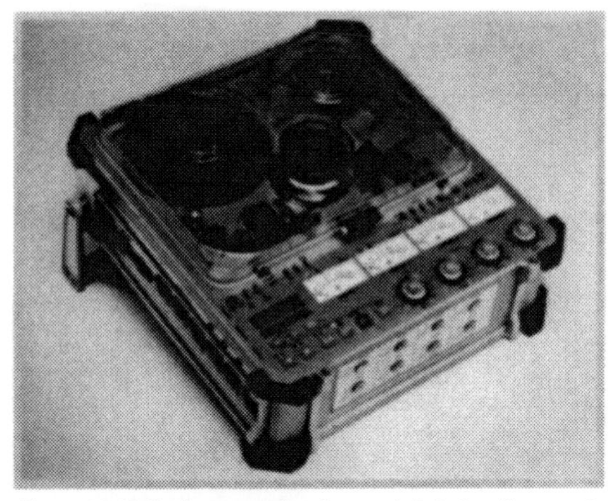

Figure 24. Helically scanned reel-to-reel digital audio recorder

Post-Production

With the arrival of the digital audio workstation (DAW), the editorial process has been revolutionized. Never before has the editor had such power and flexibility at hand. This is not to mention the speed and efficiency inherent in the DAW. In the end, it may be the practicalities of speed and efficiency, rather than vastly enhanced audio quality, that has led many of today's audio producers to make the leap into digital production.

The world of digital audio brings with it a whole new set of problems. There is much to learn at the basic level in order to successfully implement systems and practices that fully exploit the benefits of digital technology. One thing seems clear, digital audio is here to stay. Even if only because of the efficiencies of nonlinear editing, there is no going back. At the end of the day, most common practices of audio production and post-production are very similar to what they have always been.

The Whys and Hows of Time Code

Why is time code so important to the video postproduction process? The answer can be stated in two words: accuracy and repeatability. Prior to the advent of time code, electronic editing systems utilized two basic increment/decrement indexing methods for rapid, automatic location of edit points: they either counted electronic pulses from a tachometer coupled to the VTR tape transport mechanism or they counted control track pulses or mark tones recorded directly on the tape.

However, these methods rely upon maintaining an accurate count from a fixed starting point. This count can be upset by tape slippage during rewind or cueing, or by signal drop-outs on the tape. And any counting errors are cumulative, meaning that every individual counting error adds to the magnitude of the overall indexing error. The SMPTE/EBU cose solved this problem by providing each video frame with its own unique identification. Consisting of a binary pulse coded electronic signal, the SMPTE/EBU code is recorded on the videotape along with the corresponding video and audio signals. It identifies every single video frame by hour, minute second and frame. This approach produces some distinct advantages:

1. Time reference is precise. The duration of a selected scene or program interval can be determined with frame accuracy. It can be determined, to the frame, how much unrecorded tape is available for a program segment. As a program is shot, or before it is edited, a scene schedule can be blocked out so that postproduction personnel can run program tapes to the desired edit points with a minimum of time-consuming searching.

2. Time code allows interchangeability between editing systems. The IN and OUT points for edits selected on one editing system can be listed by their time code designations (either in a written list or on some type of electronic medium) and input to another editing system. The edits performed by the second system will be identical to those selected on the first, whether the two editing systems are in the same room or half a world apart.

Interchangeability is also the key to a time and money-saving process called auto-assembly. Using this process, programs can be mastered on high quality (and expensive to operate) VTRs and then dubbed down with the same time code onto an inexpensive tape format (like ¾ or ½-inch cassette) to prepare a "workprint" for editing.

Editing on low-cost equipment, the production team can work as carefully as it wishes, without regard for the amount of running time being put on the VTRs. This is called off-line editing. The edit list that results from the off-line editing session is then input to an editing system controlling high-quality VTRs on which the master tapes have been mounted (an on-line editing system).

Since the time code in the off-line edit list corresponds directly to the time code on the master tapes, the edits performed off-line will be duplicated on the master tapes. And because there is no human decisionmaking at this point, all of the on-line edits are performed as fast as the VTRs can run the tape to the designated edit locations; this reduces expensive running time on the mastering VTRs to the absolute minimum. An extra dividend of the auto-assembly process is that the irreplaceable master tapes are never touched during the actual edit decision-making process, and are thus protected from accidental erasure or over-recording.

3. Time code allows precision synchronization of one VTR to another. The time code acts as "electronic sprocket holes," providing the means for an editing system or synchronization unit to bring two or more tapes into exact sync automatically. This means perfect frame-to-frame match-ups at the edit points.

To achieve this degree of synchronization, SMPTE/EBU time code editing systems employ comparator circuits which look at the time code from each tape that is in motion. The comparators make real-time edit code calculations to judge the relative distance of each tape from the sync point at any given instant, and constantly issue slowdown/speed-up commands to the VTRs to keep all tapes in sync.

During initial synchronization, some of the VTRs involved may be sped up or slowed down as much as 50% over or under normal play speed in order to achieve sync. This initial sync-up process normally occurs during a short period just prior to reaching the edit IN point. This period is called the preroll.

With so many advantages, it is little wonder that the SMPTE/EBU time code has become so crucial to the operation of professional quality computer-assisted editing systems. These systems utilize the time code's precise indexing not only to control tape decks in the performance of cues, previews, edits and replays, but also to trigger video switchers and special effects generators in the performance of wipes, dissolves, keys, flips, and other dazzling edit transitions — all automatically and accurate to the frame.

What Does Time Code Look Like?

Now that you're familiar with the importance of SMPTE/EBU time code to postproduction systems, let's take a closer look at the code's make-up and inner workings.

To begin with, there are two versions of the SMPTE/EBU time code: one is recorded on an audio track of the video tape and is called longitudinal (serial) time code; the other is recorded in the video, and is called vertical interval time code (VITC). Despite the different recording methods, the two versions of the code are quite similar in form and content, so we will describe the longitudinal time code in detail, then extend the description to VITC by comparing the two.

Longitudinal Time Code

The longitudinal time code is an electronic signal that switches from one voltage to another, forming a string of pulses. Each one-second long chunk of this signal is "sliced" into 2,400 equal parts when the code is being used with the U.S. television standard of 30 frames per second (called NTSC), or 2000 equal parts when used with the European standard of 25 frames per second (called PAL/SECAM). Each slice of the time code signal is referred to as a bit. With some simple arithmetic, we can see that each video frame coincides with 80 time code bits:

NTSC 2400 bits/sec ∏ 30 frames/sec = 80 bits/frame

PAL/SECAM 2000 bits/sec ∏ 25 frames/sec = 80 bits/frame

Most of these 80 bits have specific values assigned to them. However, these values are counted only if the time code signal changes from one voltage to the other in the middle of the bit period, forming a ½-bit pulse. If the voltage remains at one value or the other through an entire bit period, that bit's assigned value won't be counted. In computer parlance, a ½-bit pulse represents a digital "1," while a full-bit pulse represents a digital "0."

Let's take a look at how all these bits are deciphered by examining one frame's worth of time code (80 bits).

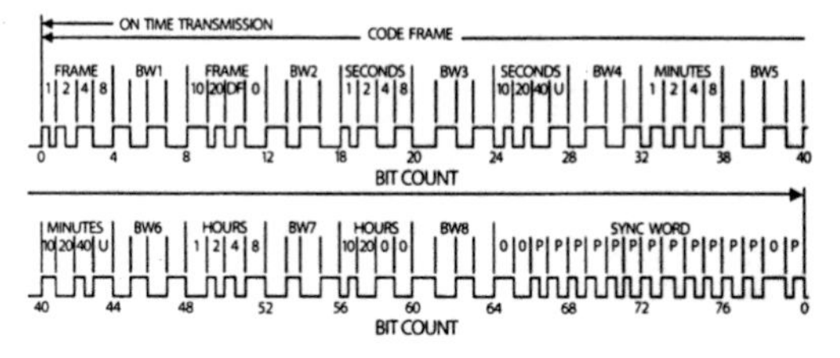

Breaking this frame down into its various parts, we get the following information:

Bits zero through 3, and 8 and 9, are assigned to the frame count. Bit zero is assigned a value of 1, bit 1 a value of 2, bit 2 a value of 4, bit 3 a value of 8, bit 8 a value of 10 and bit 9 a value of 20. Notice that in the example, bits 0, 1 and 9 contain digital "ones" (the voltage level has switched in the middle of the bits, forming half-pulses). Only the values of these "1" bits will be counted; if we add the values of these bits—1 + 2 + 20—we get 23, the frame count of this particular frame.

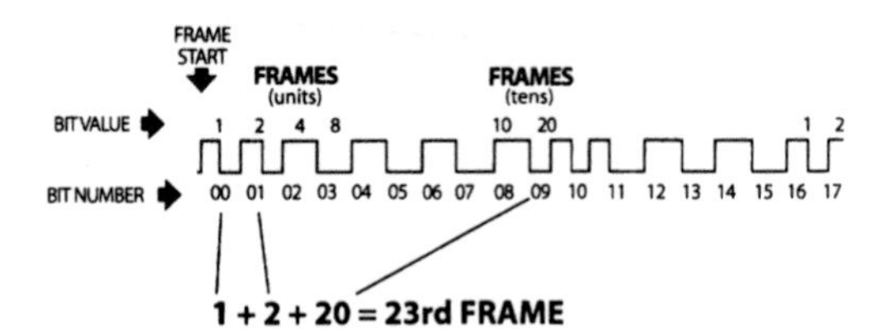

Bits 16 through 19 and 24 through 26 tell us that this is the 31st second:

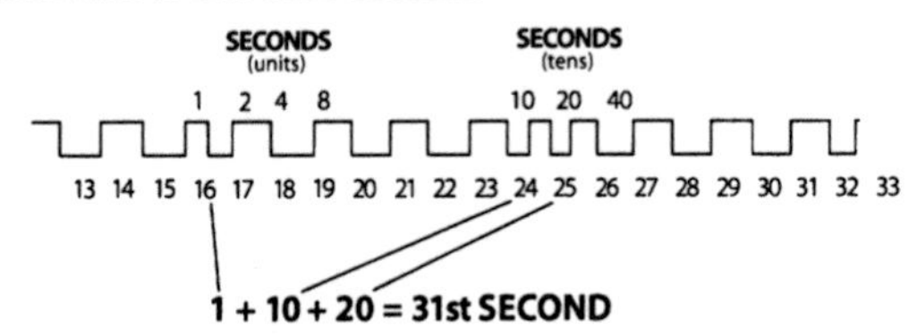

Bits assigned to the minute count show that this is the 47th minute.

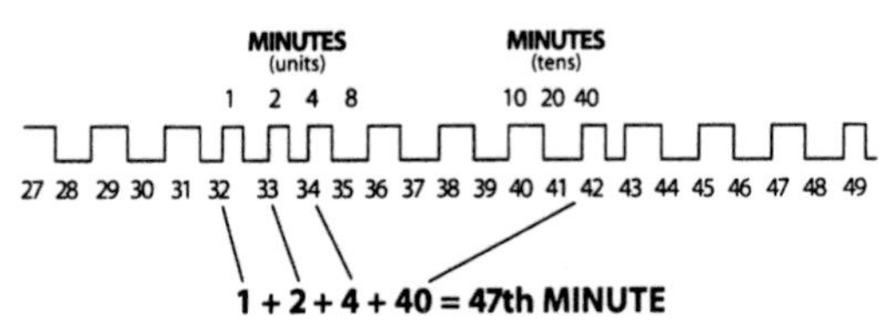

And, finally, the hours bits show us that this is the 16th hour:

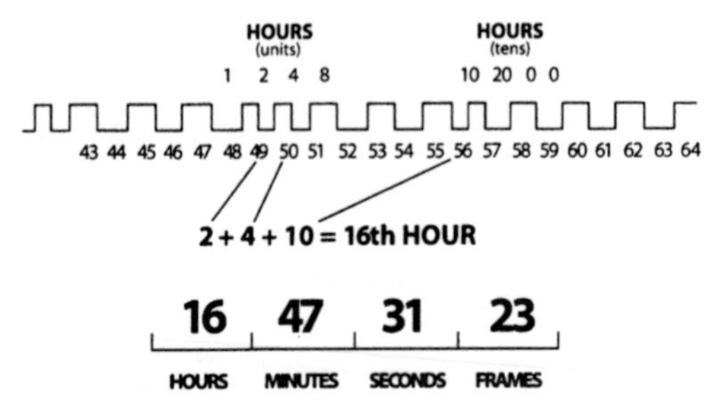

Put all this together as an electronic time code reader would, and the indexing on this particular frame reads "16th hour, 47th minute, 31st second and 23rd frame."

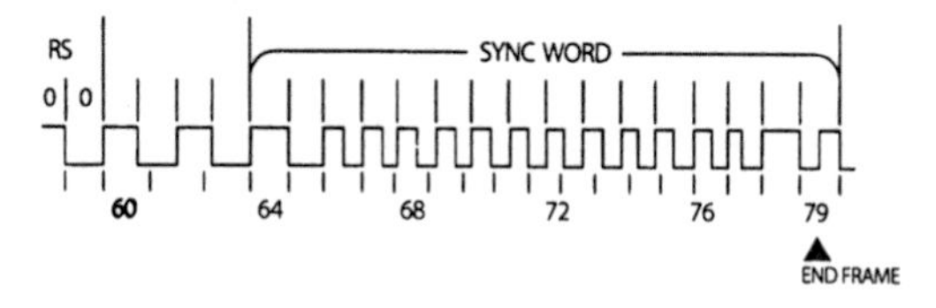

Bits 64 through 79 are always the same in every frame. They form a special pattern of "1" and "0" bits called the sync word. The sync word tells the decoding circuits in an electronic time code reader that this is the end of one frame and the start of another. It also indicates whether the tape is moving forward or in reverse.

Besides the main groups of indexing bits that we have just discussed, there are several other bits and bit groups scattered through the time code frame that have special significance to time code systems equipped to use them.

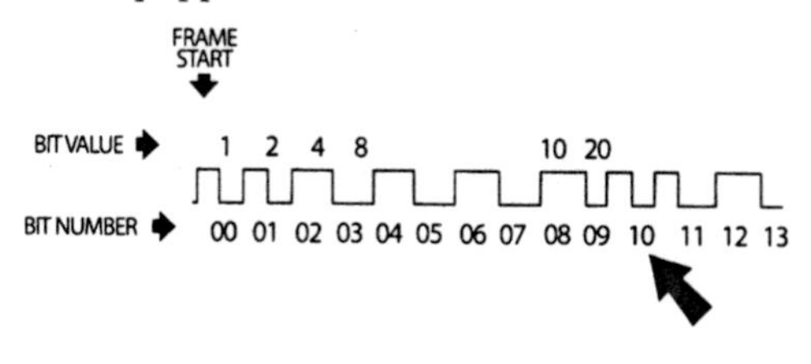

Drop-Frame

Bit number 10 is called the drop-frame bit. It tells electronic time code reading systems whether the code was recorded in drop-frame or non-drop frame format. A couple of definitions are in order here.

It's really not too tricky. The time code is normally produced by a generator which counts at 30 frames-per-second (NTSC) or 25 frames-per-second (PAL/SECAM), synchronized to the same studio sync source as the VTRs. However, NTSC color signals have an actual frequency of close to 29.97 frames-per-second. So a generator counting at 30 frames-per-second would produce an increasing error as time went on (3.6 seconds every hour).

To compensate for this error build-up, a certain number of frames are eliminated from the time code each hour to shorten the time code and make it match clock time. Since 3.6 seconds equals 108 frames, 108 frames must be eliminated from the time code each hour. To accomplish this, two frames are dropped each minute, every hour around the clock except every 10th minute. The reason for the 10th minute exception is that if two frames were dropped every minute of each hour, 120 frames would be dropped instead of the desired 108 frames.

Frame dropping occurs only at the changeover points from minute to minute. For example, when the time code changes from 01:08:59:29, the next frame number identified in drop-frame format would be displayed as 01:09:00:02. In drop-frame time code, frames 00 and 01 don't exist. This effectively shortens the time code so that it agrees with standard clock time.

Time code generated in the drop-frame format is identified by placing a digital "l" in bit 10 of every frame of code so generated, to alert the equipment used in subsequent reading and synchronizing operations to account for the missing frame numbers. If the code is generated in non-drop-frame format, a digital "0" is placed in bit 10 of every frame.

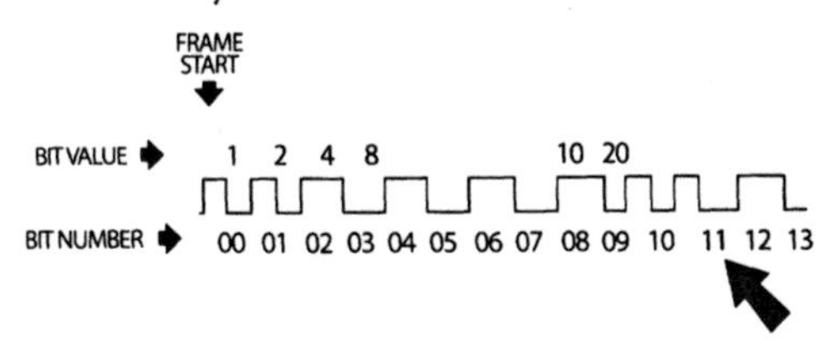

Color Frame

Bit number 11 is the color frame bit. Applicable only to color recordings, it tells electronic time code reading systems whether or not color frame indetification has been applied intentionally. A color frame is four fields—1⁄15 second—in NTSC. A color frame is eight fields—1⁄6 second—in PAL. Fields 1 and 3 are defined as color frame "A," while fields 2 and 4 are defined as color frame "B." A digital "1" is recorded in bit 11 to indicate that color frame identification has been applied to the time code.

NTSC color frame identification of the code indicates that even frame numbers coincide with color frame "A" and odd frame numbers coincide with color frame "B." This identification helps videotape editing systems to maintain the correct video signal color burst phase relationship across the edit points. The editing system corrects for improper color framing during an edit by "bumping" the servo system of the record VTR during the VTR synchronization process that occurs during the preroll.

Failure to achieve proper color framing will result in a flash or flicker in the television picture at the edit IN point. It should be noted that some VTRs have built-in color framers and that most SMPTE/EBU videotape editing systems have a color framer that needs to be set for correct color burst phasing only once when a new tape is mounted on the record VTR. In both cases, the color frame bit is not used, and should be set to digital "0" in all time code frames.

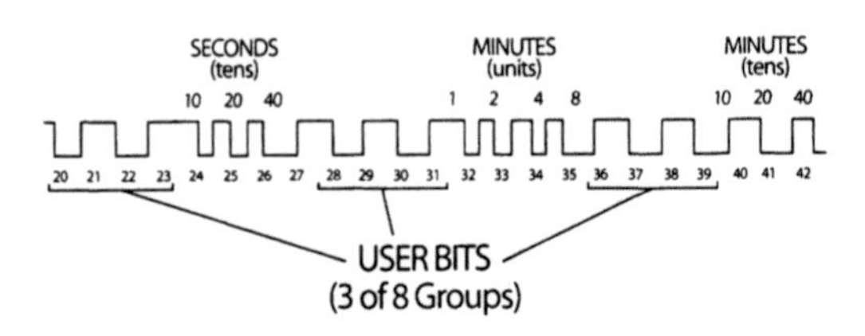

User Bits

Interspersed through each 80-bit frame of time code are eight groups of four bits each. These 32 bits are referred to as user bits. The user bits are essentially leftovers; the time code can meet all of the indexing requirements imposed on it without filling these bits with data. This leaves the user bits available for any auxiliary function the user may have in mind.

The user bits can generally accommodate data for four alphabetical characters or eight numerical digits, or a combination of the two. They can be used to designate such things as reel numbers, recording date, or any other information that can be expressed in four letters or eight digits. In order to access the user bits, you MUST use time code equipment designed to generate and read them.

User bit data must be recorded simultaneously with the recording of the rest of the time code information; it can't be added once the code is on the tape. So it's important that the time code generator be set to produce the desired user bit data at the desired time code frames. If the user bits are not used, they should all be set to digital "0."

Vertical Interval Time Code

As already noted, VITC is very similar in composition to the longitudinal time code. It does, however, include several extra "housekeeping" bits that bring its total number of bits per frame to 90.

Also note that, in the VITC, each of the nine data-carrying bit groups is preceded by two sync bits. These sync bits are always set to digital "1" and digital "0," respectively.

Another difference between VITC and longitudinal time code is that VITC includes a very useful additional utility called a field bit (bit 35).

The field bit allows VITC readers to index each video field. As we will find out in the section covering time code recording, each frame of video is actually comprised of two interlaced video fields, called the odd field (field 1) and the even field (field 2). Each field makes up half of the raster scan lines which trace the picture onto the television screen. Thus, time code readers equipped to recognize the field bit can index to a resolution of half a frame — 1⁄60 of a second. This precision resolution can be quite useful when performing tight edits.

A digital "0" recorded in the field bit denotes monochrome field 1 (color field 1 or 3); a digital "1" denotes monochrome field 2 (color field 2 or 4).

At the end of each frame of VITC is another group of bits that the longitudinal time code doesn't have. These bits (82 through 89) are called the Cyclic Redundancy Check Code (CRC). This is an error detection code, common to many types of digital data

VITC

Longitudinal Time Code

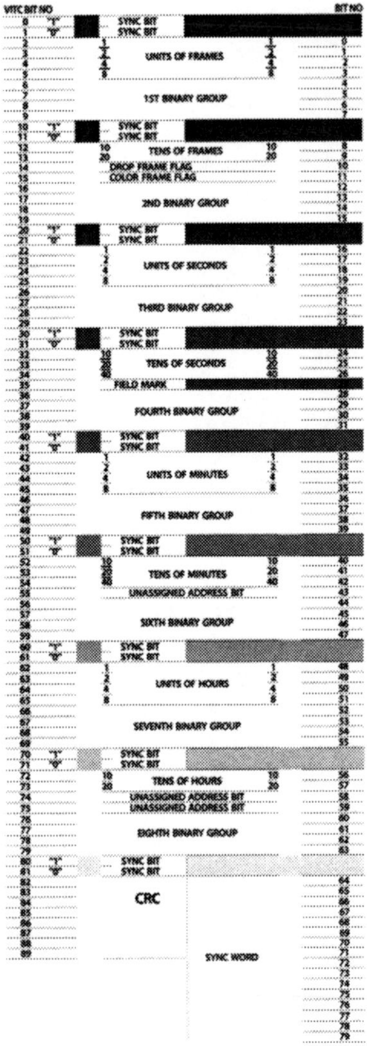

VITC BIT NO — BIT NO

"1" "0" SYNC BIT / SYNC BIT

1 2 4 8 UNITS OF FRAMES 1 2 4 8

1ST BINARY GROUP

"1" "0" SYNC BIT / SYNC BIT

10 20 TENS OF FRAMES 10 20

DROP FRAME FLAG

COLOR FRAME FLAG

2ND BINARY GROUP

"1" "0" SYNC BIT / SYNC BIT

1 2 4 8 UNITS OF SECONDS 1 2 4 8

THIRD BINARY GROUP

"1" "0" SYNC BIT / SYNC BIT

10 20 40 TENS OF SECONDS 10 20 40

FIELD MARK

FOURTH BINARY GROUP

"1" "0" SYNC BIT / SYNC BIT

1 2 4 8 UNITS OF MINUTES 1 2 4 8

FIFTH BINARY GROUP

"1" "0" SYNC BIT / SYNC BIT

10 20 40 TENS OF MINUTES 10 20 40

UNASSIGNED ADDRESS BIT

SIXTH BINARY GROUP

"1" "0" SYNC BIT / SYNC BIT

1 2 4 8 UNITS OF HOURS 1 2 4 8

SEVENTH BINARY GROUP

"1" "0" SYNC BIT / SYNC BIT

10 20 TENS OF HOURS 10 20

UNASSIGNED ADDRESS BIT

UNASSIGNED ADDRESS BIT

EIGHTH BINARY GROUP

"1" "0" SYNC BIT / SYNC BIT

CRC

SYNC WORD

recording systems, which allows the reader to electronically compare the "1"/"0" pattern of the CRC bits read off the tape against a known bit pattern. This comparison provides a verification that no bits have been lost (or added) through the entire 90-bit frame.

Not all VITC readers are capable of CRC verification. A unit unable to perform a CRC could produce erroneous or invalid time information. Units equipped with CRC verification circuitry will indicate an error if a CRC discrepancy is detected.

How Time Code Is Recorded On Tape

The chief difference between longitudinal time code and VITC is the way each are recorded on the tape. And that's become a very important difference since the advent of reel-to-reel helical scan VTRs, as we will see shortly.

Longitudinal Recording Technique

Longitudinal time code is recorded on one of the video tape's longitudinal tracks, usually an address track, the cue track or audio track 2. The code can be recorded from +3dB to -l0dB. The recording level depends largely on the type of VTR. Longitudinal time code recorded at levels above 3dB can cause crosstalk problems, resulting in a distracting "whine" in the background of the program audio.

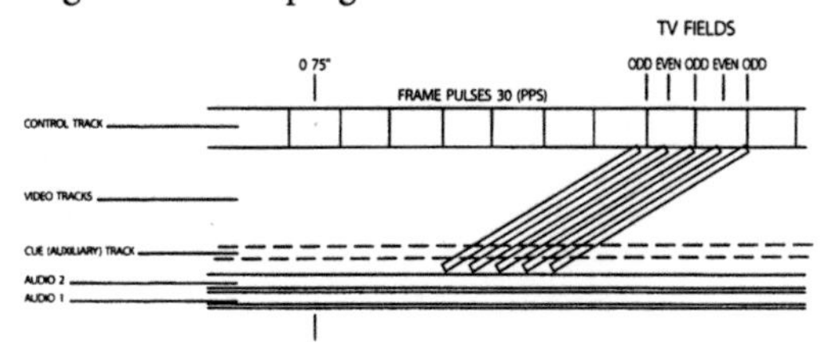

Even more important than the recording level is the quality of the time code signal. Despite the fact that the time code waveform may be kept sharp and rectangular during recording, many factors are at work during playback that may distort the time code signal to the point where electronic time code reading systems cannot reliably recognize the code's digital "1s" and "0s."

Some of these degrading factors may be: dirty audio heads; distortion introduced into the time code channel by the VTR reproduce amplifiers; misaligned reproduce heads or tape guides; or attempts to dub the time code without sufficient signal processing. And the problems get worse at speeds above and below normal play.

In order to read longitudinal time code at high wind speeds (e.g., during rapid cueing), the VTR must be equipped with wide band amplifiers and broadband reproduce heads. This is because the time code frequency increases as tape speed increases, to the point where high frequency roll-off may occur in the VTR's audio/time code reproduce system. The result is a distorted time code signal that is hard to read.

At low tape speeds, the time code frequency decreases, as does its amplitude. So the VTR's reproduce system must have good low-frequency response and may require higher gain amplifiers. At very low tape speeds or freeze-frame, the time code amplitude drops below the ambient noise level or disappears completely. This is due to the fact that the tape is moving so slowly across the reproduce heads that little or no signal voltage is induced in the head. At such times, many time code readers automatically switch to counting control track pulses or tachometer pulses to maintain indexing. And we already know that these methods don't give us the accuracy the SMPTE/EBU time code does.

VITC Recording Techniques

VITC solves many of the reading problems associated with longitudinal time code. In fact, the main impetus behind the development of the vertical interval time code recording technique was the widespread acceptance of the highly controllable VTRs with film editing features like freeze-frame and viewable pictures at very low speeds.

As we've already learned, longitudinal time code is unusable at these speeds. VITC, on the other hand, is readable at all times that the video is visible on the television screen, because the VITC records the indexing information for each field/frame in the video signal during the vertical blanking interval.

Let's digress for a moment and become a little familiar with the vertical blanking interval and the manner in which the electron beam that forms the television picture scans across the screen.

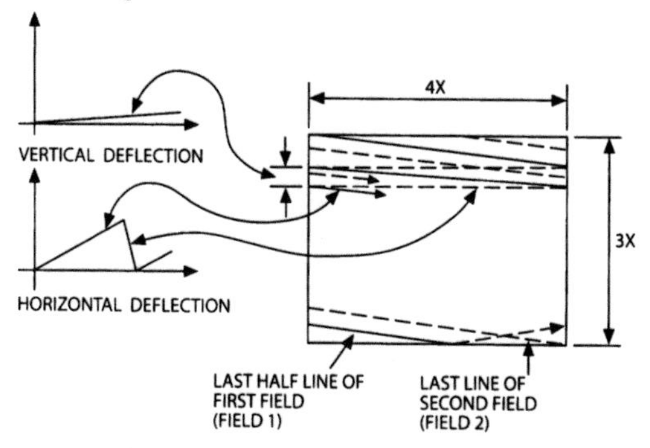

For the NTSC television standard, there are 525 lines scanned across the television screen every frame. These lines are full-width, while one consists of two half-width scans at the top and bottom of the screen. To prevent any noticeable picture flicker, interlaced scanning is employed. With this scanning technique, every other line of the picture is skipped during the first half of the frame, then filled in during the second half of the frame. The scans that occur during the first half of the frame are called "field 1," while those that occur during the second half are called "field 2."

At the end of each left-to-right scan of the raster, the electron beam returns to the lefthand side of the screen and drops down, skipping one line, to begin the next sweep. After sweeping a complete field, the beam returns to the left top corner of the screen to begin the first line of the next field.

This return to the top of the screen is referred to as flyback. Just before, during, and just after flyback, the electron beam is shut off, or "blanked." This is called the vertical blanking interval and occupies a space equivalent to 21 raster scan lines. The black bar visible on the television screen when the picture is rolling is the vertical blanking interval, and it is in this normally unseen area of the picture that the VITC is recorded.

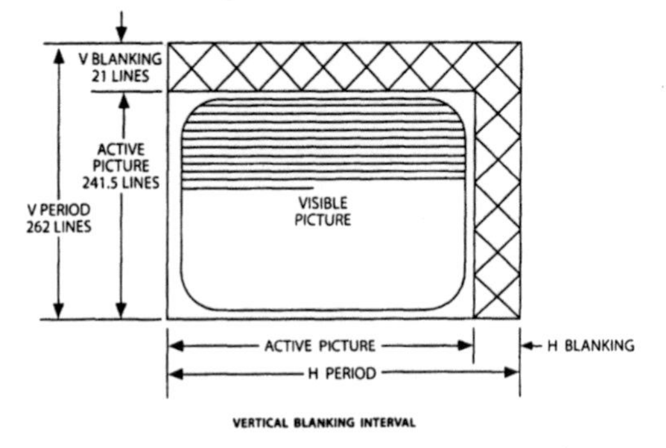

VERTICAL BLANKING INTERVAL

The VITC is normally recorded on two non-adjacent vertical blanking interval lines in both fields of each frame (lines 10 through 20 in NTSC). Recording the code four times per frame provides a redundancy factor which lowers the possibility of reading errors due to tape drop-outs. In conjunction with the CRC error checking code, this redundancy virtually eliminates reading errors.

Since the VITC is recorded in the video track of the VTR, it can be read by the rotating video heads of helical scan VTRs at all times, even when the tape is being shuttled at high speed or is stopped. Thus, frame-accurate edit decisions can be made regardless of tape speed. And once recorded, the VITC becomes an integral part of the video signal, so it doesn't have to be handled separately when the video is processed or transmitted.

Because VITC can be extracted at wind speeds and provides all of the indexing capabilities of longitudinal time code (and then some), it is possible to rely solely on the VITC for all edit indexing, dispensing with the longitudinal time code completely. This produces the distinct benefit of freeing the second audio track for other uses, such as an additional audio channel.

To recap, the major advantages of VITC over longitudinal time code are:

1. VITC doesn't require any special amplification or signal processing within the VTR during playback or dubbing. If the VTRs in use can produce a useable television picture, they can also reproduce useable VITC.

2. VITC is available whenever the program video is available, regardless of playback speed.

3. VITC provides indexing resolution down to the video field.

4. VITC doesn't require a dedicated track on the videotape.

5. Redundant recording methods and an integral error detection code give VITC a high immunity to drop-out reading errors.

In all fairness to the longitudinal time code, there are some special operating procedures that must be observed when using the VITC:

1. Tapes can't be pre-striped with VITC; the code must be recorded at the same time as the video. This makes jam sync time code regeneration on the electronically edited master tape mandatory.

Jam-sync involves using a master/slave time code generator to resynchronize time code being newly recorded onto the videotape with the time code already on the tape. In practice, the first program segment recorded on the electronically edited master tape includes VITC originating from a VITC generator or from the source tape that is supplying the program segment. At the start of the next edited interval, the last recorded frame of VITC from the previous edit interval is "jammed" into a master/slave time code clock that picks up the count from that frame with absolute synchronization.

This process is repeated at the start of every subsequent edit interval through the entire recorded program on the master tape. The result is that continuous VITC is laid down in an ascending count from start to finish. It is important that any videotape editing system utilizing VITC as the sole indexing method include jam-sync in the time code feed to the record VTR, either as an internal function of a VITC reader, or as a separate unit.

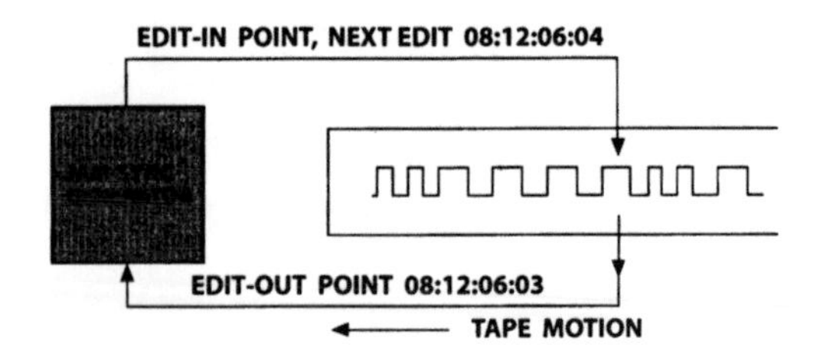

2. Associated with the jam-sync requirement described above is another important time code handling requirement: the VITC from the source VTRs must be removed from the video supplied to the record VTR. Normally, this is done by the VITC reader/generator being used to produce jam-sync VITC for the record VTR. The video input to the record VTR passes through this reader/generator prior to entering the record VTR (but downstream from any video switcher being used to mix multiple sources). Upon entering the reader/generator, the source video's vertical interval is suppressed, effectively erasing the source VITC; jam-sync record VTR VITC is then reinserted into the vertical interval as the video is output to the record VTR. This procedure prevents source VTR VITC from over-recording the VITC on the electronically edited master tape, precluding time code discontinuities on the master tape.

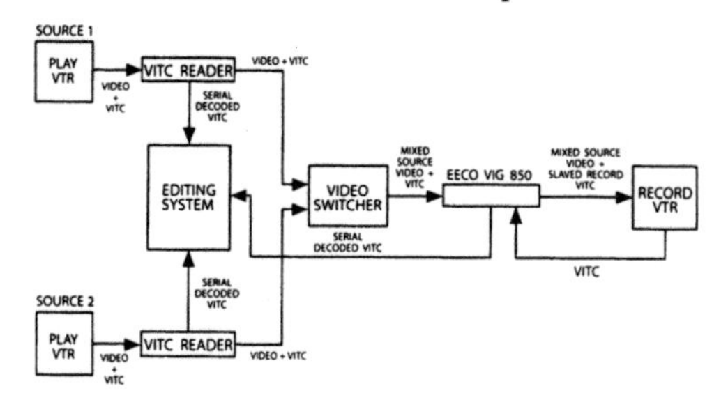

3. VITC competes for space in the vertical blanking interval with other users of this area of the video signal, such as teletext and closed captioning. This is not a major concern, however, since the time code is a postproduction tool only, and can be recorded over with teletext or closed captioning data during dubbing of the final release prints.

Guidelines for Using Time Code

Here are some practical production tips that will help with "real world" usage of time code in video applications. Many of these hints will apply to longitudinal time code only, since it is somewhat more difficult to distribute and process than VITC.

Cleanliness is Critical

To achieve optimum recording quality, the VTR tape path must be thoroughly clean. This includes all audio, video, time code and erase heads, as well as all tape guides and other tape path components that come into contact with the tape. Dirty heads can cause low reproduction levels, distortion or signal dropouts on one or more VTR output channels.

Monitor Record Levels

When recording longitudinal time code on a tape machine without an address track, it is recommended that the code be placed on the auxiliary track audio channel 2 (right channel) and the program audio on audio channel 1 (left channel). The program audio can be recorded at reference level, but the time code must be recorded at 3dB above reference level (in other words, the time code should record and play back 3dB above the zero level reference mark on the VTR's VU meter). These levels provide the best performance for editing. Since VITC is part of the video signal, it is recorded at the same level as the program video.

Recording levels may vary from one machine to another. The best way to find the correct setting is trial and error. Use the following table as a starting point for each family of machine:

REC Type	Recording Level
ATR	between -5 and -10dB
1" VTR	between 0 and -10dB
2" Quad	between +3 and 0dB
¾" U-Matic	between 0 and -5dB
M Format	between 0 and -5dB

Time Code Reading Problems

The most serious problem encountered in time code editing is poor quality time code, and this is especially true of longitudinal time code. Because longitudinal time code occupies its own track on the videotape, it is possible for the time code channel to exhibit reproduction problems independent of the program video and audio channels. This is not the case with VITC; if the video is good, the VITC will also be good.

Poor quality longitudinal time code can be caused by a number of factors, such as dirty or misaligned heads, distortion introduced by amplifiers having inadequate bandwidth, or too many generations of dubbing without suitable signal conditioning.

Occasionally, audio amplifiers used to distribute the time code may be overloaded if excessive levels are fed into them. This will cause time code distortion and erratic time code reading. To avoid these problems, use high quality amplifiers and stick to the amplifier input specifications.

Another problem that can occur with longitudinal time code is distortion produced by feeding the time code signal into an AGC (automatic gain control) amplifier or through an audio limiter. No constraints should be placed on the time code signal during either recording or playback.

Duplicating Time Code

When dubbing longitudinal time code from one tape to another, the best way to prevent distortion is to duplicate the time code through a jam-sync time code generator that produces fresh time code synchronization with the source time code (dubbing isn't a major problem with VITC, since the code is part of the video signal; again, if the dubbed video is acceptable, the time code will be too).

It is not advisable to simply copy longitudinal time code directly from tape to tape, because the quality of the time code signal deteriorates with each generation. Typically, second-generation time code will be marginal at wind speeds above six times normal play speed, but will be readable at slower speeds. Third-generation time code reads unreliably even at play speed.

FIRST

SECOND

THIRD

Distortions that arise in going through multiple generations.

Non-Synchronous Time Code

Non-synchronous time code can lead to frequent edit aborts by some editing systems during previews and edits. As the edit IN point approaches, the time code drifts out of frame synchronization and straddles two adjacent frames. The editing system can't tell which frame is the correct edit IN point and re-cues repeatedly trying to find the right frame.

Time code drift or loss of frame sync may occur during time code recording due to an interruption or transient "glitch" in the reference signal feeding the time code generator. Another cause of frame sync problems stems from not referencing the VTR to properly locked video during time code recording. The best rule of thumb for avoiding these problems is to ensure that all time code generators and VTRs within the production facility are referenced to a single high-quality house composite sync generator.

Use Ascending Time Code

Generally, time code editing systems are programmed to expect the time code on each reel of tape to go forward in time as the tape runs forward. This is not to say that time code discontinuities ("jumps") can't exist. Discontinuities are OK, as long as the time code jumps forward in time when the tape is moving forward. A typical situation where this rule must be applied is when a taping session is interrupted and then resumed on the same reel of tape.

When the taping is resumed, the time code generator need not pick-up the time code count at exactly the value where it left off when the tape was stopped. The only stipulation is that the count pick up at a time code value later in time than the code already recorded. If the code were to jump backwards in time, there would be a time code duplication on the tape which would thoroughly confuse the editing system.

Allow Enough Leader

When recording tapes that will be edited on a time code editing system, it is imperative to allow sufficient leader ahead of the first recorded material. If this is not done, the tape may run off the take-up reel as the editing system attempts to cue up for an edit involving the first few seconds of recorded material on the tape. A 20-second leader will accommodate the cueing requirements of even the least sophisticated editing systems.

(Courtesy of Paltex International)

The Care and Storage of Videotape

Many video producers assume that once a program is on tape it will stay there—indefinitely. Unfortunately, professionals have come to the conclusion that videotape is not a permanent medium. And since it is a relatively new technology, no one really knows how long a videotape will actually last.

We've had over 30 years of experience with traditional cobalt ferric oxide tape formulations. But what about the new "metal" videotape formulations? Metal particle tape, which arrived on the scene with the consumer Video 8 format in 1985, is now used in virtually every professional digital format, such as Betacam SX, Digital Betacam, D-1, D-2, D-3, D-5, D-6, DVCPRO and DVCAM. Are metal tapes chemically stable? Are these tapes subject to corrosion?

Sony Corp. conducted a series of tests comparing metal with co-oxide tape formulations. The tests were run with analog Betacam, since this half-inch format uses both types of tape. The archival stability of both tapes was extensively tested under varying conditions for magnetic properties, RF output, video signal-to-noise and dropout level.

The bottom line, according to the Sony research, is that both metal tape and co-oxide tape, when stored under normal room conditions of 77° F and 50 percent relative humidity, "are very stable and have no change in video electromagnetic performance." If stored consistently under these conditions, Sony predicts both tape formulations will last 15 years without significant degradation.

Sony noted that the life of any magnetic tape depends on the decomposition of its chemical components: plastic base film, binder polymers, back-coating materials, lubricants and dispersing agents. Degradation of these organic materials is accelerated with heat and moisture. This applies, Sony said, to both co-oxide and metal formulations.

In light of their study, released in 1991, Sony recommends the following procedures for long-term tape storage, regardless of the type of formulation:

• Pay strict attention to temperature and humidity. For storage of 10 years or more, place tapes in an environment with a constant temperature between 59° and 77° F with 40 percent to 60 percent relative humidity. There should be minimum fluctuation of temperature or humidity to prevent expansion and contraction of the base film of the tape. The storage area should also be clean and as free of dust and pollutants as possible.

• Make sure the tape is wound properly. If the tape is not neatly wound, rewind it on a VTR before storage. Unevenly-wound tape with slipped sections will stretch over time, thus causing disturbances in playback. Also make sure tape is fully wound, either onto the take-up or supply side.

• Store tapes in their cases in the upright position. Stacked tapes with no cases can be distorted due to excess collective weight. Also store tapes the same way in shipping, since this offers the best protection from vibration.

• To keep tapes ventilated, fast-forward and rewind them at least once every three years.

• Keep tapes away from magnetic fields. Don't

leave tapes near speakers, motors, high voltage transformers or other devices which generate a strong magnetic field. The magnetism can cause tape noise or even partial erasure.

• Keep your video recorder properly maintained. Since videotape incorporates a thin plastic base film, irreparable wrinkles and scratches may be incurred when playing the tape on a VTR with a faulty tape transport mechanism or tape path. Always check the degradation of the rubber on the pinch roller which grips and pulls the tape. This rubber should be replaced at regular intervals.

• Make sure you have the right kind of fire extinguisher in the tape vault. The extinguishing agent should be gaseous. Liquid or powder extinguishers can damage tapes.

At-Home Storage

These storage conditions may seem stringent, but it must be remembered that these recommendations are for optimal archival storage.

For the individual videographer who does not have access to such controlled environmental vault conditions, consider this simple rule: a videotape is content in the same kind of environment as a human being. Generally, if you are comfortable, the tape is comfortable.

If you must keep tapes at home or in the office, keep them in the area where you live or work. Don't place them in a hot attic or damp basement. Try to keep them away from smoke, moisture and dirt.

The tape manufacturer Maxell offers a suggestion for those who must keep tapes in high humidity areas: use foil-lined corrugated storage cartons; package about a dozen cassettes in a plastic bag, insert a cloth desiccant bag (calcium chloride) inside each bag and seal the bag, either with a tie-wrap or tape.

Tapes that are frozen should be allowed to warm up to normal temperatures before use. This should be accomplished gradually over a 24-hour period. Cold tapes are brittle and easily damaged. Also, any moisture on a tape can cause dropout spots if it freezes.

Consider storing special, irreplaceable tapes in an environmentally-controlled tape vault. Many vault facilities accept single tapes for storage at a reasonable cost.

It should also be remembered that not all tapes were created equal or perfect at the factory. It pays to stick with tape made by established, leading manufacturers.

Even with brand-name tape, experienced video users have encountered so-called "bad" tapes. Sometimes it's a single tape and sometimes it's an entire batch. It is good practice to do a short test recording and playback at the top of a new tape before an important shoot, just to make sure.

Finally, in spite of all the advice about tape care and storage, many producers find it a good practice to make new copies of important programs every few years. Some companies do backups of programming every five years, others every seven years. With the lack of generational losses in the new digital formats, backups can be made with no loss of video quality. The best advice concerning video preservation is: back it up regularly and store it properly.

Long-Term Storage of Magnetic Tape Recordings

Magnetic tape is a significant factor in the retention of moving picture information. It has become, by default, the archival storage medium for many individuals and organizations. Television networks alone store hundreds of thousands of recorded programs, documentaries and news stories. Even individuals with electronic cameras and VCRs have family recordings that will never be discarded or erased as long as they are playable. There are those who have made recordings with the express intention of storing the information for archival purposes.

What follows are some general ground rules and recommendations for the long-term storage of prerecorded magnetic tape.

Pertinent Tape Factors

Magnetic tape consists of magnetic material in a binder system that is coated onto backing material. Assuming the tape and recording are in good condition to begin with, success in satisfactorily retrieving the recorded information after archival storage will depend upon how adversely the storage conditions and time will affect the following:

1. The magnetic signal.

2. The binder system integrity.

3. The backing integrity.

The Magnetic Signal

The magnetic particles dispersed in the binder system of the coating are the important memory elements in the overall construction of videotape. There are literally millions of these particles. When the tape has been recorded, each particle may be considered a small magnet with a north-south polarity. The polarities have been set in specific directions by the recording signal and, as a result, their combined magnetic fields will reproduce the original signal when detected on playback.

Unless acted upon by some outside force, these individual magnets will retain their original magnetic strength and polarity indefinitely. Outside influences that can change the polarities of the individual magnets and degrade the signal include heat, magnetic fields, radiation and physical stress. It is important to know the level at which these factors become a problem.

1. The heat required to destroy the magnetism in a magnetic material is known as its curie temperature. The curie temperatures of the materials used in tapes start at 250°F. Thus, there is little danger of failure of the magnetic signal due to temperatures expected in storage conditions unless the tape is exposed to fire.

2. Obviously, external magnetic fields can affect the signal on the tape. However, what is known as the tape's coercivity must be taken into consideration when trying to determine harmful levels. The coercivity is a measure of the magnetic field strength required to affect erasure or polarity reversals in the magnetic material. Coercivity is expressed in

oersteds. Virtually all commercially made videotapes have a coercivity of 250 oersteds or higher; current videotapes rate at or above 500 oersteds.

This means that an external magnetic field of 50 oersteds or less will have very little negative effect on the tape. Because the strength of a magnetic field falls off by the square of the distance from the source, adequate spacing between the tape and the source alone offers considerable protection.

Examples of some field strengths for reference purposes are as follows:

The earth's magnetic field:	0.6 oes.
The field strength directly on the case of an electric hand drill:	10.0 oes.
The field strength 3" away from a 1500 oersted bulk deguasser:	under 50.0 oes.

Even after long-term exposure, signal deterioration from the stray magnetic fields likely to be found in a tape storage area, or on a home user's shelf, would be negligible.

One signal stability problem resulting from magnetic fields could be called an unwanted signal gain, and is more commonly referred to as *print-through.* This is a phenomenon by which long wavelength recordings, as found in the audio recording portions of the tape, will cause magnetic particles to become magnetized by the recorded signal on an adjacent layer. In effect, the recording on one layer is imprinted onto the adjacent layers in the tape pack. Although the effect is low-level, it is noticeable on playback as a pre-echo or post-echo.

Print-through occurs because some magnetic particles have a coercivity lower than the average value; as a result, they are more easily magnetized by weak signals from the adjacent layer. The level of the print-through signal is dependent on the number of low coercivity particles, distance between layers (backing thickness), recorded wavelength and time.

The ratio of the desired signal level to the print signal level with time is known as the signal-to-print characteristic of the tape. The higher the number, the better. The signal-to-print characteristic of a typical videotape reveals a loss of approximately two to three dBs per decade of time.

3. Based on tests that have purposely exposed magnetic recordings to microwave radiation and X-rays, the intensity levels below those that adversely affect a human being will have no adverse effects on recorded signals.

4. When exposed to high mechanical stresses, a magnetic tape can exhibit signal losses, but the stress level that could be reached in a storage situation would have no more effect on the signal retention than that experienced by one playback pass on the machine.

All factors considered, the probability of successfully retaining an acceptable magnetic signal after long-term storage is very high and puts very little restriction on the storage environment.

The Binder System

The videotape binder system involves very sophisticated chemical technology. The binder must facilitate full, uniform dispersion of the small magnetic particles, maintain firm anchorage to the backing material, remain flexible, and still be strong enough to withstand the buzz saw action presented by the high-speed rotating heads. The formulation of the binder system is kept a closely guarded secret by each tape manufacturer, but it is safe to say that most systems contain resin-type material, plasticizers and lubricants as necessary. The result is a strong, flexible, lubricated piece of plastic.

The strength of this plastic comes from the design of its individual molecules. These molecules may be considered long chains of atoms that give the molecule a rope-like shape. If the binder material could be seen with the naked eye, it would probably look like a bunch of long interwoven strands of spaghetti. Like most plastics, this material is very stable and will weather the tests of time; but unlike the permanent siding on a house, this application requires that the material maintain an integrity beyond mere aesthetics.

The binder material is hygroscopic, which means it will absorb or attract moisture from the air. With enough moisture, a hydrolysis action begins to take place, and at some point the long chains of spaghetti will break down into shorter chains, thus losing some of their strength. The degree to which this happens is dependent upon the moisture level, temperature and time. When degradation has proceeded far enough, the tape will be susceptible to shredding and head clogging during playback on the machine, and at some point could reach a stage of complete breakdown to the buzz saw action.

Due to the number of variables, tolerance

levels are still somewhat unclear. Studies indicate, however, that exposure to relative humidities below 50%, and temperatures below 70°F will yield optimum long-term storage results.

The Backing

Since the inception of coated magnetic tape, three types of backing material have been used in its construction: paper, acetates and various forms of polyester. The paper backings were dropped shortly after 1948, but acetates are still being used today, along with polyester. Although polyester is the predominant backing in most magnetic tape, some audio recording applications, such as mag film, are still primarily using the acetate for its cut and tear characteristics. All videotapes, past and present, use a form of polyester.

The polyester is a plastic material made from resins, most likely with some additives. Like the binder, it is hygroscopic in nature and subject to degradation due to high humidity and temperature. This degradation reduces the strength of the backing and, along with the binder deterioration, could increase the potential of adhesion failure (separation of coating from backing). Again, with temperatures below 70°F and relative humidities below 50, the probability of successful long-term storage is very good.

Another factor that must be taken into account is the dimensional stability of the backing. In the manufacture of the backing, the polyester is put through a stretching process in arriving at its carefully controlled caliper. This produces a memory effect that, along with the thermal and hygroscopic expansion characteristics, affects the dimensions of the tape after long-term storage.

When the backing is exposed to higher temperatures than those found in manufacturing, the material tends to shrink with time and the result is not reversible. This dimensional change is of little consequence before a recording is made; after recording, however, a dimensional change could cause tracking or timing error problems upon playback. This is particularly true of helical scan formats. Some manufacturers incorporate a stabilizing process during production of helical tape backings which significantly improves the tolerance to time and temperature effects.

There are two types of backing that may be encountered in the field: stabilized and non-stabilized. Based on laboratory tests conducted at 72°F over a 10-month period to compare the two backings, the non-stabilized backing tapes reached a 0.03 percent dimensional change in the 10 months, while it was projected that the stabilized tapes would not reach that level until after 100 years.

The combination of times and temperatures that will result in giving the same 0.03 percent dimensional change on the stabilized backing is shown in the following table:

80°F	or	27°C —	after 10 years
90°F	or	32°C —	after 1 year
105°F	or	40°C —	after 6 months
125°F	or	52°C —	after 24 hours
150°F	or	66°C —	after 1 hour

The degree to which this phenomenon will affect the information retrieval after long-term storage is dependent on the recording format and the machine's built-in ability to handle tracking and time base errors. In the quadruplex format this presents no tracking problem, but will increase head banding effects. In the 1-inch and other formats with auto scan tracking and time base correction, this should not present a problem.

Contamination Factors

Internal Contamination

All magnetic tape contains a certain amount of unavoidable contamination as the result of by-products from their manufacture. Contaminants are present in both the coating and backing to various degrees. The quantity of this undesirable material is very small due to design and manufacturing controls, but the presence of contaminants should not be ignored. After long periods of storage under conditions of high humidity and temperature, the internal contaminants will migrate to the surface of the tape and manifest themselves as dropouts.

If the quantity released is higher than normal, possible head clogging and noticeable ruboff could occur. In either case, it is important to recognize that no deterioration of the tape occurs with the exudation of this material, and simply passing the tape through a cleaning device will restore normal playback. High humidity and temperature storage should be avoided in order to prevent this situation, but should it occur, the chances for recovering the recorded data are still very high.

External Contaminants

The most familiar and oft-discussed form of contamination is the dirt and debris in the operations environment that usually finds its way into the tape pack. This is worth mentioning again under the subject of long-term storage, because the effects from this debris will be greatly accentuated as tension in the tape increases with high temperature or high humidity storage. Under these conditions, the wound-in debris causes impressions in multiple layers of tape and results in significant drop-out growth.

At temperature and humidity conditions above 75°F and 70 percent RH, the chances of fungus growth developing on the tape during storage is very high. While contamination may not prevent the future recovery of recorded information, it will most certainly affect the quality.

Past Results

Magnetic tape recording is a relatively new means of information storage when compared to written matter, printed matter, paintings and even photographic film.

Magnetic recording in general is less than 100 years old; magnetic tape recording is less than 60 years old; the first commercially available audio tapes and machines are 40 years old; and the first commercially available videotapes and machines are just over 30 years old. Although the time period is relatively short when considering archival storage, some of the known successes and failures that have occurred on stored audio and videotapes deserve mentioning.

Audio Tape Storage Results

In the 1970s there were some glowing reports of a few audio tape recordings made in 1938 that played back with amazingly good quality. It was judged they may have even sounded better than when first recorded due to the improvements in playback heads and electronics.

There have been reports of some audio tapes made with acetate backing that were considered unusable after 10 years storage because the backing became brittle and cracked. The storage conditions were known to have been very dry for most of the period.

A few tapes, known to have been stored for extended periods at 80°F and 80 percent RH or more, exhibited blocking (sticking between layers) and adhesion failures (separation of coating from backing) when taken out of storage after 15 years. Adhesion and blocking failures in the areas of physical splices have been reported on some tapes that presumably had been stored for approximately 25 years in good environments.

Actual signal measurements on tapes before and after many years of storage are difficult for reasons of accuracy; there is often a question as to whether the heads, the electronics, the test equipment or the tape itself has changed. However, when two signals of the same frequency are measured for level changes between them after a long period of storage, the results are meaningful.

This is the case when making signal-to-print measurements. Several reports of the print-through levels found on tapes after long term storage have confirmed the initial tests used for predicting the time vs. print characteristic.

The random subjective testing done at 3M (in St. Paul, MN) over the past several years has included reel-to-reel tapes recorded in the early '50s, '60s, '70s, and '80s. The results indicate the quality after storage to be very near the quality when first recorded, at least as far as critical subjective evaluation is concerned. The testing has also included cassettes recorded in the '60s and later, with the same result.

Videotape Storage Results

In mid-1970 a survey of television broadcast operations was conducted for the purpose of assessing the general quality of pre-recorded videotapes after time in storage. The only tapes involved were the 2-inch quadruplex type. The age of the recordings ranged from seven to 14 years, and the reported storage conditions were temperatures of 50°F to 85°F along with humidities of 30 percent RH to 70 percent RH.

The evaluations made were strictly subjective in nature. The overall conclusions were positive—the reports indicated that the quality of the stored recordings was acceptable, and was nearly equal to the quality when first recorded.

The reported problems—which may or may not have been attributable to storage time—were drop-outs, audio print level, shedding, time base errors and head clogging. The percentage of these problems were small and none of them prevented the usability of the recordings. Presumably this was helped by the use of a tape cleaning device when necessary.

Storage reports received from various operations since that time, involving pre-recorded quadruplex tapes ranging in age from 10 to 20 years, have been similar in nature and have mostly involved color recordings.

Early 1-inch tapes, utilizing non-stabilized backing and recorded on one of the older 1-inch formats, exhibited a relatively high percentage of time base error problems after only two or three years of storage. The storage conditions were believed to have exceeded 80°F on occasion, and the resultant time base error was beyond the machines' ability to correct via the tension control. This led to stabilized backings in the early 1970s.

Pre-recorded U-Matic tapes more than 10 years old have been evaluated at 3M and judged to be of acceptable quality, with only minor problems. Numerous 1-inch Type C recordings up to 8 years old have also been evaluated and found to be of high quality with virtually no problems that can be attributed to storage.

The random observations made on older Beta and VHS recordings would indicate they are capable of holding up quite well under proper storage.

Storage Recommendations

One of the most important factors in realizing the long-life capability of magnetic tape is the care and attention provided before storage. With proper compliance to SMPTE recommended practice RP-103 and technical competence, the tape should exhibit the following conditions when placed on the storage shelf:

1. Recorded with a quality VTR that meets the manufacturer's specifications and complying with the appropriate standard.

2. A smooth, even, and full-length uniform wind at proper machine tensions.
3. No bad edges.
4. Free from excessive moisture absorption.
5. Free from external contaminants.
6. In the case of reel-to-reel tape, the end properly secured with hold-down tab material.
7. In its original clean container or equivalent.
8. No visible physical distortion in the tape pack.
9. In the case of cassette tape, a properly functioning and clean cassette.
10. Proper labeling and identification.
11. No physical splices.

In order to meet some of the conditions just outlined, tapes that have been exposed to considerable usage and have been in suspect environments should, if possible, be given a cleaning pass through a properly operating tape cleaning device.

The only further effort required is to control the atmosphere in which the tape will rest. We recommend that one of the following environments be adopted, depending on the situation:

1. If only videotape is to be stored, and in an isolated area where no access to the area is expected or required during the life of the storage, we recommend maintaining a reasonably constant temperature and humidity—below 70°F and 50 percent RH.

2. If videotape is to be stored along with mag film, photographic film, or any other type of media, and no access to the area is expected or required during the storage life, we recommend maintaining a

reasonably constant temperature below 70°F, with humidity between 30 percent RH to 50 percent RH.

3. If the storage area is to be made available to frequent access, we recommend that the temperature and humidity be maintained within the same limits recommended for the operations area: 70°F plus or minus 5 percent and humidity 50 percent plus or minus 20 percent.

One further consideration is the videotape machine itself. With the rapid development of video recording technology, the possibility of the current machines being readily available in 50 to 100 years is highly unlikely. This situation therefore requires the archivist to store and maintain the machines necessary for playing back the recorded format.

The particular machine manufacturer involved may have recommendations in this regard, but the same storage and operating conditions should suffice for the machines. When given the proper attention, tape is a very viable archival storage medium.

(Courtesy of 3M Magnetic Media Division, St. Paul, MN)

Temperature and Humidity Recommendations for VTR Facilities

Does your videotape recording facility comply with the SMPTE recommended practice for care and handling of videotape? Just as hospitals control environment to help ensure the success of an operation and subsequent patient recovery, a true

Courtesy of Hollywood Vaults.

quality videotape recording facility should follow industry recommendations to help ensure the success of a program.

Many program productions run into six-digit cost figures, and the consequences of failure are dire. An operation that is environmentally out of control is taking unnecessary chances. Following the industry-recommended practices for videotape recording operations is a big step in the right direction.

The primary source of environmental information is found in the SMPTE Recommended Practice RP-103.

This document was the result of work done by experts from both user and manufacturer organizations and is based upon a broad range of data from laboratory tests and field experience. Similar information may be found in the *NAB Engineering Handbook.*

One important part of these publications is the recommended temperature and humidity control for both the operating area and the videotape storage area; namely, 21°C plus or minus 2°C (70°F ± 4°F) and 50 percent RH plus or minus 20 percent. To help reinforce the industry recommendations, and to serve as a reminder, the following information is offered as a reference.

Temperature and Humidity Effects

With temperature and humidity, the level of risk is the potential of having a quality problem, functional problem, or the possibility of complete failure. The different zone categories shown are used for reference purposes in the following comments.

Zone A - 48% to 52% RH and 68°F to 72°F

The range of temperature and humidity control used for establishing a reference.

Zone B - 30% to 70% RH and 66°F to 74°F (per SMPTE RP-103)

The maximum range of temperature and humidity allowed by the industry recommendations for minimizing risks within a facility while still permitting a practical degree of flexibility.

Zone C - Low Humidity Effects

Storage Area

Presents no increased risks for either short- or long-term storage.

Operations Area

1. Increased amounts of airborne dust and debris which could contaminate tapes.

2. Increased static attraction of debris onto exposed tape surfaces and increasing the amount of wound-in debris.
3. Increased random static discharges that may disrupt the tape machine's memory logic.
4. Potential head-to-tape interface problem creating increased video noise on playback.
5. Potential for decreased stop motion capability.

Zone D - High Humidity Effects Storage Area

1. Increased absorption of moisture in the tape pack, resulting in binder deterioration after long-term storage.
2. Increased tape pack stresses resulting in increased distortion.
3. Increased tightness of tape pack creating increased drop-out problems from wound-in foreign debris.
4. Possible exudation of minute tape contaminants after long term storage.
5. Possible fungus growth when accompanied with warm temperatures.

Operations Area

1. Increased potential toward head clogging, particularly on tapes coming from long-term storage.
2. Increased potential for stiction problems which significantly reduces the number of edit passes from the same park point.
3. Increased possibility of tape scoring.
4. Increased possibility of higher headwear.

Zone E - Low Temperature Effects

Storage Area

No problems if allowed to stabilize for 24 hours before use at normal operating temperature.

Operations Area

1. Tape wind becomes loose, creating a likelihood of cinching. This is true during shipment as well.
2. Due to change in tape dimensions the potential of interchange problems exist.
3. Increased chance of human error.

Zone F - High Temperature Effects Storage Area

1. Significant increase in tape pack tightness causing increased dropouts due to wound-in debris.
2. Significant increase in tape pack pressure resulting in tape distortion.
3. Possible layer-to-layer adhesion after long term storage.
4. The potential of interchange problems due to the change in tape dimensions.

Operations Area

1. Potential interchange problems due to tape dimensional change.
2. Increased chances of machine failure.
3. Increased chances of human error.

Zone C and E - Combined Effects of Low Temperature and Low Humidity Storage Area

Low risk for archival storage; however, the recommended environment should be followed for normal storage to avoid changing conditions for tapes going in and out of storage and saving the tape stabilization time recommended.

Operations Area

Same potential problem effects as mentioned for the individual zones, and at about the same degree of risk.

Zone D and F - Combined Effects High Temperature and High Humidity

This combination represents the worst possible conditions for both storage and operations. The risk levels should be considered additive and provides high potential for complete failure if maintained.

(Courtesy of 3M Magnetic Media Division, St. Paul, MN)

How to do an "Eyeball" Setup of a Picture Monitor

by Algie Abrams

Sometimes it is necessary to do a quick "eyeball" setup of a television picture monitor in the field. The only tool necessary is a SMPTE color bar feed—either from a live source or tape.

Before we start, two absolutely essential points should be remembered:

• If it takes longer than three or four minutes to accomplish the setup, look away from the monitor to some neutral-colored area or leave the room entirely for another three or four minutes. The eye tends to accept any color as being "normal" after a period of several minutes, and it will become very difficult to judge colors on the monitor screen accurately.

• In a given operating environment, only one person should set up all color monitors. No two people see colors in exactly the same way, therefore no two people will set up monitors in exactly the same way.

Chroma and Hue

Feed SMPTE color bars to the monitor. Locate the red, green, and blue color switches (probably located behind a door). Also locate the chroma and hue controls on the front panel.

Switch off the red and green colors. You should see four vertical blue bars with three darker bars separating them. At the bottom of each blue bar will be a small rectangular bar segment. Other things will be visible on the display, but we are only interested in the vertical bars for this step.

The object is to make the color and brightness of the vertical blue bars match the rectangular bar segments below them. You will find that the HUE control affects mainly the middle two bars. Adjusting the CHROMA control will affect mainly the two outside bars. Continue adjusting both controls until all four bars match.

Turn on the red and green colors when finished.

Brightness and Contrast

Locate the BRIGHTNESS control on the front panel. Observe the sixth (red) bar on the screen. Directly below this bar you should see three narrow vertical bars which are shades of gray. If these gray bars are not visible, turn the BRIGHTNESS control until they can be clearly seen.

Now locate the COLOR/MONOCHROME switch and set it to the MONOCHROME (no color) position.

Reduce the BRIGHTNESS setting until the center gray bar just disappears from the screen.

Locate the CONTRAST control. Adjust it until the white reference square (lower left portion of the screen) is bright enough to appear white. It should not be so bright that it is uncomfortable to look at or causes the dark squares on either side of it to "glow."

The BRIGHTNESS and CONTRAST controls

interact with one another and will probably have to be touched up more than once. When both controls are correctly set, turn the COLOR/MONOCHROME switch back to the COLOR position.

The monitor set-up is now complete.

Pulse Cross Display

A switch on many monitors activates a delay of both horizontal and vertical synchronizing pulses. This depiction, referred to as the "pulse cross" display, allows observation of the signal in a different form than that of a waveform monitor or vectorscope.

The pulse cross display is useful to the engineer in checking proper adjustment of videotape tension and for viewing the portion of scanning that precedes the vertical interval. It is especially good as an indicator of tape skew error, which is more difficult to see on a waveform monitor. Skew error shows up as a "flag waving" or "palm waving" effect at the point where the pulses cross on the screen.

***Algie Abrams** , SuperTech Field Services, Los Angeles, CA.*

How to Establish an Exposure Index for a Video Camera

by Harry Mathias

Establishing the sensitivity, or the exposure index, of a video camera is a concept that has gained international acceptance. Just as with motion picture film, a video camera's exposure index (some call it ASA, but technically, ASA applies only to film) enables the videographer to predict the lighting levels and to pre-light without the camera.

Establishing an exposure index (E.I.) allows a light meter to be used meaningfully with a video camera. Assuming the camera is on a lighted chip chart and a waveform monitor is available, the procedure takes only a few minutes.

First open the iris until the crossover chip is at 55 IRE units on the waveform monitor or the peak white chip is at 100. Check the f-stop on the lens, then take a reading with an incident light meter at the chip chart. The photosphere on the meter should be pointed at the camera. Change the slide in the meter until the f-stop reading on meter coincides with the f-stop at which the lens is set. Once you have found the slide that results in the closest approximation to the f-stop on the lens, you have determined the effective exposure index of the camera. You need only keep that slide in the meter and use it as you would with film.

Changing the gain boost setting, however, will alter the correct exposure index. If you want to know the camera E.I. at the +6 db gain setting, for example, you must repeat the process with the + 6 db gain boost switched on.

***Harry Mathais** is cinematographer and is noted for the seminars he conducts for industry professionals and advanced students.*

How to Use the Zone System to Predict Video Image Contrast

by Harry Mathias

The waveform monitor is simply a graphic display of video signal exposure levels. The vertical axis of the waveform monitor is calibrated in IRE units. On the waveform monitor's screen, IRE signal or "exposure" levels are displayed with black level at 7.5 IRE units (darkness, not a lit black surface) , and peak picture white levels at 100 IRE units.

The videographer can, with a little practice, evaluate exposure levels, image contrast and lighting contrast using a waveform monitor, alone or in conjunction with a light meter. A waveform monitor displays the picture with the correct orientation left to right; by comparing its image with that of a picture monitor, the videographer begins to develop the skill of finding picture elements on the waveform monitor's screen and evaluating their exposure level.

The most useful mode on a waveform monitor is the horizontal, or line rate mode. In this position, what is seen on the display is a composite of the signals for every line of picture information in the frame.

The zone system is often used as a tool to predict reproduction contrast when photographing a scene on film. According to the zone system, Zone II represents the darkest exposure level in which any texture may be preserved in the final print; Zone III is a dark gray in which good texture reproduction should be present; and Zone IV is a light gray. A middle gray is represented by Zone V. Zone VI is the level at which Caucasian skin is usually reproduced. Zone VII is the upper limit of white reproduction with good texture, and Zone VIII, the limit of any texture in the reproduction of white.

It is possible to correlate the scale on a waveform monitor to the zones used in the zone system. Zone I is below 7.5 units, while Zone II is from 7.5 up to 20 units. Zone III is at 20 units. Zone IV is at 40 units. Zone V, the middle grey zone, is at 55 units. Zone VI is at 80 units. Zone VII is at 100 units, while Zone VIII is at 120 units. The zone system, used in this way, becomes equally effective at predicting contrast reproduction in video as it is in film.

How to Set Up a Time Base Corrector

by Algie Abrams

Being mechanical devices, video tape recorders develop variations in timing during playback. To compensate for these variations, a time base corrector (TBC) is used.

Although common in the postproduction suite, TBCs are also used by location video crews for feeding video to other recorders or to satellite, microwave or telco links. The following checklist may be used as a guide when setting up some of the more popular cassette-based video machines for field playback.

Off-Tape Video Signal Parameters Controlled by TBC

1. H Sync Phase
a) Observed on waveform monitor
b) Adjusted to match reference H sync timing
c) No manual adjustments on some TBCs

2. Pedestal Level (also called Setup)
a) Observed on waveform monitor
b) Adjusted for a black level of 7.5 IRE

3. Video Level
a) Observed on waveform monitor
b) Adjusted for peak white level of 100 IRE

(Note: The TBC circuits which control video level and pedestal level are interactive. You may have to adjust each more than once in order to have them both correct.)

4. Chroma Level
a) Observed on waveform monitor
b) Adjusted so that the upper peaks of yellow and cyan are at 100 IRE
5. Sub-Carrier Phase
a) Observed on vectorscope
b) Adjusted to match reference SC or burst timing
c) No manual adjustment on some TBCs.
6. Hue Phase
a) Observed on vectorscope
b) Adjusted so that each color bar centers on the appropriate target.

Hiding Lavalier Microphones

One of the ever-present difficulties of hiding lavaliers under wardrobe is clothing noise. There are two different types of clothing noise: *contact* noise and *acoustic* noise.

Contact noise is the result of garments rubbing directly against either the mic itself or the leading few inches of cable (equally sensitive to friction). Contact noise can usually be controlled—if not completely eliminated—by careful positioning and taping down pf the mic and cable.

Begin by securing the clothing on both sides of the mic capsule. This can be done by sandwiching the mic between two sticky triangles of cloth camera tape or gaffer's tape. Form these triangles by folding a few inches of one-inch-wide tape corner over corner, similar to folding a flag *(see Figure 1)*.

By immobilizing the mic between both layers of clothing, you have eliminated the possibility of either layer of clothing rubbing against or flapping onto the microphone.

If the lavalier must be positioned between skin or clothing, or attached directly to skin, then a professional medical/surgical tape should be used against the skin.

Once the mic capsule has been secured, the next step is to form a strain relief for the thin cable. Make a small loop just under the mic capsule. In the case of very sensitive mics, such as the Sony ECM-77 and Sennheiser MKE 2, make the loop go around

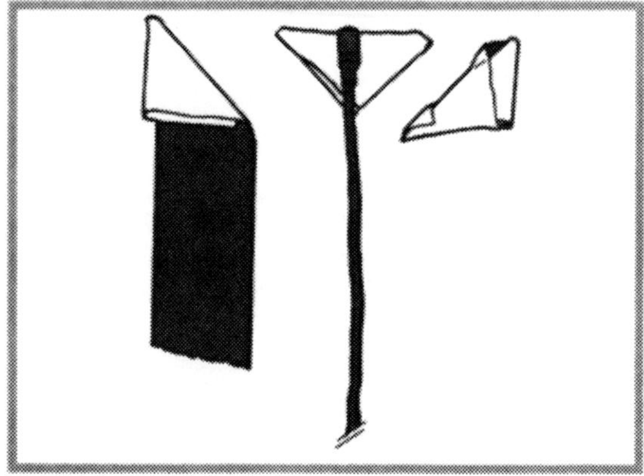

Figure 1

twice. Tie a small thread or use a thin strip of camera tape (sticky side out) to preserve the loop. Tie the loop loose enough so that it can "breathe" (change diameter to absorb tugs).

Apply a few inches of tape along the cable below the loop. Any tension on the cable will be absorbed by the garment, rather than by the microphone, which is somewhat isolated by the floating loop *(see Figure 2)*.

The remainder of the mic cable can be run under clothing and can terminate either at the waist or the ankle. The end of the mic connector should be secured so that it does not dangle freely.

During a take, it becomes a simple matter to plug in an extension XLR cable. Afterwards, the talent can easily be disconnected so that he or she is free to roam around.

When using an external "tie clip," it is still important to create a strain relief. Loop the thin cable up and under the tie clip, forming a semi-

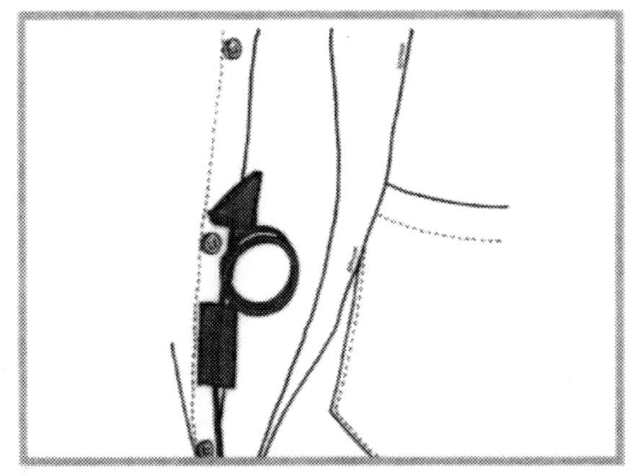
Figure 2

circle, and pass it through the wide hinge of the clip. Continue the loop behind the garment and bring the cable around and downward, thus completing the circle. As the cable loops downward, it should be inserted between the jaws of the tie clip and the back of the garment. Hide the balance of the cable behind the wardrobe.

Not only is this arrangement more pleasing to the eye than a dangling cable, but the floating loop of cable isolates the mic while the grip of the clip serves as strain relief.

Acoustic clothing noise is the sound generated by the clothing itself as garments or layers rub against each other when the actor moves. Noise is much more prevalent with synthetic fabrics than with natural cottons or wools. There is no simple remedy, only prevention, so it is wise to consult early with the wardrobe department and/or the specific on-camera talent as to what they will be wearing in the scene.

Nevertheless, here are a couple of tricks that may help. Anti-static sprays, such as "Static Guard," will reduce static electrical discharge, clinging, and friction. Dry silicon spray lubricants sometimes help, but be careful to avoid staining. Stiff or starched clothing can be softened with water or alcohol, but make sure the colors don't bleed. Saddle soap, silicon, or light oil can take the bite out of hard leather.

Another problem common to lavaliers is wind noise. Manufacturers usually supply small foam or metal mesh windscreens with their lavaliers, but these are usually more effective against breath pops than against outdoor gusts of wind.

Lavaliers used under clothing have the advantage of being partially shielded from the wind, but may still require added protection.

Clothing rubbing against windscreens can be extremely noisy, so great care must be taken when using hidden lavaliers out of doors. Surrounding the wind-screen with sticky tape and securing it to both layers of clothing, as you would a bare mic, will reduce the friction noise. However, the tape may destroy a foam windscreen when it is removed. Inexpensive, expendable foam windscreens can be made by wrapping the mic in acoustafoam or by pulling the foam booties off of video cleaning swabs.

Cheesecloth over a mic works very well against wind. Another Hollywood variation is to snip the finger tips off of children's woolen gloves and pull the wool tips over a lavalier wrapped in foam or cheesecloth.

(Courtesy of Audio Services Corp., North Hollywood, CA)

Wireless Microphone Installation Guide

Without question, the greatest difficulty encountered during the use of radio mics is correctly attaching them to the body of the user.

Body pack transmitters can be hidden almost anywhere. The most common places include the small of the back, rear hip, inside thigh, ankle, pants pocket, inside chest pocket of a jacket, or in the heroine's purse. When talent is wearing a scant bathing suit, for example, radio (wireless) mics can sometimes be hidden under straw hats, or even on the back of the neck under long tresses of hair. Leg warmers provide a convenient place to hide radios when dealing with excercise attire.

There are a number of ways transmitters may be secured. Belt clips work fine under a jacket or loose top. Special pouches or pockets can be pinned on or permanently sewn into wardrobe. Sometimes it is possible to merely hang the unit with a safety pin that has been taped onto the transmitter casing. Specially constructed elastic belts can be worn around the waist, thigh, calf, or ankle. Transmitters can also be held in place by elastic bandages.

Anytime camera and gaffer's tape is used, special care must be taken not to tape directly to skin or delicate wardrobe (such as nylon stockings). Fold the tape over itself to form a non-adhesive strip to wrap around first. Better yet, use some sort of liner, such as a strip of cloth, wide gauze, or even a length of toilet paper.

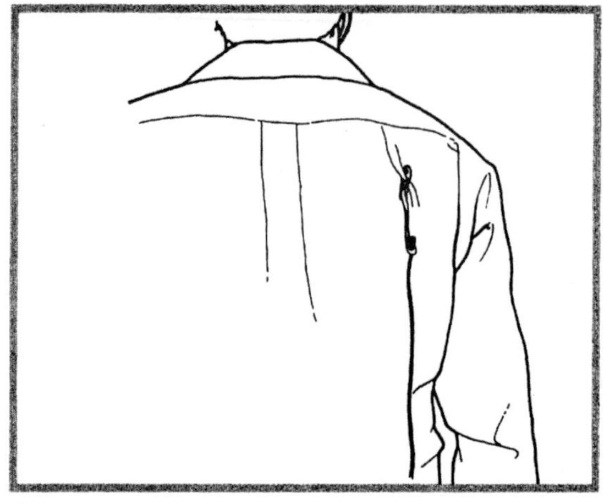

Figure 1

Avoid placing the transmitter directly against the skin, since perspiration does not get along well with fragile electronics. Many mixers have found that unlubricated condoms provide excellent protection from excess perspiration, rain or water spray.

Care should be taken in securing the flexible transmitter antenna cable. To prevent the antenna from being torn from its connector the first time the user moves or bends over, use a rubber band to provide elastic strain relief *(see Figure 1)*. Attach one end of the rubber band to the top of the antenna. The free end of the rubber band can be safety-pinned to the clothing or taped in place (use medical tape on skin). Thus, the antenna can be held reasonably straight (a little slack is okay) yet protected against tearing. Avoid running the antenna directly against the skin, since body moisture tends to interfere with the outgoing signal.

The transmitter antenna can be run vertically up or down from the body pack. If the antenna trails downward, however, then the transmitter should be mounted in an inverted position to avoid making a loop in the line. The transmitter antenna can also be run horizontally, such as partially around the waist. In these instances, the receiver antenna may need to be tilted sideways (matching the angle) to improve reception.

Under no circumstances should the mic line and antenna wire ever cross. Run the microphone cable out from the body pack in the opposite direction of the antenna. When the transmitter is mounted on the body upside-down (the antenna running downward), it is okay for the mic line to loop upward, as long as it doesn't cross the antenna.

Install a fresh alkaline battery in the transmitter every time you use it. This sounds like an obvious detail, but all too often radio mic problems boil down to a weak battery in the transmitter. Change the battery frequently—every four to six hours with most brands.

Forced Perception

There are several ways to soften the problem of forced close-up perspective. The first is to select a lavalier microphone with an open sound, such as the Tram TR-50 or Sennheiser MKE-2, rather than a lavalier that tends to isolate, such as the Sony ECM-55. Another solution is to attach the lavalier a little lower on the body than usual. When there are two people playing close to each other, it sometimes helps to mic each person off the opposite person's mic. Finally, simultaneously employ a boom microphone in order to bleed in some sound effects and background, thus taking the sterile edge off the lavalier.

Antenna Placement

The antenna of the receiver should initially be adjusted to match the angle of the transmitter antenna. Then experiment with changing the angle, for sometimes an unusual condition on the set may favor an odd combination of antenna angles to yield best signal.

A clean path between receiver antenna and transmitter is important, since almost any object or body can deflect or absorb RF. Mounting the receiver up high, such as on a wooden ladder, usually helps.

Depending on the system, it may also be possible to simply separate the receiving antenna from the receiver unit and mount the antenna in a higher place. High-quality RG-58 50-ohm cable should be used to make the connection. If the system is being used on location rather than in a permanent installation, use a brand of flexible cable. Traditional RF cable, with its hard plastic core, is brittle and may break or short after being recoiled.

Wireless mics come equipped with one of three forms of receiver antenna: the straight wire "whip"; the shorter helical "rubber duckie"; and the "limp wire." The straight whip will yield the best reception, although the rubber duckie offers more convenience in terms of mobility. Limp wires perform least effectively.

Certain special antenna systems can be used to improve reception. Dipole antennas "hear" transmitters with less regard to the angle of body pack antennas. Directional antenna systems can be cued or aimed (similar to a directional microphone) in order to reject radio interference. High-gain antenna systems with signal amplifiers can significantly increase the range of some wireless mics.

Placement and Environment

Strive to maintain minimum distance between the transmitters and receiver. Move the receiver/antenna from shot to shot in order to achieve close and clean line-of-sight placement. Don't be afraid to locate an antenna just outside the camera frame, or even to conceal it behind a prop right in the shot.

Sometimes, it may be expedient to have the boom or third man physically carry the entire receiver during the take in order to maintain proximity with the actors. Given the option, it is better to run long lengths of audio cable (from receiver to recorder) than to have long lengths of antenna cable (from antenna to receiver).

Virtually anything can interfere with good radio transmission and cause bursts of static. Check for metallic objects of any kind, such as jewelry, zippers, coins, snaps and keys. If you cannot eliminate the metal, then at least reposition the antenna on the actor.

Carefully eyeball the path of transmission between the actor and the receiver. Pay attention to lighting or grip stands that may suddenly have appeared. A new influx of crew members or spectators can also block the RF signal.

Examine the location itself. Check for additional electrical lines, especially coiled feeds, which can generate magnetic fields. Dimmers and special effects equipment (especially neons) are often a problem. Motors can also produce interference; also be aware of golf carts, forklifts, camera cranes, automobiles and kitchen appliances.

Video and computer equipment can create strange fields. Be aware of Steadicams and other camera mounts relying on high intensity video or radio controlled camera functions.

(Courtesy of Audio Services Corp., North Hollywood, CA)

Digital Glossary

ACATS (Advisory Committee on Advanced Television Service) — ACATS is an FCC-recognized committee responsible for recommending the final DTV system to the FCC.

Active Picture — The area of a television frame that carries picture information. Outside of the active area there are line and field blanking which roughly correspond to the areas defined for the original 525- and 625-line analog systems. In digital TV the blanked/active areas are defined by ITU-R 601, SMPTE RP125 AND EBU-E.

A/D (Analog to Digital Conversion) — The process of converting analog signals to digital data, normally for subsequent use in digital video production equipment. Also referred to as digitization or quantization (see Chapter I). An A/D converter is a circuit that converts an analog signal into a digital word. This "word" is represented by a binary number. D/A represents the reverse translation.

AES/EBU — The digital audio standard that permits a variety of sampling frequencies.

Aliasing — Undesirable "beating" effects caused by sampling frequencies being too low to faithfully reproduce image detail. The "steppiness" of unfiltered lines presented at an angle to the TV raster is also referred to as aliasing.

Aliens — A term for alias effects such as ringing, contouring and jaggy edges caused by a lack of resolution in a raster image. Some can be avoided by careful filtering or dynamic rounding.

Alpha channel — Another name for a key channel, a channel to carry a key signal.

Analog — An electrical signal is referred to as either analog or digital. DTV uses digital signals. Analog signals are those signals directly generated from a stimulus such as a light striking a camera picture tube. You can convert an analog signal to a digital signal by using an analog to digital converter (A/D).

Analog audio — A signal where the instantaneous voltage is proportional to the diaphragm velocity at the microphone.

Anamorphic — Refers to the use of 16 : 9 aspect ratio pictures in a 4:3 system.

Anti-aliasing — Smoothing of aliasing effects by filtering and other techniques.

Anti-aliasing filter — A filter that restricts the frequency range of an analog signal to less than one half the sampling rate.

Aperture — The opening that allows light to pass through a camera lens. An adjustable diaphragm is used to control the size of the opening. Also, a cross-sectional area of the antenna which is exposed to the satellite signal.

API (Application Programming Interface) — A set of interface definitions that provide a convenient interface to the functions of a subsystem. They simplify the work by insulating the application programmer from minutiae of the implementation.

Arbitrated Loop — A technique used on computer networks to ensure that the network is clear before a fresh message is sent. When it is not carrying data frames, the loop carries "keep-alive" frames. Any node that wants to transmit places its own ID into a keep-alive frame. When it receives that frame back it knows that the loop is clear and that it can send its message.

Areal Density — The density of data held on an area of the surface of a recording medium. This is one of the parameters that manufacturers of disk drives and tape recorders strive to increase.

Artifact — A side effect in video or audio caused by any unnatural component. In video, artifact is usually a term describing distortion or a flaw in the image. These visible deffects are a direct result of some technical limitation. Examples include cross-color artifacts, cross-luminance artifacts, jitter, blocking, ghosts, etc.

ASCII (American Standard Code for Information Interchange) — This is a standard computer character set used throughout the industry to represent keyboard characters as digital information. There is an ASCII table containing 127 characters covering all the upper and lower case characters in normal and non displayed controls such as carriage return, line feed, etc. Variations and extensions of the basic code are used in special applications.

ASIC (American Specific Integrated Circuit) — A custom designed integrated circuit with functions specifically tailored to a particular application. This effectively replaces the many discrete devices that could otherwise do the job but its performance will be superior. Being far more compact than the separate components, the single chip can work faster than an array of separate chips. Often a ten-fold increase in speed is achieved, while the power consumption can drop by a similar factor and reliability is greatly increased.

Aspect Ratio — The ratio of the width of an image to its height. A standard NTSC image has a 4:3 (1.33) aspect ratio. Most digital television (DTV) and high definition video systems have a 16:9 (1.78) aspect ratio.

Asynchronous — A system where various signals are unlocked. Switching between signals results in unpredictable results.

ATM (Asynchronous Transfer Mode) — A high speed switched data communications system potentially capable of both local area network (LAN) and wide area network (WAN) operation. Twenty-five, 155 and 622 Mbps ATM links are currently available.

ATSC (Advanced Television Systems Committee) — Established in 1982 to coordinate the development of voluntary national technical standards for the generation, distribution and reception of high definition television.

ATV (Advanced Television) — This term is used in North America to describe television with capabilities beyond those of analog NTSC. It includes digital television (DTV) and high definition (HDTV).

Auditory Masking — The psycho-acoustic phenomenon of human hearing where what can be heard is affected by the components of the sound. Audio compression systems such as Dolby Digital and MPEG audio use auditory masking as their basis and only code what can be heard by the human ear.

Aural — The sound portion of a total television system.

Average Picture Level (APL) — The average signal level with respect to blanking during the active picture time. APL is expressed as a percentage of the difference between the blanking and reference white levels.

Axis (x, y, z) — Used to describe the three dimensional axes available in DVE manipulations. At normal (clear) x lies across the screen left to right, y up the screen bottom to top and z points into the screen. Depending on the power of the equipment and the complexity of the DVE move, several sets of xyz axes may be in use at one time.

Azimuth recording — The twisting of alternate magnetic heads left and right to record adjacent tracks which can be read without crosstalk. Also called "guard-band-less" recording. A technique used in most DVTRs and RDAT machines.

Background Task — An operation that is completed while the main operation continues uninterrupted.

Backtiming — Providing a reference clock from a destination so that a source can provide a synchronous transmission. Also called "genlocking."

Bandwidth — The amount of information that can be passed in a given time, measured by the range between the lowest and highest limiting frequencies of an electronic system. In video, the term — measured in megahertz (MHz) — is used to describe the technical boundaries of equipment. NTSC and DTV television channels have a bandwidth of 6 MHz. The greater the bandwidth, the more information a television system can carry. Bandwidth is also known as the range between the lowest and highest limiting frequencies in an electronic system. In digital audio, the term represents the maximum digital information which can be stored in a system.

Bandwidth compression — Reducing the bandwidth that is required for transmission of a given digital data rate. Reducing gigabits of raw data into a DTV signal of 19 Megabits per second allows this signal to be transmitted over the 6 Mhz bandwidth.

Baseband — Any signal in its original form prior to modulation or after demodulation.

Beam — The directed flow of bombarding electrons in a television picture tube.

Beam-Splitter Prism — The optical block in a video camera onto which three CCD sensors are mounted. The optics split the red, green and blue wavelengths of light for the camera.

B-frames — Bi-directional predictive frames created by assessing the difference between the previous and the next frames in a television picture sequence.

Binary — The base of mathematics used in digital systems and computing. It is a mathematical representation of a number to base 2.

Bit (b) — Binary Digit = bit. The smallest increment of digital information. One mathematical bit can define two levels or states: on or off, black or white, 0 or 1, etc., two bits can define four levels, three bits eight, and so on.

Bitstream — 1) A flow of data or 2) Name of a supplier of text fonts.

Bit rate reduction (BRR) — see compression

Blocking and "Blockiness" — Artifact of compression generally showing momentarily as rectangular areas of picture with distinct boundaries. This is one of the major defects of digital compression, especially MPEG. Its visibility generally depends on the amount of compression used, the quality and nature of the original pictures as well as the quality of the coder.

Blocks — Rectangular areas of pictures, usually 8 x 8 pixels in size, that are individually subjected to DCT coding as part of a digital picture compression process.

BNC Connector — Standard twist-connector for attaching coaxial cable to professional video equipment.

Bus — An internal pathway for sending digital signals from one part of a system to another.

Byte — (B), Kilobyte (kB), Megabyte (MB), Gigabyte (GB), Terabyte (TB) and Petabyte (PB) -

1Byte (B) = 8 bits (b) which can describe 256 discrete values (brightness, color, etc.). The values kilo, mega, giga, etc. can be described by 2 raised to the power 10, 20, 30, etc.. They then become 1,024, 1,048,576, 1,073,741,824, respectively. A full frame of digital television, according to ITU-R 601, requires just under 1 MB of storage. HDTV frames are around 5-6 times larger -and digital film frames larger again.

Capstan Servo — The regulating device of the capstan as it passes tape through a video tape recorder.

CCD (Charge-Coupled Device) — A light-sensitive semiconductor used as an image sensor in video cameras for memory storage or as a light pickup device.

CCIR (Comite Consultatif International des Radiocommunications) — The International Radio Consultative Committee. This standardization committee is now called ITU-R.

CCU (Camera Control Unit) — The remote control device used to set parameters for one or more television cameras.

CDDI (Copper Data Distributed Interface) — A high speed data interface - like FDDI, but using copper.

CDTV (Conventional Definition Television) — The analogue NTSC, PAL, SECAM television systems with normal 4:3 aspect ratio pictures.

Checksum — A simple check value of a block of data, calculated by adding all the bytes in a block.

Chroma Keying — The process of overlaying one video signal over another with the areas of overlay being defined by a specific range of color or chrominance on the foreground signal.

Chrominance — The color information in a television picture. Chrominance can be further broken down into two properties of color: hue and saturation. It's often referred to as part of a signal, relating to the hue and saturation but not the brightness of luminance of the signal. Also called chroma.

Chrominance-to-Burst Phase — The difference between the expected phase and the actual phase of the chrominance portion of the video signal relative to burst phase.

Chrominance-to-Luminance Delay — The difference in time that it takes for the chrominance portion of the video signal to pass through a system relative to the time it takes for the luminance portion. Also called relative chroma time.

Chrominance-to-Luminance Gain — The difference between the gain of the chrominance portion of the video signal and the gain of the luminance portion as they pass through a system.

Clip — A segment of sequential frames made during the taping of a scene. A clip can be a single video segment or a series of video segments spliced together.

Clipping — A type of sound distortion that occurs when the signal level exceeds the headroom of the mixing console or other piece of audio processing equipment. In video, clipping refers to a circuit that blocks highlights in the video signal which exceed 100 IRE units.

Coaxial Cable — A single conductor, braid-shielded cable used to carry video signals. It normally has a 75 ohm impedance.

Coefficient Recording — A form of data bit-rate reduction used by Sony in its Digital Betacam format and with its D-2 component recording accessory, the DFX-C2. Coefficient recording uses a discrete cosine transformation (DCT) and a proprietary information handling scheme to lower the data rate generated by a full bit-rate component digital signal. Such a data bit-rate reduction system allows component digital picture information to be recorded more efficiently on VTRs.

Color Balance — Adjustment of the color circuitry of a television camera to the color temperature of the light source for a given scene.

Color Bars — An electronically-generated test signal usually consisting of six vertical strips of color.

Color Burst — The burst of color subcarrier added to the back porch of the composite video signal. It serves as a frequency and phase reference for the chrominance signal.

Color Space — The color range between specified references. Usually three references are quoted in television: RGB, Y, R-Y, B-Y and Hue Saturation and Luminance (HSL). Operating across different media, such as print, film, TV and computer to TV, will require conversions in color space.

Color Temperature — A measurement of the proportional amounts of the three primary colors (green, red, blue) in a light source.

Composite Video — A single video signal containing all of the necessary information to reproduce a color picture. Luminance and chrominance are combined with the timing reference 'sync' information using one of the coding standards - NTSC, PAL or SECAM - to make composite video. The process restricts the bandwidths (image detail) of components. In the composite result color is added to the monochrome (luminance) information using a visually acceptable technique.

Compression (audio) — Reduction of bandwidth or data rate for audio. This is generally beneficial where bandwidth and storage are limited, such as in delivery systems to the home.

Compression (video) — The process of reducing the bandwidth or data rate of a video stream. Digital compression systems analyze their picture sources to remove redundancy within and between picture frames. The compression techniques currently in use include ETSI, JPEG, Motion JPEG, MPEG-1 and MPEG-2.

Compression ratio — The ratio of the data in the non-compressed digital video signal to the compressed version.

Concatenation — The linking together of systems. In digital television this refers to the concatenation of compression systems which is currently a subject of concern because any compression beyond about 2:1 results in the removal of information that cannot be recovered. As the use of compression increases, so too does the likelihood that material will undergo a number of compressions between acquisition and transmission. Although the effects of one compression might not be very noticeable, the impact of multiple decompressions and recompressions, with the material returned to baseband in between - can cause considerable damage. The damage is likely to be greatest where different compression schemes are concatenated in a particular signal path.

Contouring — An unwanted artifact similar to posterisation. Digital systems exhibit contouring when insufficient quantizing levels are used or inaccurate processing, or truncation occurs.

Contrast — The range in brightness between the darkest and brightest areas of a picture.

Corner pinning — A technique for defining the position and rotation of pictures in a DVE, by dragging their corners to fit a background scene.

Co-Sited sampling — This is a sampling technique applied to color difference a component video signal (Y, Cr, Cb) where the color difference signals, Cr and Cb, are sampled at a sub-multiple of the luminance, Y, frequency—for example, as in 4:2:2. Co-sited sampling is the "norm" for component video as it ensures the luminance and the chrominance digital information is coincident, minimizing chroma/luma delay.

CRC (Cyclic Redundancy Check) — an advanced checksum technique. It uses a check value calculated for a data stream by feeding it through a shifter with feedback terms "EXORed" back in.

CRT (Cathode Ray Tube) — Display device, or picture tube, for video information.

CSDI (Compressed Serial Data Interface) — This protocol is in the process of being ratified by the SMPTE. It uses the same signal format as DVCPRO and, as this is a compressed format, enables video data to be transferred at four times real time rate over SDI links.

D-7 — This has been assigned to DVCPRO.

D-16 — A recording format for digital film images making use of standard D-1 recorders. The scheme was developed specifically to handle Quantel's Domino (Digital Optical for Movies) pictures and record them over the space that sixteen 625 line digital pictures would occupy. This way three film frames can be recorded or played every two seconds. Playing the recorder allows the film images to be viewed on a standard monitor; running at x16 speed shows full motion direct from the tape.

D/A (digital-to-analog) Converter — A circuit which converts a digital word—made up of a binary number — into analog voltage.

DAT (also known as R-DAT) — Stands for digital audio tape. The "R" for rotary head drum. Though the term DAT can apply to any means of digital audio recording, it is generally used to refer to the Japanese two-track miniature cassette standard for professional and consumer use.

Data recorders — Machines designed to record and replay data. Usually includes a high degree of error correction to ensure that the output data is absolutely correct and not easily editable. This compares with video recorders which will conceal missing or incorrect data by repeating adjacent areas of picture and are designed to allow direct access to every frame for editing.

DCT (Compression) — Discrete Cosine Transform - widely-used as the first stage of compression of digital video pictures. DCT operates on blocks of the picture (usually 8 x 8 pixels) resolving them into frequency, amplitudes and colors. By itself, DCT may not reduce the amount of data but it prepares it for following processes that will. JPEG and MPEG depend on DCT.

DD2 — Using D2 tape, data recorders have been developed offering (by computer standards) vast storage of data (that may include images). A choice of data transfer rates is available to suit computer interfaces. Like other computer storage media, images are not directly viewable, and editing is difficult..

Decibel (db) — A measurement standard of sound intensity and signal strength. These are units of measurement expressing ratios using logarithmic scales to give results related to human aural or visual perception. Many different attributes are given to a reference point termed 0 dB, for example a standard level of sound or power - subsequent measurements then being relative to that reference. Many performance levels are quoted in dB - for example signal to noise ratio (S/N). A logarithmic unit that expresses the ratio between a signal and a reference signal. For voltages, dB = 20 log (Vmeasured/Vnominal).

Depth of Field — The portion of an image which is in focus.

Diagnostics — Tests to check the correct operation of hardware and software. As digital systems continue to become more complex, built-in automated testing becomes an essential part of the equipment. Some extra hardware and software has to be added to make the tests operate. Digital systems with such provisions can often be quickly assessed by a trained service engineer, thus speeding repair.

Differential Gain — Variation in the gain of the chrominance signal as the luminance signal on which it rides affecting saturation, is varied from blanking to white level.

Differential Phase — Variation in the phase of the chrominance subcarrier as the luminance signal on which it rides is varied from blanking to white level.

Digital disk recorder (DDR) — Disk systems that record digital video. Their application is often as a replacement for a VTR or as video caches to provide extra digital video sources for far less cost than a DVTR. They have the advantage of not requiring pre-rolls or spooling, however, their operation is not true random access.

Digital keying and chroma keying — Digital chroma keying differs from analog in that it can key uniquely from any one of the 16 million colors of component digital video. It is then possible to key from relatively subdued colors, rather than relying on highly saturated colors which can cause color-spill problems on the foreground. A high quality digital chroma keyer examines each of the three components (Y,B-Y,R-Y) of the picture and generates a linear key for each. These are then combined into a composite linear key for the final keying operation. The use of three keys allows much greater subtlety of selection than with a chrominance-only key.

Digital Mixing — Digital mixing requires "scaling" each of two digital signals and then adding them. Mathematically this can be shown as:

$$A \times K = (\text{Mix})\ 1$$

$$B\,(1 - K) = (\text{Mix})\ 2$$

$$\text{Result} = (\text{Mix})\ 1 + (\text{Mix})\ 2$$

where A and B represent the two TV signals, and K the positional coefficient or value at any point of the mix. In a digital system, K will also be a number, normally an 8-bit value, to provide a smooth mix or dissolve.

When two 8-bit numbers are multiplied together, the result is a 16-bit number. When mixing, it is important to add the two 16-bit numbers to obtain an accurate result. This result must then be truncated or rounded to 8 bits for transmission to other parts of the digital system.

Truncation by simply dropping the lower bits of the partial result (Mix) 1 or (Mix) 2, to 10 bits, or even 12 or 14 bits, will introduce inaccuracies. Hence it is important that all partial results, e.g. (Mix) 1 and (Mix) 2, maintain 16-bit resolution. The final rounding of the result to 8 bits can reveal visible 1-bit artifacts - but these can be avoided with Dynamic Rounding.

Digital Signal Processing (DSP) — In audio, digital technology is used to perform traditionally analog audio processing functions. DSP can be used for equalization, compression and expansion, level adjustment, surround sound and general mixing functions. When applied to video cameras, DSP means that the analog signal from the CCD sensors is converted to a digital signal. It is then processed for signal separation, bandwidth settings and signal adjustments. After processing, the video signal either remains in the digital domain for recording by a digital VTR or is converted back into an analog signal for recording or transmission. DSP is also being used in other parts of the video chain, including VTRs, and switching and routing devices.

Digital Sound — A process of converting analog sound to numerical digits and returning those digits to analog sound.

Distortion — A deformity in a sound signal, normally caused by excessively high signal levels.

Digitizer — A system that converts an analog input into a digital representation.

Digitizing time — Time taken to record footage into a disk-based editing system. Digitizing time is often regarded as "dead" or "down time" but it can be reduced if some ititial selection of footage has been made—this is usually done during logging.

Direct Editing — Editing at a workstation that directly edits material stored in a server. This workstation depends totally on the server store. It allows background loading of new material, via several ports if required, and playout of finished results, while removing the need to duplicate storage or transfer material to/from the workstation and allowing any number of connected workstations to share work.

Discrete 5.1 Audio — This reproduces six separate (discrete) channels - Left, Center, Right, Left Rear, Right Rear and sub-woofer. All the five main channels have full frequency reponse which, together with a separate low-frequency sub-woofer, create a three-dimensional effect. Ths Dolby Digital (AC-3) standard for DTV employs 5.1 discrete channels.

Distortion — A deformity in a sound signal, normally caused by excessively high signal levels

Dither — In digital television, original analog pictures are converted to digits: a continuous range of luminance and chrominance values are translated into a set range of numbers. While some analog values will correspond exactly to numbers, others will fall in between. Given that there will always be some degree of noise in the original analog signal, the numbers may "dither" by one Least Significan Bit (LSB) between the two nearest values. This has the advantage of allowing the digital system to describe analog values between LSBs to give a very accurate digital rendition of the analog world.

Dolby Digital (also known as AC-3) — A digital audio compression system that uses auditory masking for compression. It works with from 1 to 5.1 channels of audio and can carry Dolby Surround coded two-channel material. It applies audio masking over all channels and dynamically allocates bandwidth from a 'common pool'. Dolby Digital is a constant bit rate system supporting from 64 kbps to 640 kbps rates; typically 64 kbps mono, 192 kbps two-channel, 320 kbps 35mm Cinema 5.1, 384 kbps Laserdisc/DVD 5.1 and DVD 448 kbps 5.1.

Dolby Noise Reduction — A group of systems designed to reduce noise in analog audio recordings. Dolby A, B, C and SR are each encode/decode systems that are incompatible with each other. Each has been incorporated in video recording systems.

Dominance — Field dominance defines whether a field type 1 or type 2 represents the start of a new TV frame. Usually it is field 1 but there is no fixed rule.

DRAM (Dynamic RAM (Random Access Memory)) — High-density, cost-effective memory chips (integrated circuits). The Japanese call them the "rice of electronics." DRAMs are used extensively in computers and generally in digital circuit design. In digital video equipment they make up stores to hold pictures. Being solid state, there are no moving parts and they offer the fastest access for data. Each bit is stored on a single transistor, and the chip must be powered and clocked to retain data. Current sizes available are 16 and 64 Mb (per chip), with 256 Mb now becoming commercially available.

Drop-frame (timecode) — The 525/60 line/field format used with the NTSC color coding system does not run exactly 60 fields per second but 59.94, or 29.97 frames per second—a difference of 1:1000. Timecode identifies 30 frames per second. Drop-frame timecode compensates by dropping two frames at every minute except the tenth. Note that the 625/50 PAL system is exact and does not require drop-frame. (see the chapter on Time Code).

DSS (Digital Satellite Service) — A term no longer used to describe DTV services distributed via satellite.

DTT (Digital Terrestrial Television) — The term used in Europe to describe the broadcast of digital television services using terrestrial frequencies.

DTV (Digital Television) — Everything that can be broadcast to the home digitally whether by cable, satellite or terrestrially.

DV (Digital Video)— This digital VCR format is a co-operation between Hitachi, JVC, Sony, Matsushita, Mitsubishi, Philips, Sanyo, Sharp, Thomson and Toshiba. It uses 6.35 mm (1/4-inch) wide tape in a range of products to record 525/60 or 626/50 video for the consumer (DV) and professional markets (Panasonic's DVCPRO and Sony's DVCAM). All models use digital intra-field DCT-based DV compression (about 5:1) to record 8-bit component digital video based on 13.5 luminance sampling. The consumer versions and DVCAM sample video at 4:1:1 (525/60) or 4:2:0 (625/50) video and provide two 16-bit/48 or 44.1 kHz, or four 12-bit/32 kHz audio channels onto a 4 hour 30-minute standard cassette (125 x 78 x 14.6 mm) or smaller 1 hour 'mini' cassette (66 x 48 x 12.2 mm). The video recording rate is 25 Mbps.

DVB (Digital Video Broadcasting) — The group, with over 200 members in 25 countries, that developed the preferred scheme for digital broadcasting in Europe. The DVB Group has put together a satellite system—DVB-S—that can be used with any transpopnder, current or planned, a matching cable system—DVB-C—and a digital terrestrial system (DVB-T).

DVB-T — The DVB-T is a transmission scheme for terrestrial digital television. Its specification was approved by ETSI in

February 1997 and DVB-T services are being deployed both within Europe and elsewhere.

DVD (Digital Versatile Disk) — A high-density development of the Compact Disk. It is the same size as a CD but stores from 4.38 GB (seven times CD capacity) on a single sided, single layer disk. DVDs can also be double sided or dual layer, storing even more data.

DVD-Video — DVD-Video uses MPEG-2 video compression, has multi-channel audio, subtitles and copy protection to record live video on a CD-sized disc. To maximize quality and playing time DVD-Video movies use Variable Bit Rate (VBR) coding where the bit rate varies with the demands of the material. A typical 525/60 TV format movie would have an average bit rate of 3.5 Mbps, but for sections with a great deal of movement it could peak at 8 or 9 Mbps. Even with 30 fps material, only 24 fps are recorded onto the disk—with the conversion back to 30 fps being performed in the player. This allows a 120-minute 24 fps movie to fit on a DVD-5. For continuous playback of long movies, DVD-9 can employ a "reverse spiral" technique so that the second layer starts where the first layer ends.

DVE (Digital Video Effects (systems)) — These have been supplied as separate machines but increasingly are being included as an integral part of a multipurpose system. The list of effects varies but will always include picture manipulations such as zoom and position and may go on to rotations, 3D perspective, page turns, picture bending, blurs, etc. Picture quality and control also vary widely.

DVTR (Digital Video Tape Recorder) — The first DVTR for commercial use was shown in 1986, complying with the ITU-R 601 component digital standard and the associated D-1 standard for DVTRs. It uses 19 mm cassettes recording 34, 78 or (using thinner tape) 94 minutes.

EBU (European Broadcasting Union) — An organization comprising European broadcasters that co-ordinates production and technical interests of European broadcasting. It has within its structure that a number of committees can make recommendations to ITU-R.

ECC (Error Check and Correct) — This system appends check data to a data packet in a communications channel or to a data block on a disk. It allows the receiving or reading system both to detect small errors in the data stream (caused by line noise or disk defects) and—provided they are not too long—correct them.

EDL (Edit Decision List) — A list of the commands and time code locations that which describe a series of edits that are often recorded on a floppy disk. EDLs can be produced during an off-line session and passed to the on-line suite to control the conforming of the final edit. In order to work across a range of equipment there are some widely adopted standards such as CMX 3400 and 3600.

Embedded audio — Audio that is carried within an SDI connection and simplifies cabling and routing. The standard (ANSI/SMPTE 272M-1994) allow up to four groups, each of four mono audio channels. Generally VTRs only support Group 1 but other equipment may use more.

Encoder — The circuit in a television camera that combines the red, blue and green information into composite color video. NTSC, PAL and SECAM have different encoding systems.

Encryption — The process of coding data so that a specific code or key is required to restore the original data. In conditional access broadcasts, this is used to make transmissions secure from unauthorized reception—for example, in satellite or cable systems.

ENG (Electronic News Gathering) — Term applied to a small portable outfit, with a broadcast quality TV camera, VTR and/or microwave link, usually used for news. The term was originated to distinguish between news gathering on film and video tape (electronic). Also refers to compatible studio or portable editing equipment.

Entry point — A point in a coded bit stream from which a complete picture can be decoded without first having to store data from earlier pictures. In the MPEG-2 frame sequence this can only be at an I-frame—the only frames encoded with no reference to others.

Equalization — The relative level of various frequency ranges in an audio path, controlled through adjustment of highs, mid-range and bass.

Ethernet — A form of Local Area Network (LAN) widely used for interconnecting computers and standardized in IEEE 802.3. It allows a wide variety of manufacturers to produce compatible interfaces and extend capabilities.

EXOR — The mathematical operation of EXclusively ORdering a number of data bits. The EXOR is widely used in data recovery. If the EXOR of a number of blocks of data is stored, when one of those blocks is lost, its contents can be deduced by EXORing the undamaged blocks with the stored EXOR.

FDDI (Fiber Data Distribution Interface) — A high-speed, fiber-optic data interface operating at up to 100 Mbps. FDDI is most commonly used as backbone data distribution for lower bandwidth networks such as Ethernet or Token Ring.

Fiber Channel — An integrated set of standards being developed by ANSI that is designed to improve data speeds between workstations, supercomputers, storage devices and displays while providing one standard for networking storage and data transfer.

Field — Half of the information in a frame of interlaced video. It represents one complete vertical scan of an image. The NTSC system rate is 59.94 fields per second.

Field Sequence — A television frame, or picture, comprises two fields. Each successive frame of component 525 and 625 line television repeats a pattern and so can be edited to frame boundaries—for example, film editing.

FireWire (IEEE 1394) — A serial interface, introduced by Apple Inc. in 1987, offering transfer rates of 100, 200 and 400 Mbps. Initially used to transfer data between mainframes without reformatting, it can now be extended to over 70 meters and 16 nodes.

Fragmentation — The scattering of data over a disk store caused by successive recording and deletion operations. This will eventually result in the store becoming slow—a situation that is not acceptable for video recording or replay. The slowing is caused by the increased time needed to access randomly distributed data.

Frame — Two fields of 262.5 interlaced scanning lines. In NTSC, 30 frames make up one complete video picture.

Frequency — The rate of occurrence of events in a system. The frequency of electrical signals is measured in Hertz, or cycles per second. Also referred to as the number of oscillations of a signal over a given period of time (usually one second). In audio, it refers to the tone or pitch of sound.

Frequency Response — A system's gain characteristic versus frequency. Frequency response is often stated as a range of signal frequencies over which gain varies by less than a specified amount.

FTP (File Transfer Protocol) — The high level Internet standard protocol for transferring files from one machine to another, FTP is usually implemented at application level.

Gamma — A term that describes the tonal reproduction characteristics of a video signal.

Gateway — A device connecting between two computer networks.

Generation (loss) — The signal degradation caused by successive recordings. Newly recorded material is first-generation, one re-recording, second, etc. This is a major concern in analog linear editing but less so using a digital suite. Non-compressed component DVTRs should provide at least 20 generations before any artifacts become noticeable but the very best multi-generation results are possible with disk-based systems. These can be re-recorded millions of times without causing dropouts or errors. Generations are effectively limitless.

In addition to the limitations of recording, the action of processors such as decoders and coders will make a significant contribution to generation loss. The decode/recode cycle of NTSC and PAL is well known for its limitations but equal caution is needed for digital video compression systems, especially those using MPEG, and the color space conversions that typically occur between computers handling RGB and video equipment using Y, Cr, Cb.

Global (control) — The top level of control in a multi-channel DVE system. A number of objects (channels) can be controlled at one time, for example to alter their opacity or to move them all together relative to a global axis - one which may be quite separate from the objects themselves. This way the viewing point of all the assembled objects can be changed. For example a cube assembled from six channels could be moved in 3D space as a single action from a global control.

GOP — Group Of Pictures. In an MPEG signal the GOP is a group of pictures, or frames between successive I-frames; the others being P and/or B-frames.

GPI (General Purpose Interface) — This is used for cueing equipment, usually by a contact closure. It is simple, frame accurate and can be easily applied over a wide range of equipment. Being electro-mechanical it cannot be expected to be as reliable as pure electronic controls.

Grand Alliance (Digital HDTV) — The United States grouping, formed in May 1993, to propose "the best of the best" HDTV systems. The participants were AT&T, General Instrument Corporation, Massachusetts Institute of Technology, Philips Consumer Electronics, David Sarnoff Research Center, Thomson Consumer Electronics and Zenith Electronics Corporation. The Grand Alliance has played a big part in arriving at the ATSC digital television standard that uses MPEG-2 video compression and the audio surround-sound compressed with Dolby AC-3. So that a wide variety of source material, including that from computers, can be best accommodated, two line standards are included, each operating at 24, 30 and 60 HZ.

Graphic Equalizer — A device with a group of volume faders, each assigned to adjust a portion of the audio frequency spectrum.

Graticule — The calibrated scale for quantifying information on a waveform monitor or vectorscope screen. The graticule can be silkscreened onto the CRT face plate (internal graticule), silk-screened onto a piece of glass or plastic that fits in front of the CRT (external graticule), or it can be electronically generated as part of the display.

Grid Compression — A proprietary video compression system developed and used by manufacturer Quantel in its editing product line.

GUI (Graphical User Interface) — A means of operating a system through the use of interactive graphics displayed on a screen.

HD D5 — A compressed recording system developed by Panasonic that uses compression at about 4:1 to record HD material on standard D5 cassettes. HD D5 supports both the 1080 and the 1035 interlaced line standards at both 60 Hz and 59.94 Hz field rates. Four uncompressed audio channels sampled at 40 kHz, 20 bits per sample are also supported.

HDCAM — A means of recording compressed high definition video on a tape format which uses the same cassette shell as Digital Betacam, although with a different tape formulation. The technology is aimed specifically at the USA and Japanese 1125/60 markets and supports both 1080 and 1035 active line standards. Quantization from 10 bits to 8 bits and DCT intra-frame compression are used to reduce the data rate. Four uncompressed audio channels sampled at 48 kHz, 20 bits per sample, are also supported.

HDTV Production Standard — An existing standard, known as SMPTE 240M, has been established for the production of high definition television programming. The standard has 1125 lines, 2:1 interlace, a 16:9 aspect ratio and is frame and field compatible with NTSC.

Headroom — The measurement in decibels (db) above 0 db a piece of equipment can process before clipping.

Helical Recording — A video recording method in which the information is recorded in diagonal tracks. Also known as slant-track recording.

Hertz (Hz) — One cycle per second. The term was derived from the name of the 19th Century German physicist, Heinrich Hertz.

High frequency — The treble or high end of the audio frequency spectrum.

HiPPI — High Performance Parallel Interface. Capable of transfers of up to 100 Mbps, it is targeted at high performance computing and optimized for applications involving streaming large volumes of data, rather than bursts of network activity. The parallel connection is limited to a short distance.

Horizontal Resolution — The number of vertical lines that can be observed by a video camera in a horizontal direction on a TV test chart.

Huffman coding — This compresses data by assigning short codes to frequently-occurring sequences and longer ones to those less frequent. Assignments are held in a Huffman Table. The more likely a sequence is to occur the shorter the code will be that replaces it. It is widely used in video compression systems where it contributes a 2:1 reduction in data.

ICMP (Internet Control Message Protocol) — The part of the Internet Protocol that handles the error and control messages data link layer. The second layer of the Open Systems Interconnect (OSI) communications model. It puts messages together and co-ordinates their flow.

IDTV (Integrated Digital TV Receiver) — For viewers to receive DTV services they will require a new type of receiver either in the form of a new television set (IDTV) or a set top box.

I-frames — Contain data to construct a whole picture as their compression is intra-frame, very similar to JPEG.

Illegal colors — Colors that force a color system to go outside its normal bounds. Usually a result of electronically painted images rather than direct camera outputs.

Image Enhancer — A device used to sharpen transition lines in a video picture.

Insertion Gain — The gain (or loss) in overall signal amplitude introduced by a piece of equipment in the signal path. Insertion gain is expressed as a percent (Vout – Vin)/Vin x 100.

Integrated system — Single system that contains enough tools to complete a whole area of operation.

Inter-frame (compression) — Compression that involves more than one frame. Inter-frame compression compares consecutive frames to remove common elements and arrive at "difference" information. MPEG-2 uses two types of inter-frame processed pictures—the "P" (predictive) and "B" (bi-directional) frames. As B and P frames are not complete in themselves (but relate to other adjacent frames), they cannot be edited independently.

Interlaced Scanning — A display technique in which each TV picture, or frame, is produced using two sequential fields. One field contains the off-numbered lines of the frame, and the other the even-numbered lines. The TV tube is scanned twice, with the lines of two fields interleaved, or interlaced. The technique eliminates visible flicker which can be annoying at low frame rates. For analog systems this is the reason for having odd numbers of lines in a pictures, e.g. 525 and 625, so that each field contains a half-line, causing the constant vertical scan to place the lines of one field between those of the other. The technique improves the portrayal of motion and reduces picture flicker without having to increase the picture rate. Disadvantages are that it reduces vertical definition to 70 or 80 percent (known as the "Kell Factor") of the progressive or non-interlaced definition and tends to cause horizontal picture detail to dither.

Interpolation (spatial) — When repositioning or resizing a digital image, more, less or different pixels are required from those in the original image. Replicating or removing pixels causes unwanted artifacts. For better results the new pixels have to be interpolated—calculated by making weighted averages of adjacent pixels—to produce a more transparent result. The quality of the results will depend on the techniques used and the number of pixels or area of original picture used to calculate the result.

Interpolation (temporal) — Interpolation between the same point in space on successive frames. It can be used to provide motion smoothing and is extensively used in standard converters to reduce the judder caused by the 50/60 Hz field rate difference. The technique can also be adapted to create frame averaging for special effects.

IRE — A relative unit of measure (named for the Institute of Radio Engineers) on a waveform monitor. One IRE equals 1/140th of the composite video signal's peak-to-peak voltage.

ISDN (Integrated Services Digital Network) — Allows data to be transmitted at high speed over the public telephone network. ISDN operates from the Basic Rate of 64 kbps to the Primary Rate of 2 Mbps.

ISO (International Standards Organization) — An international organization that specifies international standards, including those for networking protocols, compression systems, disks, etc.

ISO layer — A model containing seven conceptual layers, with each providing a set of services that are used in network operations.

ITC (Independent Television Commission) — It is responsible as a regulator, both legally and technically, for all independent programming in the United Kingdom.

ITS (The Association of Imaging Technology and Sound) — A United States-based international association of members from the industry dedicated to promoting and furthering the use of video as a medium of communication.

ITU (International Telecommunications Union) — The United Nations regulatory body covering all forms of communication. The ITU sets mandatory standards and regulates the radio frequency spectrum. ITU-R (previously CCIR) deals with radio spectrum management issues and regulation while ITU-T (previously CCITT) deals with telecommunications standardization.

ITU-R 601 — (Full title: ITU-R Rec. BT. 601-5.) This standard defines the encoding parameters of digital television for studios. It is the international standard for digitizing component television video in both 525- and 625-line systems and is derived from the SMPTE RP125. ITU-R 601 deals with both color difference (Y, R-Y, B-Y) and RGB video and defines sampling systems, RGB/Y, R-Y, B-Y matrix values and filter characteristics. It does not define the electro-mechanical interface. ITU-R 601 is normally taken to refer to color difference component digital video (rather than RGB), for which it defines 4 : 2 : 2 sampling at 13.5 Mhz with 720 luminance samples per active line and 8 or 10-bit digitizing.

Some headroom is allowed with black at level 16 (not 0) and white at level 235 (not 255) - to minimize clipping of noise and overshoots. Using 8-bit digitizing approximately 16 million unique colors are possible. The sampling frequency of 13.5 Mhz was chosen to provide a politically acceptable common sampling standard between 525/60 and 625/50 systems, being a multiple of 2.25 Mhz, the lowest common frequency to provide a static sampling pattern for both.

ITU -R 656 — Interfaces for digital component video signals in 525-line and 625-line television systems. The international standard for interconnecting digital television equipment operating to the 4 : 2 : 2 standard defined in ITU-R 601. It defines blanking, embedded sync words, the video multiplexing formats used by both the parallel (now rarely used) and serial interfaces, the electrical characteristics of the inter face and the mechanical details of the connectors.

Java — A general purpose programming language developed by Sun Microsystems and known for its widespread use on the World Wide Web. Unlike other software, programs written in Java can run on any platform type, so long as they contain a Java Virtual Machine.

JPEG (Joint Photographic Experts Group) — JPEG is a standard for the data compression of still pictures (intra-frame). Its work has been involved with pictures coded to the ITU-R 601 standard. It offers data compression of between two and 100 times and three levels of processing are defined: the baseline, extended and lossless encoding.

JPEG baseline compression coding, which is the most common in both the video post-production and computer environments, starts with applying DCT to 8 x 8 pixel blocks of the picture, transforming them into frequency and amplitude data. This itself may not reduce data but then the generally less visible high frequencies can be divided by a high factor (reducing many to zero), and the more visible low frequencies by a lower factor. The factor can be set according to data size or picture quality requirements - effectively adjusting the compression ratio. The final stage is Huffman coding which is lossless but can further reduce data by about 2 : 1.

Baseline JPEG coding is very similar to the I-frames of MPEG. The main difference is that they use slightly different Huffman tables. (see Huffman Coding)

Keycode — A machine-readable bar-code printed along the edge of camera negative stock outside the perforations. It gives key numbers, film type, film stock manufacturer code, and offset from zero-frame reference mark (in perforations). It has applications in telecine for accurate film-to-tape transfer and in editing for conforming negative cuts to EDLs.

Keyframe — A set of parameters defining a point in a transition, e.g. of a DVE effect. For example, a keyframe may define a picture size, position and rotation. Any digital effect must have a minimum of two keyframes, start and finish, although more complex moves will use more—maybe as many as 100. Increasingly, more parameters are becoming "keyframeable," e.g., they can be programmed to transition between two or more states. Examples are color correction to make a steady change of color and keyer settings to make an object slowly appear or disappear.

Keying — The process of selectively overlaying an area of one picture (or clip) onto another. If the switch between the overlaid and background pictures is simply a hard switch this can lead to jagged edges of the overlaid or keyed pictures. They are usually subjected to further processing to give a cleaner more convincing result. The whole technology of deriving a key signal has expanded through the use of digital technology, so that many operations may be used together.

Kilohertz (kHz) — One thousand cycles per second.

Latency — The delay between requesting and accessing data. For disk drives, it refers to delay due to disk rotation. The faster a disk spins the quicker it will be at the position where the required data can start to be read. As disk diameters have decreased, rotational (spindle) speeds have tended to increase, but there is still much variation. Modern 3 1/2-inch drives typically have spindle speeds of between 3,600 and 7,200 revolutions per minute. So, one revolution is completed in 16 or 8 ms respectively. This is represented in the disk specification as average latency of 8 or 4 ms. This is reduced to 3 ms in the latest drives operating at 10,000 RPM.

Layer(ing) — A collection or "pack" of clip layers can be assembled to form a composite layered clip. Layers may be background video or foreground video with its associated matte element. The ability to compose many layers simultaneously means the result can be seen as it is composed and adjustments made as necessary.

Level — Picture source format ranging from about VHS quality to full HDTV.

Linear (editing) — The process of editing footage that can only be accessed or played in the sequence recorded. Tape is linear in that it has to be spooled for access to any material and can only play pictures in the order they are recorded.

Linear (keying) — Selective overlay of one video signal over another, the ratio of foreground to background at any point being determined on a linear scale by the level of the key (control) signal. This form of keying provides the best possible edges and anti-aliasing. It is essential for the realistic keying of semi-transparent effects such as transparent shadows, through windows and partial reflections.

Low frequency — The bass or low end of the audio frequency spectrum.

Low-Frequency Amplitude Distortion — A variation in amplitude level that occurs as a function of frequencies below 1 Mhz.

LSB (Least Significant Bit) — Binary numbers are represented by a series of ones and zeros. For example:

Binary 1110 = Decimal 14

In this example the right-most binary digit, 0, is the LSB—the least significant bit—here representing the absence of 20 i.e. 1.

LTC (Longitudinal Timecode) — Timecode recorded on liner track on tape and read by a static head. (see Chapter on Time Code.)

Luminance — A component—the black and white or brightness element—of an image. It is written as Y, so the Y in Y (B-Y) (R-Y), YUV, YIQ, Y, Cr, Cb is the luminance information of the signal.

The luminance signal amplitude varies in proportion to the brightness of the televised scene and is therefore capable of producing a complete monochrome picture. In a color TV system, the luminance signal is usually derived from the RGB signals, originating from a camera or telecine, by matrix or summation of approximately:

$$Y = 0.3R + 0.6G + 0.1B$$

Luminance Nonlinearity — The degree to which the luminance signal gain is affected by changes in luminance level.

Main Level (ML) — A range of allowed picture parameters defined by MPEG-2 with maximum resolution equivalent to ITU-R 601.

Macroblock — A group of picture blocks, usually four (16 x 16 pixels overall), that are analyzed during MPEG coding to give an estimate of the movement of particular elements of the picture between frames. This generates the motion vectors that are then used to place the macroblocks in decoded pictures.

Metadata — Data about data. Data about the video but not the video bits themselves. This is important for labeling and finding data—either in a "live" data stream or an archive. Within the studio, digital technology allows far more information to be added. Some believe metadata will revolutionize every aspect of production and distribution. Metadata existed long before digital networks: video time code and film frame numbers are two examples.

Megahertz (MHz) — A frequency of (M) millions of cycles (or samples) per second.

Moore's Law — A prediction for the rate of development of modern electronics. This has been expressed in a number of ways but in general states that the density of information storable in silicon roughly doubles every year. Or, the performance of silicon will double every 18 months, with proportional decreases in cost. For more than two decades this prediction has held true. Moore's law initially talked about silicon but it could be applied to disk drives: the capacity of disk drives doubles every two years.

Motion vectors — Direction and distance information used in MPEG coding and some standards converters to describe the movement of macroblocks (of picture) from one picture to the next.

MPEG (Moving Picture Experts Group) — MPEG is involved in defining standards for the data compression of moving pictures. Its work follows on from that of JPEG to add inter-frame compression, the extra compression potentially available through similarities between successive frames of moving pictures.

Four MPEG standards were originally planned but the accommodation of HDTV within MPEG-2 has meant that MPEG-3 is now redundant. MPEG-4 is intended for non-broadcast applications, so interest for the television industry lies mainly with MPEG-2, and partly with MPEG-1.

MPEG-1 — A compression scheme designed to work at 1.2 Mbps, the data rate of CD-ROM, so that video could be played from CDs. Its quality is not sufficient for TV broadcast.

MPEG-2 — A family of inter- and intra-frame compression systems designed to cover a wide range of requirements from "VHS quality" all the way to HDTV through a series of compression algorithm "profiles" and image resolution "levels." With data rates between 4 and 100 Mbps, the family includes the compression system that delivers digital TV to the home and that puts video onto DVDs.

MSB (Most Significant Bit) — Binary numbers represented by a series of ones and zeros.

M-S Stereo — A recording technique that uses "mid" and "side" sound information to create a mono-compatible stereo sound image.

MTBF (Mean Time Between Failure) — A statistical assessment of the average time taken for a unit to fail, or, a measure of predicted reliability. The MTBF of a piece of equipment is dependent on the reliability of each of its components. Generally the more components the lower the MTBF, so packing more into one integrated circuit can reduce the component count and increase the reliability. Modern digital components are highly reliable. Even complex electro-mechanical assemblies such as disk drives now offer MTBFs of up to 1,000,000 hours—some 110 years.

Multiplex — A term for the group of compressed video channels multiplexed into single transmission feed. The term "Bouquet" has also been used in this context.

Network layer — 1) In TCP/ICP, the network layer is responsible for accepting IP (Internet Protocol) datagrams and transmitting them over a specific network. 2) The third layer of the OSI reference model of data communications.

NFS (Network File System) — Developed by Sun Microsystems, NFS allows sets of computers to access each other's files as if they were locally stored. NFS has been implemented on many platforms and is considered an industry standard.

Nibble — 8 binary bits = 1 Byte

4 binary bits = 1 Nibble

NICAM (Near Instantaneously Companded Audio Multiplex) — This digital audio system used in Europe uses compression techniques to present "very near CD" quality stereo into the transmitted TV signal.

Noise (Random) — Irregular level fluctuations of a low order of magnitude. All analog video signals contain random noise. Ideally for digital sampling the noise level should not occupy more than on the LSB of the digital dynamic range. Pure digitally generated signals however do not contain any noise—a fact that can be a problem under certain conditions. Generally, in ITU-R 601 systems fine noise is invisible; coarse or large area noise may be perceptible under controlled viewing conditions.

Non-additive mix — A mix of two pictures that is controlled by their luminance levels relative to each other as well as a set mix value K (between 0 and 1): e.g. the position of a switcher lever arm. A and B sources are scaled by factors K and 1-K but the output signal is switched to that which has the greatest instantaneous product of the scaling and the luminance values. The output of any pixel is either signal A or B but not a mix of each. So if K = 0.5, where picture A is brighter than B, then only A will be seen. Thus, two clips of single subject shot against a black background can be placed in one picture.The term has also come to encompass some of the more exotic types of picture mixing available today: for example, to describe a mix that could add smoke to a foreground picture (also known as an additive mix).

Non-drop-frame timecode — Timecode that does not use drop-frame and always identifies 30 frames per second. This way the timecode running time will not exactly match normal time. (See chapter on Time Code.)

Non-linear (editing) — Non-linear means not linear; that the recording medium is not tape and editing can be performed in a non-linear sequence—not necessarily the sequence of the program. It describes editing with quick access to source clips and record space (usually using computer disks to store footage). This removes the spooling and pre-rolls of VTR operations.

Notch Filter — A device that allows the lowering of the level of a narrow portion of frequency spectrum. Useful in cutting out unwanted sounds.

NTSC (National Television Systems Committee) — National Television Systems Committee. A broadcast (U.S.) engineering group that developed a black & white television standard in the early 1940s and a color standard in the early 1950s. Those standards — now called NTSC — are currently used in the United States, Canada, Mexico and Japan. The bandwidth of the NTSC system is 4.2 MHz for the luminance signal and 1.3 and 0.4 MHz for the I and Q color channels.

NVOD — Near video on demand. Rapid access to program material on demand achieved by providing the same program on a number of channels with staggered start times. Many of the hundreds of TV channels soon to be readily available will be made up of NVOD services. These are typically delivered by a disk-based transmission server.

Operating system — The base program that manages a computer and gives control of the functions designed for general purpose usage - not for specific application.

Pack — A set of clips, mattes and settings for DVE, color corrector, keyer, etc., that are used together to make a video layer in a composited picture.

PAL (Phase Alternating Line) — The European color television system using a 50 cycle power source, 625 scan lines per frame and 25 frames per second. It was derived from the NTSC system but by reversing the phase of the reference color burst on alternate lines (Phase Alternating Line), the system is able to correct for hue shifts caused by phases errors in the transmission path. Bandwidth for the PAL-I system is typically 5.5 MHz luminance and 1.3 MHz for each color difference signals, U and V.

PAL-M — a version of the PAL standard using a 525 line 60-field structure. Used only in parts of South America.

PALplus — A widescreen encoding system compatible with existing 4:3 PAL receivers as well as new 16:9 PALplus receivers. PALplus uses the normal 626/50 line/field structure as well as PAL color coding so that existing 4:3 receivers can show the 16:9 wide aspect color picture in letterbox format spread over 432 TV lines (instead of the normal 576). The 16:9 PALplus receivers display the full 576 lines with the additional high frequency detail added to the pictures from the Helper signal transmitted above and below the central band of 432 lines. The Helper appears as black on normal receivers. The system relies on digital processing in the encoder and in each widescreen PALplus receiver.

One of the aims of the system is to give a soft start to new TV formats and resolutions. In the studio the normal ITU-R 601 signal with 13.5 MHz sampling is recommended, thus allowing much existing production equipment, including component digital VTRs, to be used with no change (the shape of the picture has changed but the nature of the signal has not). Mixers, character generators, DVEs and graphics systems need to take account of the geometry change but the core electronics—including framestores—are unaffected. The biggest alterations come with picture monitors and cameras, where existing units can be used with anamorphic lenses or wide (16:9) CCD chips.

Parallel processing — Using several processors simultaneously with the aim of increasing speed over single processor performance. It often refers to array processor computer hardware that carries out multiple (often identical), mathematical computations at the same time. Generally array processors are designed with specific tasks in mind and thus are not suitable for running complex operational software. Due to system administration and the fact that not all processors will complete their tasks at the same moment, causing waiting time, the increase in speed gained by sharing the task is generally not proportional to the number of channels available. Due to the very different structure of a parallel processing computer, software designed to run on a single processor system may well need very major changes to run on a parallel system.

Parametric Equalizer — In addition to controlling bass and treble, it has the ability to raise and lower the level of a certain frequency. A parametric equalizer is useful in pulling certain frequencies above the noise in a tape.

Pedestal — Two meanings in video. It can mean the portion of the video signal that reproduces black or a camera mounting device which allows "up" or "down" camera movement.

P-frames — Used from Main Profile video compression upwards, these contain only predictive information (not a whole picture) generated by looking at the difference between the present frame and the previous one.

Pixel (or Pel) — A shortened version of "Picture cell' or "Picture element." The name given to one sample of picture information. Pixel can refer to an individual sample of R, G, B luminance or chrominance, or sometimes to a collection of such samples if they are co-sited and together produce one picture element. CCD semiconductors used in today's best NTSC cameras have in excess of 1,000,000 pixels.

Processing Amplifier — An analog circuit that allows the luminance and chrominance parameters in a video camera to be controlled.

Progressive Scanning (also known as Sequential Scanning) — A video format in which each scanning line follows the previous in progression. Unlike interlace scanning, the field and frame rate are identical in a progressive scanning system. This method of scanning lines down a screen is used with computers monitors, where all the lines of a picture are displayed in one vertical scan. There are no fields or half pictures as with interlace scans. A high picture rate is required to give good movement portrayal and to avoid a flicker display. For television applications this implies a high bandwidth or data rate. The vertical definition is equal to its number of lines and does not show the dither of detail associated with interlaced scans.

Positioning time — The time taken for the read/write heads of a disk drive to be positioned over a required track. Average positioning time is the time to reach any track from any track. A high performance modern disk will offer around 7 ms for the former and 14 ms for the latter.

Quantizing — The process of sampling an analog waveform to provide packets of digital information to represent the original analog signal.

RAID (Redundant Array of Independent Disks) — A grouping of standard disk drives together with a RAID controller to create storage that acts as one disk to provide performance beyond that available from individual drives. Primarily designed for operation with computers, RAIDs can offer very high capacities, fast data transfer rates and much increased security of data. The latter is achieved through disk redundancy so that disk errors or failures can be detected and corrected.

A series of RAID configurations is defined by levels and they start counting from zero. Different levels are suited to different applications.

Level 0—No redundancy—benefits only of speed and capacity—generated by combining a number of disks.

Level 1—Complete mirror system featuring two sets of disks (both reading writing the same data). This has the benefits of level 0 plus the security of full redundancy, but at twice the cost. Some performance advantage can be gained in read because only one copy need be read, so two reads can be occurring simultaneously.

Level 2—An array of nine disks. Each byte is recorded with one bit on each of eight disks and a parity bit recorded to the ninth. This level is rarely used.

Level 3—An array of n+1 disks recording 512 byte sectors on each of the n disks to create n x 512 'super sectors' + 1 x 512 parity sector on the additional disk which is used to check the data. The minimum unit of transfer is a whole superblock. This is most suitable for systems in which large amounts of sequential data are transferred—such as for audio and video. For these it is the most efficient RAID level since it is never necessary to read/modify/write the parity block. It is less suitable for database types of access in which small amounts of data need to be transferred at random.

Level 4—Similar to level 3 but individual blocks can be transferred. Where data is written it is necessary to read the old data and parity blocks before writing the new data as well as the updated parity block which reduces performance.

Level 5—As level 4, but the role of the parity disk is rotated for each block in level 4 the parity disk receives excessive load for writes and no load for reads. In level 5 the load is balanced across the disks.

Soft RAID—A RAID system implemented by low level software in the host system instead of a dedicated RAID controller. While saving on hardware, operation consumes some of the host's power.

Relative Chroma Level — See chrominance-to-luminance gain.

Resolution — The measure of image detail in a television system.

Calculated in resolvable lines per picture width and height. Although it is influenced by the number of pixels in the display (e.g. high definition approximately 2000 x 1000, broadcast SDTV 720 x 576 [PAL] or 720 x 487 [NTSC]) note that the pixel numbers do not define the resolution but merely the resolution of that part of the equipment. The quality of lenses, display tubes, film processes, edit systems and film scanner, etc. must be taken into account.

Resolution Independent — A term used to describe the notion of equipment that can operate at more than one resolution. Most dedicated video equipment is designed to operate at a single resolution although some modern equipment, especially that using the ITU-R 601 standard, can switch between the specific formats and aspect ratios of 525/60 and 625/50.

RF Output — RF stands for radio frequency. An RF output on a video recorder allows picture and sound to be played over a vacant channel in a conventional television receiver.

RGB — The red, green and blue components of the video signal.

RIP — Raster Image Process. The method of converting vector data into raster image form, making it suitable for use in a television picture. Vector data is size independent and so has to be RIPped to a given size. RIPping to produce high quality results requires significant processing, especially if interactive operation is required.

Rotoscoping — The practice of using frames of live footage as reference for painting animated sequences. While the painting will always be down to the skill of the artist, modern graphics equipment, integrated with a video disk store, makes rotoscoping quick and easy.

RP 125 — SMPTE Recommended Practice 125. The bit-parallel digital interface for component video signals. One of the forerunners of ITU-R 656.

RS 232 — A standard for serial data communications defined by EIA standard RS-232 and designed for short distances only (up to 10 meters). It uses single-ended signaling with a conductor per channel plus a common ground which is easy to arrange but susceptible to interference—hence the distance limitation.

RS 422 — Not to be confused with 4:2:2 sampling, this is a standard for serial data communications defined by EIA standard RS-422. It uses current-loop, balanced signaling with a twisted pair of conductors per channel; two pairs for bi-directional operation. It is more costly than RS 232 but has a high level of immunity to interference. It can also operate over reasonably long distances (up to 300m/1000ft). RS 422 is widely used for control links around production and post areas for a range of equipment.

Run-length coding — A system for compressing data. The principle is to store a pixel value along with a message detailing the number of adjacent pixels with that same value. This gives a very efficient way of storing large areas of flat color and text. It's not so efficient with pictures from a camera, where the random nature of the information, including noise, may mean that more data is produced than was needed for the original picture.

Saturation — The variable property of color that is determined by its purity, or its lack of dilution by white light. Highly saturated colors are vivid, while less saturated colors appear pastel.

Scaling — Analog video signals have to be scaled prior to digitizing in an A/D converter so that the total amplitude of the signal makes full use of the available levels in the digital system. The ITU-R 601 digital coding standard specifies black to be set at level 16 and white at 235. Computer systems tend to operate with a different scaling: black set to level 0 and white at 255, but for color they usually use RGB from 0-255. Going between computers and TV requires processing to change color space and scaling.

SCH — Subcarrier to horizontal sync timing relationship. Chrominance information in PAL and NTSC is created by a color subcarrier whose frequency is mathematically related to the line and field scanning rates. PAL and NTSC expect this relationship to remain fixed otherwise the picture may hop, jump or be subjected to further processing that may change its quality.

Scrub (audio) — Replay of audio tracks at a speed and pitch corresponding to jog speed; as heard with analog audio tape"'scrubbing" past an audio head. This feature, which is natural for fixed-head analog recorders may be provided on a digital system recording on disks to help set up cues.

SCSI (The Small Computer Systems Interface) — This is a very widely used high data rate, general purpose parallel interface. A maximum of eight devices can be connected to one bus. For example a controller, and up to seven disks or devices of different sorts (e.g., Winchester disks, optical disks, tape drives, etc.) may be shared between several computers.

SCSI specifies a cabling standard (50 way), a protocol for sending and receiving commands and their format. It is intended as a device-independent interface so the host computer needs no details about the peripherals it controls. But with two versions (single-ended and balanced), two types of connector and numerous variations in the level of implementation of the interface, SCSI devices are not "plug-and-play" on a computer with which they have not been tested. Also, with total bus cabling for the popular single ended configuration limited to 6 meters, all devices must be close.

SCSI has continued development over a number of years resulting in the following range of maximum transfer rates:

Standard SCSI	5 M transfer/sec. (max)
Fast SCSI	10 M transfer/sec. (max)
Ultra SCSI	20 M transfer/sec. (max)
Ultra SCSI 2 (LVD)	40 M transfer/sec. (max)

For each of these there is the 8-bit "narrow" bus (1 byte per transfer) or the 16-bit Wide bus (2 bytes per transfer), so Wide Ultra SCSI 2 is designed to transfer data at a maximum rate of 80 MBps. Continuous rates achieved from the disk drives will be considerably less—currently 12-17 MBps is top performance. Also, achieving this will depend on the performance of the connected device.

SDDI (Serial Digital Data Interface) — This is designed for serial digital information to be carried over a standard SDI (video) path. Although the information contained in the SDDI stream will often include video, it can also carry non-video data.

SDTI (Serial Digital Transport Interface) — Based on SDI, this does not define the format of the signals carried but brings the possibility to create a number of packetized data formats for broadcast use. Currently these are expected to include a Sony native format, a MPEG-2 transport stream format, and MPEG-2 audio/video/metadata elementary stream format, a DVCAM format (QSDI), and a DVCPRO format (CSDI).

SDTV (Standard Definition Television) — A digital television system in which the quality is approximately equivalent to that of NTSC or PAL. Pictures might be derived from an ITU-R 601 source which has been subjected to bit-rate compression. Currently, 480-lines is considered the most popular SDTV format.

SECAM (Sequential Color And Memory) — A color television system using a 50 cycle power source, 625 scan lines per frame and 25 frames per second. Color signals are encoded differently from PAL system. Used in France, parts of the Commonwealth of Independent States.

Serial control — Generally used to describe remote control of a device via a data line. The control data is transmitted down the line in serial form, i.e. one control signal after another.

Serial Digital Interface (SDI) — The standard based on a 270 Mbps transfer rate. This is a 10-bit, scrambled, polarity independent interface, with common scrambling for both component ITU-R 601 and composite digital video and four groups each of four channels of embedded digital audio. Most new broadcast digital equipment includes SDI, which greatly simplifies its installation and signal distribution. It uses the standard 75 ohm BNC connector and coax cable as is commonly used for analog video and can transmit the signal over 200 meters (depending on cable type).

Signal-to-noise-ratio (S/N or SNR) — The ratio of noise to picture signal information, usually expressed in dB. Digital source equipment is theoretically capable of producing pure noise-free images that would have an infinite signal to noise ratio. But these, by reason of their purity, may cause contouring artifacts if processed without special attention.

To express the realistic signal to noise capability of a digital system the equation given is: S/N (dB) = 6N + 6, where N is the number of bits. Hence an 8-bit system gives 54 dB S/N. This would be the noise level of continuous LSB dither and would only be produced over the whole picture by digitizing a flat field (i.e. equal gray over the whole picture) set at a level to lie midway between two LSBs. Other test methods give a variety of results, mostly producing higher S/N figures. Generally, the higher the ratio, the better.

SMPTE (Society of Motion Picture and Television Engineers) — An industry organization which sets technical standards and specifications in the film and television industries.

SRAM (Static Random Access Memory) — This type of memory chip in general behaves like dynamic RAM (DRAM) except that static RAMs retain data in a six transistor cell needing only power to operate (DRAMs require clocks as well). Because of this, current available capacity is lower than DRAM, and costs are higher, but speed is also greater.

Statistical multiplexing — Increases the overall efficiency of a multi-channel digital television transmission multiplex by varying the bit-rate of each of its channels to take only that share of the total multiplex bit-rate it needs at any one time. The share apportioned to each channel is predicted statistically with reference to its current and recent-past demands.

Storage capacity (for video) — Using the ITU-R 601 4:2:2 digital coding standard, each picture occupies a large amount of storage space, especially when related to computer storage devices such as DRAM and disks. So much so, that the numbers can become confusing unless a few benchmark statistics are remembered. Fortunately the units of mega, giga and tera make it easy to express the vast numbers involved. Storage capacities for video can all be worked out directly from the 601 standard. Bearing in mind that sync words and blanking can be re-generated and added at the output, only the active picture area need be stored. In line with the modern trend of may disk drive manufacturers, here kilobyte, megabyte and gigabyte are taken as 103, 106 and 109 respectively.

Subcarrier — The 3.58 MHz signal that is modulated by color information to form a chrominance signal.

Sub-pixel — A spatial resolution smaller than that of pixels. Although digital images are composed of pixels, it can be very useful to resolve image detail to smaller than pixel size, i.e. sub-pixel. For example, the data for generating a smooth curve on the screen needs to be created to a finer accuracy than the pixel grid itself - otherwise the curve will look jagged. Again, when tracking an object in a scene or executing a DVE move, the size and position of the manipulated picture must be calculated, and the picture resolved, to a finer accuracy than the pixels—otherwise the move will appear jerky.

Sweep Signal — A signal whose frequency is varied through a given frequency range.

Sync — A –40 IRE pulse used to ensure correct timing relationships throughout the television system.

TBC (Time Base Corrector) — This is often included as a part of a VTR to correct the timing inaccuracies of the pictures coming from tape. Early models were limited by their dependence on analog storage devices, such as glass delay lines. This meant that VTRs, such as the original quadruplex machines, had to be mechanically highly accurate and stable to keep the replayed signal within the correction range (window) of the TBC (just a few microseconds). The introduction of digital techniques made larger stores economic so widening the correction window and reducing the need for specially accurate mechanics. The digital TBC has had a profound effect on VTR design.

Tracking (image) — Following a defined point, or points, in a series of pictures in a clip. Initially this was performed by hand, using a DVE. Not only was this laborious but it was also difficult or impossible to create sufficiently accurate results. This is usually due to the DVE keyframe settings being restricted to pixel/line accuracy. More recently, image tracking has become widely used, thanks to the availability of automatic point tracking operating to sub-pixel accuracy. Used within an integrated system the tracking data can be applied to control DVE picture moving for such applications as removal of film weave, replacing objects in moving video, etc.

Truncation — Removal of the least significant bits (LSB) of a digital word, as might be necessary when connecting 10-bit into 8-bit equipment, or handling the 16-bit result of a digital video mix. If not carefully handled it can lead to unpleasant artifacts on video signals.

Uncommitted editing — Editing where the decisions are made and the edits completed but any can still be easily changed. This is only possible in a true random access edit suite where the edits need only comprise the original footage and the edit instruction. Nothing is re-recorded so nothing is committed. This way, decisions about any aspect of the edit can be changed at any point during the session, regardless of where the changes are required.

Vaporware — Software or hardware that is promised or talked about but is not yet completed—and my never be released.

Variable bit-rate (VBR) compression — While some video compression schemes are designed to produce fixed sized image files, VBR offers the possibility of fixing, or controlling picture quality by varying the bit-rate. This allows the images that require little data, like still frames in MPEG-2, to use little data and to use more for those that need it, to maintain quality. The result can be an overall saving in storage (as on DVDs), or more efficient allocation of total available bit-rate in a multi-channel broadcast multiplex.

Vector fonts — Fonts that are stored as vector information (or sets of lengths and angles to describe each character). This offers the benefits of using relatively little storage and the type can be cleanly displayed at virtually any size. However, it does require that the type is RIPped before it can be used, thus requiring significant processing power if it is to be used interactively for sizing and composing into a graphic.

VITC (Vertical Interval Timecode) — Timecode information in digital form, added into the vertical blanking of a TV signal. This can be read by the video heads from tape at any time pictures are displayed, even during jogging and freeze but not during spooling. This effectively complements LTC ensuring timecode can be read at any time. (See chapter on Time Code.)

VU Meter — VU means volume unit. A VU meter displays these units on an audio device. Used for monitoring audio levels.

WAV — An audio file format developed by Microsoft that carries audio which can be coded in many different formats. Metadata in WAV files describes the coding used. To play a WAV file requires the appropriate decoder to be supported by the playing device.

Wavelet — A compression technique in which the signal is broken down into a series of frequency bands. This can be very efficient but, as the processing is slow, it is not well suited to video.

White Balance — The color balancing procedure for a video camera. Allows the camera to "see" white under a given lighting condition.

Widescreen — A TV picture display that has a wider aspect ratio than the normal 4:3 and uses the normal 525/60 or 625/50 line/field scans. Widescreen 16:9 is also the aspect ratio used for HDTV. The widescreen aspect ratio is usually 16:9 but there are some intermediate schemes, such as 14:9. Widescreen is used on some analog transmissions as well as many digital transmissions.

Winchester disks — A form of hard disk where several disk platters and their associated heads are sealed within a case in a clean room. They offer very reliable operation with MTBFs of 1,000,000 hours and more. The absence of dust allows the read/write heads to be kept close to the disk surface so that data can be packed more tightly than otherwise possible.

Word Clock — Clock information associated with AES/EBU digital audio channels. Synchronous audio sampled at 48 kHz is most commonly used in TV. The clock is needed to synchronize the audio data so it can be read.

WORM — Write Once/Read Many - describes storage devices on which data, once written, cannot be erased or re-written. Being optical, WORMs offer very high recording densities and are removable, making them very useful for archiving.

Y, Cr, Cb — The digital luminance and color difference signals in ITU-R 601 coding. The Y luminance signal is sampled at 13.5 MHz and the two color difference signals are sampled at 6.75 MHz co-sited with one of the luminance samples. Cr is the digitized version of the analog component (R-Y), Cb is the digitized version of (B-Y).

Y, (R-Y), (B-Y) — These are the analog luminance, Y and color difference signals (R-Y) and (B-Y). Y is luminance information and the two color difference signals together provide color information. The color difference signals are the difference between a color and luminance: red-luminance and blue-luminance.

YUV — Shorthand commonly used to describe the analog luminance and color difference signal in component video systems. However, U and V are incorrect, they actually describe the two subcarrier modulation axes used in the PAL color coding system.

XLR Connector — Multi-pin connector commonly used for audio cable interconnects.

Zebra Pattern — A camera viewfinder display that places "stripes" over the parts of an image which has reached a pre-determined video level. Usually set at about 70 IRE units and used to assure correct exposure of skin tones.

Zoom lens — A lens which has a continuously variable focal length from wide angle to telephoto.

(Some definitions courtesy of Tektronix, Inc. and Quantel, Inc.)

Index